MONETARY ALTERNATIVES

MONETARY ALTERNATIVES

RETHINKING GOVERNMENT FIAT MONEY

Edited by
James A. Dorn

CATO
INSTITUTE
Washington, D.C.

ISBN: 978-1-944424-44-2
eBook ISBN: 978-1-944424-45-9

Library of Congress Cataloging-in-Publication Data available.

Printed in the United States of America
Cover design: Jon Meyers

Cato Institute
1000 Massachusetts Avenue, N.W.
Washington, D.C. 20001

www.cato.org

CONTENTS

FOREWORD
George Selgin

My, things have changed! In 1986, when the earliest of the papers gathered here first appeared in print, interest in alternatives to government fiat money was already limited to a small set—not to say a fringe—of monetary economists and policymakers. Subsequent events only tended to reduce that interest still further. Paul Volcker's Fed had managed to rein inflation back to a modest level last seen in the 1960s. On the heels of that success came the "Great Moderation"—a decline in the severity of business cycle fluctuations that many experts, after a decade or so, considered permanent. By 2000 Alan Greenspan, who had presided over most of that moderation, had been dubbed the "Maestro." So far as Fed officials and many academic economists were concerned, after three quarters of a century of stumbling, the Federal Reserve System had at last found its sea legs. If it wasn't the best of all possible monetary systems, surely it was close enough.

Subsequent events have left that confident view in tatters. The Great Moderation ended, suddenly and harrowingly, with the outbreak of the 2008 financial crisis. The accompanying "Great Recession" was, among all U.S. downturns, second only to the Great Depression itself in its overall severity. In responding to it, the Federal Reserve found it necessary to altogether abandon its traditional methods of monetary policy— the stirrups and reins that saw it through the glory days of the 1980s and 90s—in favor of untested alternatives.

George Selgin is Director of the Cato Institute's Center for Monetary and Financial Alternatives.

To say that those alternatives failed to bring about a rapid, or even a complete, recovery from the crisis, is putting things diplomatically. The unvarnished truth is that disappointment with the Fed's post-crisis experiments—and also with its handling of the crisis itself—have raised doubts concerning its ability to perform the duties Congress has assigned to it.

To appreciate the Fed's shortcomings is one thing; to propose ways to improve upon it is quite another. The complacency wrought by the Great Moderation, not to mention the limited interest in fundamental monetary reform before then, resulted in a dearth of serious inquiries into potentially superior arrangements. The Cato Institute was, until recently, practically alone among think tanks in stepping into the breach. Throughout the 1980s and 90s, while journalists and most academic economists celebrated the Fed's mastery of scientific monetary management, and other think tanks avoided the topic of monetary reform, Cato kept the subject alive, offering a safe haven, in the shape of its Annual Monetary Conference, for the minority of experts that continued to stress the need for fundamental monetary reform.

Although fundamental reform has been a consistent theme of Cato's monetary conferences, those conferences have never been dominated by any one approach to reform. The articles in this book present a variety of ideas for improving the monetary regime—including proposals for a formal "monetary constitution," various monetary rules, competing currencies, and establishing a new gold standard. The intent of the conferences has always been to encourage serious discussion of not one but many possible alternatives to discretionary government fiat money. The same purpose also informed the establishment and naming, in 2014, of Cato's Center for Monetary and Financial Alternatives.

Any idea for fundamental reform is bound to be controversial; and the proposals offered here are certainly no exception. Their authors do not agree with one another, and neither I nor Jim Dorn nor anyone else at Cato agrees—or could possibly agree—with all of them. But while I'm not inclined to agree with, much less to defend, all of the ideas put forward here, I do want to counter the suggestion that proposals for doing away with the Fed, or fiat money, or both, amount to a plea to "roll back the clock" to some bygone era. Just as there's nothing new under the sun, there are few ideas for monetary reform that might not have this complaint hurled at them. Champions of the Federal Reserve Act might, for example, have been accused of attempting to "turn back the clock" to the days of the Second Bank of the United States. Of course the complaint would have been fatuous, because the Fed, whatever its shortcomings, was not simply a replica of the Second Bank of the United States.

Similarly, while some of the alternatives proposed here, and especially those that recommend dispensing with the Fed, or establishing a new gold standard, or both, are necessarily informed by past experience, it doesn't follow that their authors regard any past arrangement as ideal, let alone as an ideal that can be replicated today. In proposing sometimes radical departures from the status quo, their aim is, not to reverse genuine progress, but to help us move beyond a system that has repeatedly, and often cataclysmically, failed to deliver the stability its champions promised.

Editor's Preface

Wen the Federal Reserve was created in 1913, its powers were strictly limited and the United States was still on the gold standard. Today the Fed has virtually unlimited power and the dollar is a pure fiat money.

A limited constitutional government calls for a rules-based, free-market monetary system, not the topsy-turvy fiat dollar that now exists under central banking. This book examines the case for alternatives to discretionary government fiat money and the reforms needed to move toward free-market money.

Central banking, like any sort of central planning, is not a panacea. Concentrating monetary power in the hands of a few individuals within a government bureaucracy, even if those individuals are well intentioned and well educated, does not guarantee sound money. The world's most important central bank, the Federal Reserve, is not bound by any strict rules, although Congress requires that it achieve maximum employment and price stability. The failure of the Fed to prevent the Great Recession of 2009, the Great Depression of the 1930s, and the stagflation of the late 1970s and early 1980s raises the question, can we do better?

In questioning the status quo and widening the scope of debate over monetary reform, the fundamental issue is to contrast a monetary regime that is self-regulating, spontaneous, and independent of government meddling versus one that is centralized, discretionary, politicized, and has a monopoly on fiat money. Free-market money within a trusted network of private contracts differs fundamentally from an inconvertible fiat money supplied by a discretionary central bank that has the power to create money out of thin air and to regulate both banks and nonbank financial institutions.

There are many types of monetary regimes and many monetary rules. The classical gold standard was a rules-based monetary system, in which the supply of money was determined by market demand—not by central bankers. Cybercurrencies, like bitcoin, offer the possibility of a private non-commodity monetary base and the potential to realize F. A. Hayek's vision of competitive free-market currencies. Ongoing experimentation and technological advances may pave the way for the end of central banking—or at least the emergence of new parallel currencies.

The distinguished authors in this volume examine the constitutional basis for alternatives to central banking, the role of gold in a market-based monetary system, the obstacles to fundamental reform and how they might be overcome, and the advent of cryptocurrencies.

In making the case for monetary reform and thinking about rules versus discretion in the conduct of monetary policy, it is important to take a constitutional perspective. As early as 1988, James M. Buchanan argued, at an international monetary conference hosted by the Progress Foundation in Lugano, Switzerland: "The dollar has absolutely no basis in any commodity base, no convertibility. What we have now is a monetary authority [the Fed] that essentially has a monopoly on the issue of fiat money, with no guidelines that amount to anything; an authority that never would have been legislatively approved, that never would have been constitutionally approved, on any kind of rational calculus."

In 1980, just after Ronald Reagan's election, Buchanan recommended that a presidential commission be established to discuss the Fed's legitimacy. There was some support within the Reagan camp, but Arthur Burns, a former chairman of the Federal Reserve Board, nixed it. As Buchanan explained at the Lugano conference, Burns "would not have anything to do with any proposal that would challenge the authority of the central banking structure."

Buchanan's aim was "to get a dialogue going . . . about the basic fundamental rules of the game, the constitutional structure." There is, he said, "a moral obligation to think that we can improve things." That is the spirit of this volume and Cato's newly established Center for Monetary and Financial Alternatives.

I would like to thank The George Edward Durell Foundation for its long support of Cato's annual monetary conferences from which all the articles in this book stem. I also would like to thank George Selgin for writing the foreword, Kevin Dowd for commenting on various aspects of the project, and Ari Blask for helping to bring this volume to fruition.

This year marks Cato's 40th anniversary and the 35th anniversary of the monetary conference. It is thus an appropriate time to bring out a collection of articles devoted to rethinking government fiat money and to offer alternatives consistent with limited government, the rule of law, and free markets.

—J. A. Dorn

Reference

Buchanan, J. M. (1988) "Comment by Dr. Buchanan." *Economic Education Bulletin* 28 (6): 32–35.

1
INTRODUCTION
TOWARD A NEW MONETARY REGIME
James A. Dorn

> The only adequate guarantee for the uniform and stable value of a paper currency is its convertibility into specie—the least fluctuating and the only universal currency. I am sensible that a value equal to that of specie may be given to paper or any other medium, by making a limited amount necessary for necessary purposes; but what is to ensure the inflexible adherence of the Legislative Ensurers to their own principles and purposes?
>
> —James Madison (1831)

Rethinking Government Fiat Money

Today we live a world of pure discretionary government fiat monies. Any link of the dollar to gold ended in August 1971, when President Nixon closed the Treasury's "gold window," which had allowed foreign central banks to freely covert their dollars for gold at the official exchange rate. The end of convertibility left the dollar without an anchor except for the Federal Reserve's promise to maintain price stability. That objective, however, has often been sacrificed in the vain attempt to promote full employment.

James A. Dorn is Vice President for Monetary Studies and a Senior Fellow at the Cato Institute.

The global financial crisis of 2007–08, increased the Fed's discretionary authority and ushered in unconventional policies—notably, largescale asset purchases known as quantitative easing (QE), and ultra-low interest rates with a lower bound on the federal funds rate near zero. Macro-prudential regulation was also added to the policy mix. By suppressing interest rates, the Fed has increased risk taking, misallocated capital, and inflated asset prices. Other central banks have followed suit. When rates rise, bubbles will burst—and the hoped for wealth effect of monetary stimulus will be recognized as a pseudo wealth effect.

The politicization of monetary policy and the failure of central banks to generate robust economic growth have led to calls for rethinking the current monetary regime and for recognizing the limits of monetary policy. The U.S. Congress has constitutional authority to "coin money" and "regulate the value thereof" (Article 1, Section 8). Using that authority, some members of Congress have advocated establishing a bipartisan Centennial Monetary Commission to review the Fed's performance and to consider ways to reduce uncertainty, safeguard the long-run value of the dollar, and mitigate financial crises.

The debate over rules versus discretion—and the choice of alternative monetary rules—is at the heart of this volume. Before discussing those issues, however, the book begins with an overview of the current state of central banking and the case for restoring a monetary constitution.

Central Banking at a Crossroads

The persistence of near-zero interest rates and the failure of the Fed to reduce the size of its balance sheet pose serious problems for policymakers. If the Fed waits too long to raise rates and end discretionary credit allocation, distortions in capital markets will worsen. But if it moves too fast, another recession could occur.

More fundamentally, if central banks are guided by erroneous monetary theory, the damage to the real economy could be substantial. Experiments with unconventional monetary policy need to be questioned and alternatives proposed. The authors in Part 1 do so.

Claudio Borio, who heads the Monetary and Economic Department at the Bank for International Settlements, revisits three "intellectual pillars of monetary policy": (1) the natural or equilibrium interest rate is best understood as one consistent with price stability and full employment; (2) money is neutral in the medium to long run; and (3) deflation is always costly. He argues that none of these beliefs are sufficient to understand current monetary policy or to guide future policy.

First, the definition of the equilibrium interest rate would be improved by including financial and macroeconomic stability, not just price stability and full employment. Second, monetary disequilibrium, as reflected in distorted interest rates and misallocated credit, can persist for 10–20 years; it is not just a short-run phenomenon. Third, one should distinguish between deflation caused by deficient aggregate demand (as during the Great Depression) and deflation due to productivity gains. The former should be avoided, but the latter should be welcomed. The Fed and other central banks typically treat any deflation as bad, while striving to increase inflation. That is a recipe for trouble. A positive agenda for reform, argues Borio, requires that central bankers recognize that "easy monetary policy cannot undo the resource misallocations" brought about by distorted interest rates, and that the focus should be on "facilitating balance sheet repair and implementing structural reforms."

Jeffrey Lacker, president of the Federal Reserve Bank of Richmond, argues that central banks should not be in the business of credit allocation and income redistribution. Instead, they should focus on achieving long-run price stability through traditional open-market operations. He is concerned about the same distortions discussed by Borio. According to Lacker, intervention in credit markets "can redirect resources from taxpayers to financial market investors and, over time, can expand moral hazard and distort the allocation of capital." In addition, such intervention is "a threat to financial stability."

By engaging in credit/fiscal policy, rather than pure monetary policy, the Fed threatens its independence and credibility. Thus, Lacker prefers a "Treasuries-only" policy, which he believes would enable the Fed to better honor its commitment to supply "an elastic currency."

John Allison, former chairman and CEO of BB&T, is highly critical of the growing power of the Fed as a result of the financial crisis. He thinks interest rates should be set by markets, not manipulated by central banks. The Fed's ultra-low interest rate policy has increased borrowing for housing consumption, but has had a negative effect on productive private investment. Meanwhile, burdensome financial regulations have been a poor substitute for strong capital requirements and market discipline.

The public needs to recognize the limits of central banks and expose the "fatal conceit" that a centrally planned monetary system can outperform a system based on free markets, individual responsibility, and well-enforced private property rights. More telling, when central banks try to allocate credit, they are bound to reduce economic and personal freedom. That is why Allison favors making "it illegal for the Fed to bail out insolvent firms." He also advocates eliminating government deposit insurance and constraining central banks by a monetary rule. Ideally, he would do away with central banks and adopt free banking under a commodity standard.

Bennett McCallum, professor of economics at Carnegie-Mellon University, is "appalled" by the Fed's "major excursions into credit policy. . . and thereby into the unauthorized exercise of fiscal policy." He favors a rules-based monetary regime that reduces uncertainty and provides a framework for price level stability. In that regard, he examines several alternatives to discretionary government fiat money: the gold standard, private competitive currencies, and the Yeager-Greenfield proposal for stabilizing a broad price index. McCallum recognizes that there is no perfect system, and "the best that can be done . . . is to adopt institutions that are less subject to temptation than others and that promise to provide stability of a broad price index."

As a first step toward monetary reform, McCallum would end the Fed's dual mandate and have Congress amend the Federal Reserve Act to make the Fed accountable for a single mandate—long-run price stability. That recommendation is consistent with his earlier proposal for a monetary feedback rule that would stabilize nominal income growth (McCallum 1989: 336–51; also see White 1999: 223–24).

Restoring a Monetary Constitution

Preoccupation with the conduct of monetary policy within a given monetary regime can easily detract from the more fundamental issue of a monetary constitution—that is, the rules of the game that underlie any monetary regime. Although the Federal Reserve is based on an act of Congress, there is a higher law of the Constitution that is meant to safeguard the public's property right in a stable-valued money. It is clear from a careful reading of the U.S. Constitution's monetary clauses that the Framers had in mind a monetary system based on convertibility to the precious metals, not one based on fiat money under a discretionary central bank. In that regard, Milton Friedman (1984: 47) told members of Congress, "As I read the original Constitution, it intended to limit Congress to a commodity standard."

In December 1913, when Congress passed the Federal Reserve Act, the United States was still on the gold standard. World War I put an end to the old monetary order. At first the Federal Reserve was narrowly limited, but over time its powers grew, especially during periods of crisis. The authors in Part 2 emphasize the need for a monetary constitution to safeguard the value of money and facilitate mutually beneficial exchanges. They discuss both the case for restoring the Framers' monetary constitution as well as searching for monetary rules that can improve upon the current discretionary government fiat money regime.[1]

Richard Timberlake, an emeritus professor of economics and finance at the University of Georgia, and author of *Constitutional Money: A Review of the Supreme Court's Monetary Decisions* (2013), provides a concise history of the metallic (gold-silver) standard in the United States, the origins of the Federal Reserve, and the drift toward a pure fiat money system as the Supreme Court and Congress eroded the Framers' Constitution. He argues that although it may not be politically possible to restore the original constitutional monetary system, Congress should remove the Fed's discretion by imposing a single mandate: price level stability.

James Buchanan, recipient of the Nobel Memorial Prize in Economic Sciences in 1986, the cofounder of the public choice school of economics, and a long-time adherent of "constitutional economics," argues for adopting a monetary constitution that has as its primary objective "predictability in the value of the monetary unit."

---

[1]On the search for a monetary constitution, see Yeager (1962), Dorn and Schwartz (1987), and White, Vanberg, and Köhler (2015).

He views this as a responsibility of government akin to protecting private property rights and enforcing contracts. Under current U.S. monetary law, notes Buchanan, "There exists no monetary constitution . . . . What does exist is an institutionally established authority charged with an ill-defined responsibility to 'do good,' as determined by its own evaluation."[2]

Buchanan contends that modern macroeconomics has diverted attention from the rules needed to bring about monetary and economic order, and instead has focused on models that operate in an institutional vacuum. He does not seek to define the optimal monetary rule, but rather to escape conventional thinking and engage in constitutional dialogue to increase the chances of improving the monetary regime. By reducing transactions costs, an improved monetary regime would enlarge the scope for voluntary exchange and increase the wealth of the nation.

Peter Bernholz, an emeritus professor of economics at the University of Basel, relies on his extensive knowledge of monetary history to explore the problem of implementing and maintaining a monetary constitution. He argues that long-run price stability "can be maintained only if politicians and central bankers have no discretionary authority to influence the stock of money."

In thinking about how to design a monetary constitution and maintain it, Bernholz recommends six measures, including "a mechanism limiting the stock of money," a requirement that the monetary constitution can only be amended by a supermajority vote, and a prohibition against the use of "emergency clauses." The money supply could be limited by either a convertibility rule or a quantity rule. Bernholz favors the former under a pure gold standard—or what Milton Friedman (1961) called a "real gold standard" (as opposed to a "pseudo gold standard"). In moving to a pure gold standard, Bernholz would abolish central banks, institute free banking with unlimited liability for shareholders, and outlaw state-owned banks. Such a laissez-faire monetary system has historical precedents, argues Bernholz, and would facilitate "innovation in the field of money."

---

[2]Buchanan's statement is reminiscent of Clark Warburton's argument that "monetary law in the United States is ambiguous and chaotic, does not contain a suitable principle for the exercise of the monetary power held by the Federal Reserve System, and has caused confusion in the development of Federal Reserve Policy" (Warburton 1966: 316).

Rules versus Discretion

The long-standing debate over rules versus discretion in the conduct of monetary policy has been energized by the 2007–08 financial crisis, which caught nearly all economists and policymakers by surprise. That crisis has led to more powerful central banks with significantly more discretion, which has increased uncertainty about the direction of monetary policy. The authors in Part 3 argue for limiting central bank discretion and adopting a rules-based monetary regime.

Charles Plosser, former president of the Federal Reserve Bank of Philadelphia, draws on work of Kydland and Prescott (1977) to emphasize the importance of having policymakers commit to a rules-based monetary regime that anchors expectations about the future path of monetary policy. Plosser is interested in "institutional design" and strategies to limit the scope of central banks and increase their credibility. Rather than rely solely on legislated rules, which might politicize monetary policy, he prefers to have central bankers reform from within. In the case of the Fed, he recommends that the Federal Open Market Committee release quarterly reports to inform the public on how well actual policy complies with various monetary rules.

George Selgin, director of Cato's Center for Monetary and Financial Alternatives, distinguishes between "real and pseudo monetary rules." The former refer to rules that are "strict" (i.e., rigidly enforced either by contract or design) and "robust," in the sense that the "monetary system itself automatically implements the rule." In contrast, pseudo monetary rules are neither rigorously enforced nor robust. Monetary authorities are not subject to penalties for failing to meet targets, policymaking is myopic, and time inconsistency is endemic. Thus, "a pseudo rule is as likely as discretion to turn monetary policy into a plaything of politics." Selgin provides examples of the two types of rules and concludes that the line between them "is a very fine one, the difference ultimately being one, not in kind, but in degree to which adherence to a rule is regarded as unbreakable."

John B. Taylor, a professor of economics at Stanford University, has long argued in favor of monetary rules over discretion. When he first introduced the famous Taylor Rule in 1993, it was intended to guide monetary policy, not be enforced by law. "The objective," notes Taylor, "was to help central bankers make their interest rate decisions in a less discretionary and more rule-like manner, and thereby achieve the goal of price stability and economic stability." Now, with the increase in the Fed's discretion and power as a result of the financial crisis, and the Fed's entry into credit allocation and unconventional monetary policies, Taylor favors enacting a monetary rule. He believes it is time for Congress to exercise its constitutional authority over monetary policy but in a way that does not lead to politicization.

Prior to the Great Recession, central banks gained experience and success using the Taylor Rule, which can be viewed as a nominal income rule, and inflation targeting. That success, argues Taylor, should be utilized in designing legislation to improve monetary policy. The key objective should be "to restore a more strategic rule-like monetary policy with less short-term oriented discretionary actions." Taylor proposes legislation that would increase accountability and reduce the temptation to engage in credit allocation and fiscal policy.

Scott Sumner, director of the Program on Monetary Policy at George Mason University's Mercatus Center, is a strong proponent of nominal GDP targeting. One benefit of NGDP targeting is that it bypasses the issue of assigning weights under the Fed's dual mandate to achieve price level stability and maximum employment. All that needs to be done is to set a target path for nominal GDP, which is the product of the general price level and real output. There is ready data on total spending (or domestic final sales if that metric is used).[3] So if the target is set at 5 percent trend growth, then market forces will determine real growth and the Fed will supply the monetary base sufficient to hit the designated nominal GDP target. This strategy avoids having to fine tune monetary policy.

To improve the operation of this monetary rule, Sumner and other "market monetarists" would rely on a futures market for nominal GDP contracts to keep actual GDP in line with the target. "The market, not the central bank, would be setting the monetary base and the level of interest rates." Once nominal GDP was on a stable growth path, argues Sumner, there would be more transparency, less chance of contagion from financial crises, and less political pressure on the Fed. Keeping nominal GDP on a stable growth path would also weaken the case for bailing out large banks, "because proponents of

---

[3]Niskanen (1992, 2001) prefers to target nominal domestic final sales.

'too big to fail' could no longer claim that failing to bail out banks would push us into a recession."

Leland Yeager, emeritus professor of economics at the University of Virginia and Auburn University, favors a price level rule over a nominal income rule.[4] However, he wants to decentralize and privatize money, define the unit of account "by a comprehensive bundle of goods and services," and let competition among private issuers "keep meaningful the denomination of their bank notes and deposits (and checks) in the stable, independently defined unit." Those steps would take us much closer to a forecast-free monetary regime than our current government fiat money system under a highly discretionary central bank. The reason is simple: absence of high-powered money in Yeager's scheme means there would be no "problem of injection effects," and thus no "need for central forecasting."[5] Monetary equilibrium would prevail and "any forecasting functions that did remain would be healthily decentralized under free banking."

Alternatives to Government Fiat Money

The authors in Part 4 provide a detailed discussion of the case for alternatives to government fiat money, the types of alternatives that may emerge if the U.S. monetary constitution is restored, and the legal barriers that need to be removed to permit free entry. Greater monetary freedom would allow competition and experimentation with alternative currencies, which in turn would produce a more robust monetary system.

Edwin Vieira Jr., an attorney and author of *Pieces of Eight: The Monetary Powers and Disabilities of the United States Constitution* ([2002] 2011), defends a bimetallic standard as consistent with the original U.S. Constitution. He thus views gold and silver as "constitutional alternative currencies," which could be introduced either by private or government action. His preference, which has constitutional backing, is to have states (rather than the federal

---

[4]Bradley and Jansen (1989: 40) contend that changes in the assumptions about the labor market can make a price level rule theoretically superior to a nominal income rule. Also, "ignorance of the correct equations, parameter values and lag structure that characterize the U.S. economy reduces the appeal of nominal GNP targeting."

[5]For a more detailed discussion, see Greenfield and Yeager (1983), and Yeager and Greenfield (1989).

government) facilitate the transition to constitutional money by offering "electronic gold and silver currencies." He provides a blueprint for doing so and explains the benefits of experimentation among the 50 states. If states were successful in introducing redeemable currencies, private banks would follow suit, and eventually the Fed would become obsolete.

Lawrence H. White, professor of economics at George Mason University, explains the steps that would have to be taken to introduce a "new gold standard," why those steps are theoretically possible, and the benefits of a "parallel gold standard." First and foremost, Congress would have to remove various legal restrictions that prevent the emergence of a gold-based monetary regime. Legal tender laws would have to be changed, taxes on gold and silver coins would have to be ended, private suppliers would have to be allowed to offer metallic currencies, and financial institutions would have to be free to service a gold-based monetary system. The impetus for such a system would depend on whether the public losses confidence in the current government fiat money regime, which would be the case if there were runaway inflation. Otherwise, network effects would make it very difficult to change regimes.

In addition to calling for legalizing a new gold standard, White advocates restoring "a gold definition of the U.S. dollar." What he does not recommend is moving to a 100 percent gold backing for outstanding U.S. currency and demand deposits. The benefit of establishing a new gold standard is that it would eliminate the need for monetary policy and thus for a central bank. Under a real gold standard, the money supply responds to money demand—markets not governments determine the quantity of money. Without a central bank, private competitive banks will have an incentive to keep redemption promises under binding contracts. As White notes, "competing private banks, which *do* face legal and competitive constraints, have a better historical track record than central banks for maintaining gold redemption." Those who oppose a new gold standard, such as Barry Eichengreen (2011), fail to recognize that a real gold standard simply defines the dollar as a fixed amount of gold; it does not peg any relative price. Moreover, a gold-based regime breeds fiscal prudence and is feasible given the existing U.S. real gold stock. White concludes that if the political consensus for a parallel gold standard exists, present-day financial innovations would facilitate the transition to a new gold standard.

Roland Vaubel, emeritus professor of economics at the University of Mannheim, makes the case for currency competition as opposed to governmental money monopolies. He begins by examining barriers to currency competition from both foreign central banks and private issuers. Allowing international currency competition among central banks, argues Vaubel, would lower inflationary expectations and thus provide the public with more stable-valued currencies. Likewise, he sees the benefits of private competitive currencies, based on the Hayekian idea that "the monopoly of government of issuing money . . . has . . . deprived us of the only process by which we can find out what would be good money" (Hayek 1978a: 5; also see Hayek 1978b).

Vaubel gives a rigorous defense for allowing free entry of private issuers. He also thinks that "if currency competition is to serve as a mechanism of discovery, government must not prescribe the characteristics of the privately issued currencies or the organization of the private issuing institutions." Finally, he holds that "there is no independent public-good justification for the government's money monopoly. The public good argument is redundant."

Lawrence H. White explores the growing market for cryptocurrencies, which are best understood as "transferable digital assets, secured by cryptography." Although bitcoin is the best-known digital currency, there are now numerous non-bitcoin currencies, collectively known as "altcoins." The market for these "competing private irredeemable monies (or would-be monies)" presents an opportunity to study the feasibility of Hayek's theory of competitive private currencies. The key features of bitcoin are its strict quantity constraint and its open source code with a public ledger. It is also used as a "vehicle currency," and thus a unit of account, for most altcoins—dollars exchange for bitcoins that are then used to buy altcoins.

At present cryptocurrencies are a small part of the monetary universe, but White sees a large potential, especially for use in international remittances. The important point is that experimentation with digital currencies is likely to improve their monetary characteristics and speed up their adoption, provided there is free entry. The problem will be to get the public to trust the new currencies and keep the government from intervening in the emergent market for cryptocurrencies.

Kevin Dowd, professor of finance and economics at Durham University, concludes Part 4 by critiquing the argument that free-market currencies are inherently unstable and inferior to a government-directed monetary system. He begins by constructing a hypothetical model of a laissez-faire monetary regime—asking how a free-market in currencies would emerge absent any central bank—and finds that its operating properties are consistent with stability and optimality. The harmony that emerges under a market-based monetary system, argues Dowd, stems from the freedom to choose alternative currencies and the rule of law that binds the system together.

After discussing "the idealized evolution of a free-banking system," Dowd describes its two key features: stability and optimality. "Stability" means a laissez-faire monetary system is "self-sustaining," the supply of its liabilities is "perfectly elastic," and the price level is well anchored. "Optimality" means that "all feasible and mutually beneficial trades take place." These features stem from the fact that there are no "outside guardians" to upset the spontaneous free-banking order. It is the lack of monetary freedom, notes Dowd, that leads to crises. Thus, what is needed for monetary harmony is monetary freedom.

Conclusion

The current system of pure government fiat monies, managed by discretionary central banks, is inconsistent with monetary freedom and stability. The lack of a rules-based monetary regime and the barriers to competitive private currencies limit freedom and needlessly and dangerously enhance the power of central bankers.

The contributors to this volume question the status quo and offer a deeper understanding of the case for rules versus discretion in the conduct of monetary policy, examine the characteristics and benefits of alternative rules, and provide a blueprint for making the transition to a free-market monetary system. It is hoped that their insights will help guide the public and policymakers to rethink current monetary arrangements and help shape a new monetary order based on freedom and the rule of law.

References

Bradley, M. D., and Jansen, D. W. (1989) "Understanding Nominal GNP Targeting." Federal Reserve Bank of St. Louis *Review* 71 (6): 31–40.

Dorn, J. A., and Schwartz, A. J., eds. (1987) *The Search for Stable Money: Essays on Monetary Reform*. Chicago: University of Chicago Press.

Eichengreen, B. (2011) "A Critique of Pure Gold." *The National Interest* (September-October). Available at http://national interest .org/article/critique-pure-gold-5741.

Friedman, M. (1961) "Real and Pseudo Gold Standards." *Journal of Law and Economics* 4 (October): 66–79.

_____ (1984) "Monetary Policy Structures." In *Candid Conversations on Monetary Policy*, 32–50. Washington: House Republican Research Committee.

Greenfield, R. L., and Yeager, L. B. (1983) "A Laissez-Faire Approach to Monetary Stability." *Journal of Money, Credit, and Banking* 15 (August): 302–15.

Hayek, F. A. (1978a) "Towards a Free Market Monetary System." *Journal of Libertarian Studies* 3: 1–8.

_____ (1978b) *Denationalisation of Money*. 2nd ed. London: Institute of Economic Affairs.

Kydland, F. E., and Prescott, E. C. (1977) "Rules Rather than Discretion: The Inconsistency of Optimal Plans." *Journal of Political Economy* 85 (3): 473–92.

Madison, J. (1831) "[Letter] to Mr. Teachle" (Montpelier, March 15). In S. K. Padover (ed.), *The Complete Madison: His Basic Writings*, 292. New York: Harper and Bros. (1953).

McCallum, B. T. (1989) *Monetary Economics: Theory and Policy*. New York: Macmillan.

Niskanen, W. A. (1992) "Political Guidance on Monetary Policy." *Cato Journal* 12: 281–86.

_____ (2001) "A Test of the Demand Rule." *Cato Journal* 21 (2): 205–09.

Taylor, J. B. (1993) "Discretion versus Policy Rules in Practice." *Carnegie-Rochester Conference Series on Public Policy* 39: 195–214.

Timberlake, R. T. (2013) *Constitutional Money: A Review of the Supreme Court's Monetary Decisions*. New York: Cambridge University Press.

Vieira, E. Jr. ([2002] 2011) *Pieces of Eight: The Monetary Powers and Disabilities of the United States Constitution*. Gold Money Special Edition. Chicago: R. R. Donnelley & Sons.

Warburton, C. (1966) *Depression, Inflation, and Monetary Policy: Selected Papers, 1945–1953.* Baltimore: The Johns Hopkins University Press.

White, L. H. (1999) *The Theory of Monetary Institutions.* Malden, Mass.: Blackwell.

White, L. H.; Vanberg, V. J.; and Köhler, E. A., eds. (2015) *Renewing the Search for a Monetary Constitution.* Washington: Cato Institute.

Yeager, L. B., ed. (1962) *In Search of a Monetary Constitution.* Cambridge, Mass.: Harvard University Press.

Yeager, L. B., and Greenfield, R. L. (1989) Can Monetary Disequilibrium Be Eliminated?" *Cato Journal* 9 (2): 405–21.

PART 1

CENTRAL BANKING AT A CROSSROADS

2

REVISITING THREE INTELLECTUAL PILLARS OF MONETARY POLICY
Claudio Borio

The Great Financial Crisis has triggered much soul-searching within the economic profession and the policymaking community. The crisis shattered the notion that price stability would guarantee macroeconomic stability: financial markets are not self-equilibrating, at least at a price that society can afford. And it showed that prudential frameworks focused on individual institutions viewed on a stand-alone basis were inadequate: a more systemic perspective was needed to avoid missing the forest for the trees. Hence, the welcome trend of putting in place macroprudential frameworks. But has this soul-searching gone far enough?

I shall argue that it has not. More specifically, I would like to revisit and question three deeply held beliefs that underpin current monetary policy received wisdom. The first belief is that it is appropriate to define equilibrium (or natural) rates as those consistent with output at potential and with stable prices (inflation) in any given period—the so-called Wicksellian natural rate. The second is that it is appropriate to think of money (monetary policy) as neutral—that is, as having no impact on real outcomes over medium- to long-term horizons relevant for policy: 10–20 years or so, if not longer. The third is that it is appropriate to set policy on

Claudio Borio is Head of the Monetary and Economic Department at the Bank for International Settlements in Basel, Switzerland. This article is reprinted from the *Cato Journal*, Vol. 36, No. 2 (Spring/Summer 2016).

the presumption that deflations are always very costly, sometimes even to regard them as a kind of red line that, once crossed, heralds the abyss.

From these considerations, I shall draw two conclusions. First, I shall argue that the received interpretation of the well-known trend decline in real interest rates—as embodied, for example, in the "saving glut" (Bernanke 2005) and "secular stagnation" (Summers 2014) hypotheses—is not fully satisfactory. Instead, I shall provide a different/complementary interpretation that stresses the decline is, at least in part, a disequilibrium phenomenon that is inconsistent with lasting financial, macroeconomic, and monetary stability. Second, I shall suggest that we need to make adjustments to current monetary policy frameworks in order to have monetary policy play a more active role in preventing systemic financial instability and, hence, in containing its huge macroeconomic costs. This would call for a more symmetrical policy during financial booms and busts—financial cycles. It would mean leaning more deliberately against financial booms and easing less aggressively and, above all, persistently during financial busts.

Equilibrium (Natural) Rates Revisited

Interest rates, short and long, in nominal and inflation-adjusted (real) terms, have been exceptionally low for an unusually long time, regardless of benchmarks. In both nominal and real terms, policy rates are even lower than at the peak of the Great Financial Crisis. In real terms, they have now been negative for even longer than during the Great Inflation of the 1970s (Figure 1, left-hand panel). Turning next to long-term rates, it is well known that in real terms they have followed a long-term downward trend—a point to which I will return. But between December 2014 and end-May 2015, on average no less than around $2 trillion worth of long-term sovereign debt, much of it issued by euro area sovereigns, was trading at *negative* yields. At their trough, French, German, and Swiss sovereign yields were negative out to a respective 5, 9, and 15 years (Figure 1, right-hand panel). While they have ticked up since then, such negative nominal rates are unprecedented. And all this has been happening even as global growth has not been far away from historical averages, so that the wedge between growth and interest rates has been unusually broad.

FIGURE 1
INTEREST RATES HAVE BEEN EXCEPTIONALLY AND PERSISTENTLY LOW

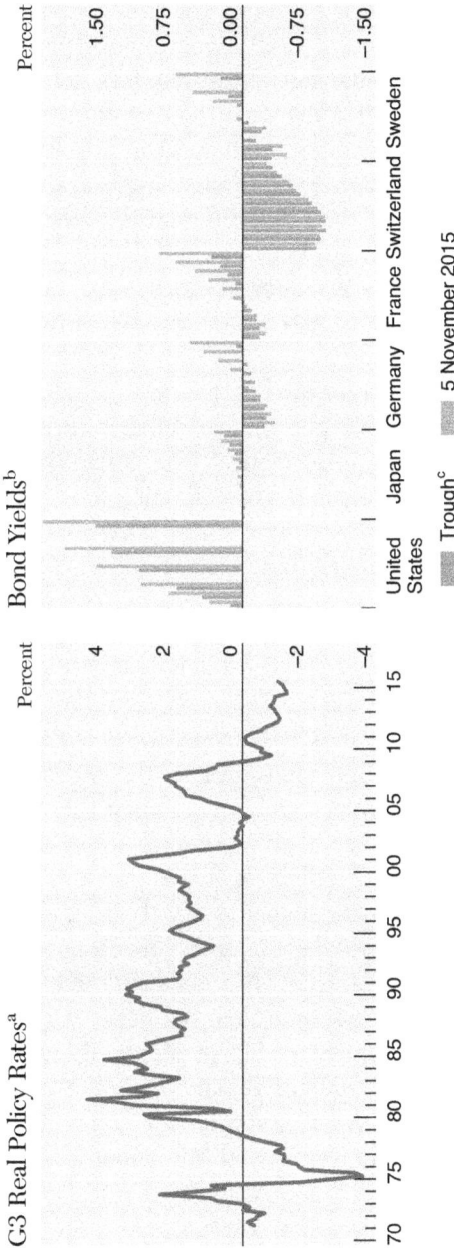

[a]Nominal policy rate less consumer price inflation excluding food and energy. Weighted averages for the euro area (Germany), Japan, and the United States based on rolling GDP and PPP exchange rates. [b]Yield per maturity; for each country, the bars represent the maturities from 1 year to 10 years. [c]For the United States, January 30, 2015; for Japan, January 19, 2015; for Germany, April 20, 2015; for France, April 15, 2015; for Switzerland, October 27, 2015; for Sweden, April 17, 2015.
SOURCES: Bloomberg; national data.

How should we think of these market rates and of their relationship to equilibrium ones? Both the received perspective and the one
offered here agree that market interest rates are determined by a
combination of central banks' and market participants' actions.
Central banks set the nominal short-term rate and, for a given outstanding stock, they influence the nominal long-term rate through
their signals of future policy rates and their asset purchases. Market
participants, in turn, adjust their portfolios based on their expectations of central bank policy, their views about the other factors driving long-term rates, their attitude toward risk, and various balance
sheet constraints. Given nominal interest rates, actual inflation determines ex post real rates and expected inflation determines ex ante
real rates. So far, so good.

But how can we tell whether market rates are at their equilibrium
level from a macroeconomic perspective—that is, consistent with
sustainable good economic performance? The answer is that if they
stay at the wrong level for long enough, something "bad" will happen,
leading to an eventual correction. It is in this sense that many economists say that the influence of central banks on short-term real rates
is only transitory.

But what is that something "bad"? Here the two perspectives
differ. In the received perspective, it is the behavior of inflation that
provides the key signal. If there is excess capacity, inflation will fall; if
there is overheating, it will rise. This corresponds to what is often also
called the Wicksellian natural rate—that is, the rate that equates
aggregate demand and supply at full employment (or, equivalently,
the rate that prevails when actual output equals potential output).

The perspective developed here suggests that this view is too
narrow. Another possible key signal is the build-up of financial
imbalances, which typically take the form of strong increases in
credit, asset prices, and risk-taking. Historically, these have been the
main cause of episodes of systemic financial crises with huge economic costs. Think, for instance, of Japan and the Nordic countries
in the late 1980s, Asia in the mid-1990s, and the United States ahead
of the Great Financial Crisis or, going back in time, ahead of the
Great Depression (see Eichengreen and Mitchener 2003).

The reasoning is straightforward. Acknowledge, as indeed some of
the proponents of the received view have, that low interest rates are
a factor in fueling financial booms and busts. After all, intuitively, it
is hard to argue that they are not, given that monetary policy operates

by influencing credit expansion, asset prices and risk-taking. Acknowledge further that financial booms and busts cause huge and lasting economic damage—in fact, no one denies this, given the large amount of empirical evidence. Then it follows that if we think of an equilibrium rate more broadly as one consistent with sustainable good economic performance, rates cannot be at their equilibrium level if they are inconsistent with financial stability.

This is partly an issue of the time frame envisaged for the disequilibria to cause damage. In the received view, it is relatively short, as the focus is on output deviations from potential at business cycle frequencies. In the view proposed here, it is longer, as the focus is on the potentially larger output fluctuations at financial cycle frequencies. As traditionally measured, the duration of the business cycle is up to eight years; by contrast, the duration of financial cycles since the early 1980s has been 16–20 years (continuous and dashed lines, respectively, in Figure 2) (Drehmann, Borio, and Tsatsaronis 2012).[1]

It is not uncommon to hear supporters of the "saving glut" and "secular stagnation" hypotheses say that the equilibrium or natural rate is very low, even negative, and that this rate generates financial instability.[2] Seen from this angle, such a statement is somewhat misleading. It is more a reflection of the incompleteness of the analytical frameworks used to define and measure the natural rate concept—frameworks that do not incorporate financial instability—than a reflection of an inherent tension between natural rates and financial stability. There is a need to go beyond the full employment-inflation paradigm to fully characterize economic equilibrium.

What I have said applies just as much to the short-term rate, which the central bank sets, as to long-term rates. For there is no guarantee that the combination of central banks' and market participants' decisions will guide long-term rates toward equilibrium. Just like any other asset price, long-term rates may be misaligned for very long periods, except that their misalignments have more pervasive effects.

---

[1]For a novel empirical analysis that digs deeper into the dynamics of financial cycles and assigns a key role to interest rates, see Drehmann and Juselius (2015). The analysis does a remarkably good job of tracing, out of sample, the behavior of U.S. output around the Great Recession.

[2]For an in-depth analysis along these lines, see Bean et al. (2015). In contrast to others, however, these authors do see monetary policy playing a role in leaning against financial imbalances in order to limit the risk of financial instability.

FIGURE 2

FINANCIAL AND BUSINESS CYCLES IN THE UNITED STATES

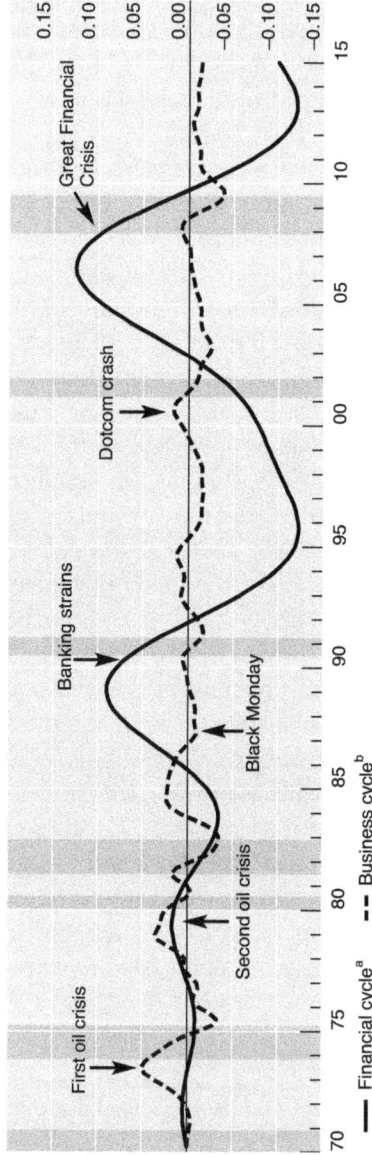

[a]The financial cycle as measured by frequency-based (bandpass) filters capturing medium-term cycles in real credit, the credit-to-GDP ratio and real house prices; Q1 1970 = 0. [b]The business cycle as measured by a frequency-based (bandpass) filter capturing fluctuations in real GDP over a period from one to eight years; Q1 1970 = 0.

SOURCE: Drehmann, Borio, and Tsatsaronis (2012), updated.

Importantly, the point about how to think of equilibrium rates is not purely semantic. It has first-order implications for monetary policy, since we all agree that the central bank's task is precisely to set the policy rate so as to track the natural or equilibrium rate. I will come back to this point.

Monetary Neutrality Revisited

Let me now turn to the second pillar of received wisdom: the notion of money (monetary policy) neutrality. The previous analysis already suggests that this notion is problematic. The reason is that there is a large body of evidence indicating that the costs of financial (banking) crises are very long-lasting, if not permanent: growth may return to its pre-crisis long-term trend, but output remains below its pre-crisis long-term trend (BCBS 2010, Ball 2014).[3] Thus, as long as one acknowledges that monetary policy can fuel financial booms and their subsequent bust, it is logically dubious to argue that it is neutral.

More recent evidence uncovered by BIS research confirms this point and sheds further light on it. It does so by investigating the mechanisms through which financial booms and busts cause so much lasting damage. The work shifts attention from the demand side of the equation, which is where the literature has gone (e.g., Reinhart and Reinhart 2010, Drehmann and Juselius 2015, Rogoff 2015), to the supply side, which is just as important (e.g., Cecchetti and Kharroubi 2015). It is well known that financial busts weaken demand as the interplay of asset prices falls and overindebtedness causes havoc in balance sheets. But what about the neglected nexus between financial booms and busts, resource misallocations, and productivity?

By examining 21 advanced economies over the period 1969–2013, our research produces three findings (Borio et al. 2015b). First, financial booms tend to undermine productivity growth as they occur (Figure 3). For a typical credit boom, just over a quarter of a percentage point per year is a kind of lower bound. Second, a good chunk of this, almost 60 percent, reflects the shift of factors of production (labor) to lower productivity growth sectors. Think, in particular, of

---

[3]The studies reviewed in BCBS (2010) that allow for the possibility of permanent effects point to a loss equivalent to some 6 percent of GDP on average. Reviewing the experience with the recent crisis, Ball (2014) estimates a permanent decline in potential output of over 8 percent among OECD countries.

FIGURE 3

FINANCIAL BOOMS SAP PRODUCTIVITY BY MISALLOCATING RESOURCES[a]

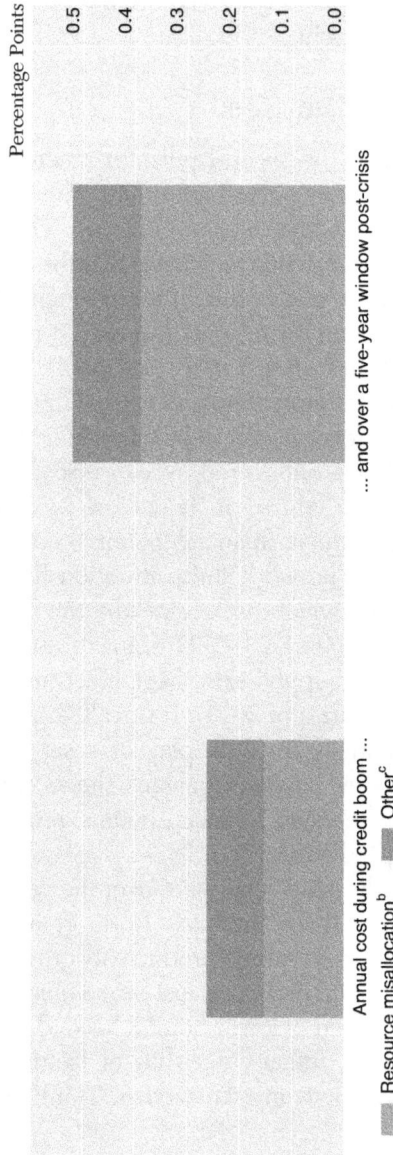

[a]Estimates calculated over the period 1969–2013 for 21 advanced economies. [b]Annual impact on productivity growth of labor shifts into less productive sectors during the credit boom, as measured over the period shown. [c]Annual impact in the absence of reallocations during the boom.
SOURCE: Based on Borio et al. (2015b).

shifts into a temporarily bloated construction sector. The rest is the impact on productivity that is common across sectors, such as the shared component of aggregate capital accumulation and total factor productivity. Third, the impact of the misallocations that occur *during a boom* is much larger if a crisis follows. The average loss per year in the five years after a crisis is more than twice that during a boom, around half a percentage point per year. Taking, say, a five-year boom and five post-crisis years together, the cumulative impact would amount to a loss of some 4 percentage points. Put differently, for the period 2008–13, we are talking about a loss of some 0.5 percentage points per year for the advanced countries that saw booms and crises. This is roughly equal to their actual average productivity growth during the same window. Now, the point is not to take these figures at face value, but to note that these factors are material and should receive much more attention. The length of the periods and orders of magnitude involved are definitely large enough to cast doubt on the notion of monetary policy neutrality.

In addition to the implication for the notion of neutrality, the role of misallocations highlights three further points. First, it is worth broadening the mechanisms behind "hysteresis" to include those that work through resource misallocations linked to financial booms and busts. The allocation of credit, over and above its overall amount, deserves much greater attention.

Second, the well-known limitations of expansionary monetary policy in tackling busts appear in a new light. It is not just that agents wish to deleverage and the transmission through banks is broken; easy monetary policy cannot undo the resource misallocations.[4] For instance, it cannot, and should not, bring back to life idle cranes when there is oversupply of buildings. In other words, not all output gaps are born equal, amenable to the same remedies. During financial busts, after the financial system has been stabilized (crisis management), removing the obstacles that hold back growth is key. This means first and foremost facilitating balance sheet repair and implementing structural reforms (Borio, Vale, and van Peter 2010; Borio 2014a; BIS 2014, 2015).

---

[4]For these reasons, post-financial boom recessions are best regarded as "balance sheet recessions." The term was probably coined by Koo (2003). While the spirit is similar, in BIS work we have embedded it in a somewhat different analysis, which does not imply the same policy conclusions, especially with regard to fiscal policy (e.g., Borio 2014a; BIS 2014, 2015).

Finally, there is a need for macro models to go beyond the "one good" standard benchmark. To be sure, a number of models do, and the time-honored distinction between tradables and nontradables is the best known example. But the workhorse models that underlie policy are, in effect, one-good models. Unless we overcome this drawback, there is a risk of throwing out the baby with the bathwater.

The Costs of Deflation Revisited

Let me now turn to the third notion I wish to question: what might be called the deflation "bogeyman" (Rajan 2015). Is deflation always and everywhere very costly for output? This is indeed the premise that seems to have underlain monetary policy for quite some time now.

In fact, if one looks at the evidence carefully, the notion does not seem to hold water. Empirical work, some of it carried out at the BIS, had already reached this conclusion pre-crisis, leading to the distinction between "good" and "bad" deflations (e.g., Bordo and Redish 2004, Borio and Filardo 2004, Atkeson and Kehoe 2004, Bordo and Filardo 2005). A more comprehensive and systematic study we carried out this year has confirmed and extended this conclusion (Borio et al. 2015a).

What did we do? We used a newly constructed data set that spans more than 140 years (1870–2013), covers up to 38 economies, and includes equity and house prices as well as debt, although still not for all countries in all periods. We then apply a variety of statistical techniques to examine across monetary regimes the link between deflation and (per capita) output growth and the relative impact of deflation and asset price declines. We consider both transitory and, even more importantly, persistent deflations.

We reach three basic conclusions. First, before controlling for the behavior of asset prices, we find only a weak association between deflation and growth; the Great Depression is the main exception (Figure 4). Second, we find a stronger link with asset price declines, and controlling for them further weakens the link between deflations and growth. In fact, the link disappears even in the Great Depression (Figure 5). Finally, we find no evidence of a damaging interplay between deflation and debt (Fisher's "debt deflation"; Fisher 1933). By contrast, we do find evidence of a damaging interplay between

FIGURE 4

OUTPUT COST OF PERSISTENT GOODS AND SERVICES PRICE DEFLATIONS[a]

(THIRTY-EIGHT ECONOMIES,[b] 1870–2013, VARIABLE PEAK[c] YEAR = 100)

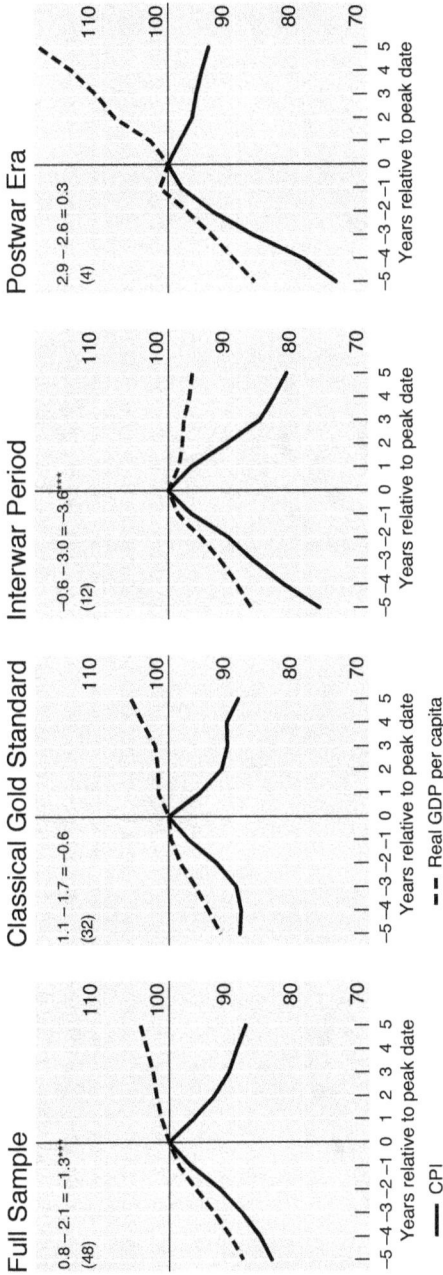

NOTES: The numbers in the graph indicate five-year averages of post- and pre-price peak growth in real GDP per capita (in percent) and the difference between the two periods (in percentage points); */**/*** denotes mean equality rejection with significance at the 10, 5, and 1 percent level. In parentheses is the number of peaks that are included in the calculations. The data included cover the peaks, with complete five-year trajectories not affected by observations from 1914–18 and 1939–45. For Spain, the Civil War observations are also excluded (1936–39).

[a]Simple average of the series of CPI and real GDP per capita readings five years before and after each peak for each economy, rebased with the peaks equal to 100 (denoted as year 0). [b]As listed in Borio et al. (2015a: Table 1). [c]Includes only persistent deflations in the price of goods and services (consumer prices) identified as periods following price peaks associated with a turning point in the five-year moving average and peak levels exceeding price index levels in the preceding and subsequent five years.

SOURCE: Borio et al. (2015a).

FIGURE 5
CHANGE IN PER CAPITA OUTPUT GROWTH AFTER PRICE PEAKS[a]
(IN PERCENTAGE POINTS[b])

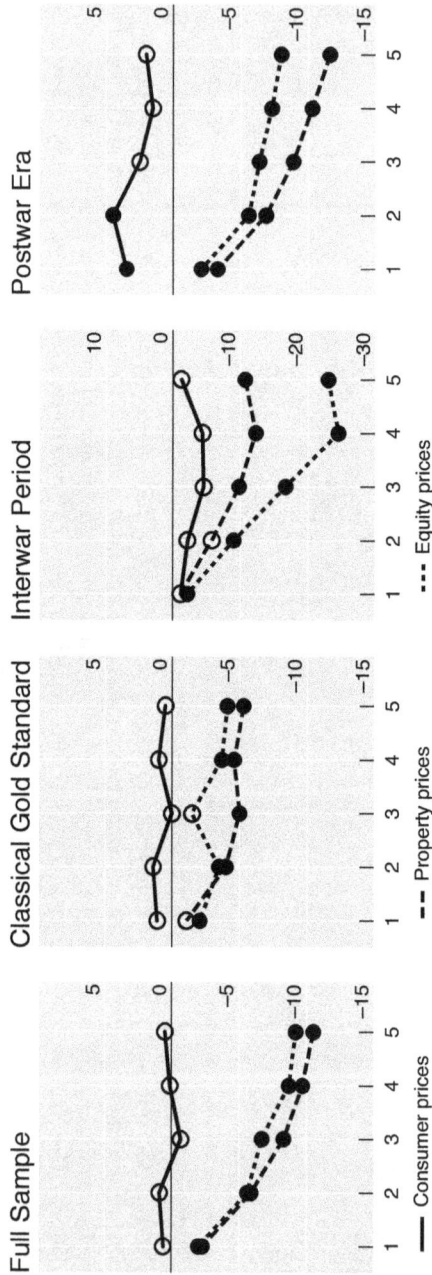

NOTES: The approach underlying the estimated effects shown in the graph is described in Borio et al. (2015a); a circle indicates an insignificant coefficient, and a filled circle indicates that a coefficient is significant at least at the 10 percent level. Estimated effects are conditional on sample means (country fixed effects) and on the effects of the respective other price peaks (e.g., the estimated change in h-period growth after CPI peaks is conditional on the estimated change after property and equity price peaks). For the respective country samples, see Borio et al. (2015a).
[a]The graph shows the estimated difference between h-period per capita output growth after and before price peak. [b]The estimated regression coefficients are multiplied by 100 in order to obtain the effect in percentage points.
SOURCE: Borio et al. (2015a).

private sector debt and property (house) prices, especially in the postwar period.

Some might argue that the recent Japanese experience contradicts this, but in fact it does not. The key is to adjust for demographics (growth per working age population), which cloud analyses based on headline growth figures and which are clearly exogenous. On this basis, Japan did very badly in the 1990s, when deflation had not yet set in but asset prices were collapsing following the outsize financial boom in the 1980s. And it did comparatively well in the 2000s, once the banking system got fixed and deflation set in, raising real interest rates as policy rates got stuck at the zero lower bound. While, on a per capita basis, average growth was roughly similar at some 0.8–0.9 percent in 1991–2000 and 2000–13, it rose from 1.0 percent to 1.6 percent on a per working age population basis. A comparison with the United States is quite telling. Between 2000 and 2013, cumulative growth per working age population exceeded 20 percent in Japan, compared with roughly 11 percent in the United States. This picture does not change if one excludes the Great Financial Crisis. Japan lost one decade, in the 1990s, not two.

How should we interpret these results? To my mind, they are consistent with the distinction between supply-driven and demand-driven deflations: the former depress prices while boosting output (i.e., they may be regarded as "good"); the latter coincide with both price declines and weak output (and, hence, may be regarded as "bad").[5] The results are also consistent with the different size and nature of the falls in the price level and asset prices: the former are typically smaller and essentially redistributional; the latter are typically much larger and are normally perceived as nondistributional.

From this viewpoint, there are grounds to believe that a sizable chunk of the secular disinflationary forces since the 1990s have been of the good variety. They may well reflect the globalization of the real economy and, possibly, technological innovation. The integration of China and former communist countries into the global economy has surely been critical. It has made labor and goods markets much more contestable, eroding producers' pricing power and labor's bargaining power as well as reducing the risk of upward wage-price spirals. BIS research has found evidence to that effect. It has uncovered a larger

---

[5]George Selgin was an early proponent of the distinction between "good" and "bad" deflation (see Selgin 1988, 1997).

role played by global factors at the expense of domestic ones in driving both wages and prices (Borio and Filardo 2007, BIS 2014).[6]

This analysis hints at some broader policy conclusions. It suggests that it may be worth rebalancing the policy focus, away from exclusive attention to deflation threats and toward financial cycle threats.

Reinterpreting the Long-Term Decline in Real Interest Rates

Consider next the implications of the analysis for how to interpret the long-term decline in real interest rates (Figure 6). The analysis helps provide a complementary interpretation to the received one. It suggests that the decline is not just an equilibrium phenomenon but, in part, a disequilibrium one.

In the received view, central banks and market participants have been pushing short- and long-term real interest rates toward their equilibrium, Wicksellian level. In turn, this natural rate is determined by deep exogenous forces, such as technology, demographics, and income distribution. A common narrative is that these have led to a structural, or at least long-lasting, deficiency in aggregate demand.

In the view offered here, the long-term decline reflects, in part, asymmetrical monetary policy over successive financial and business cycles. Global disinflationary forces, in the wake of the globalization of the real economy and technological innovations, have kept a lid on inflation. Monetary policy has failed to lean against unsustainable financial booms. The booms and, in particular, subsequent busts have caused long-term economic damage. Policy has responded very aggressively and, above all, persistently to the bust, sowing the seeds of the next problem. Over time, this has imparted a downward bias to interest rates and an upward one to debt, as indicated by the steady rise in total debt-to-GDP ratios (Figure 6).

This can contribute to a kind of "debt trap" (Borio and Disyatat 2014, BIS 2014). Over time, policy runs out of ammunition. And it becomes harder to raise rates without causing economic damage, owing to large debts and the distortions generated in the real economy. It is as if the whole economic system adjusted to such low rates

---

[6]That said, there is no consensus on this point. While some empirical studies have reached similar conclusions (e.g., Bianchi and Civelli 2013, Ciccarelli and Mojon 2010, Eickmeier and Moll 2009), others have not (e.g., Ihrig et al. 2010 and Martínez-García and Wynne 2012).

FIGURE 6

INTEREST RATES SINK AS DEBT SOARS

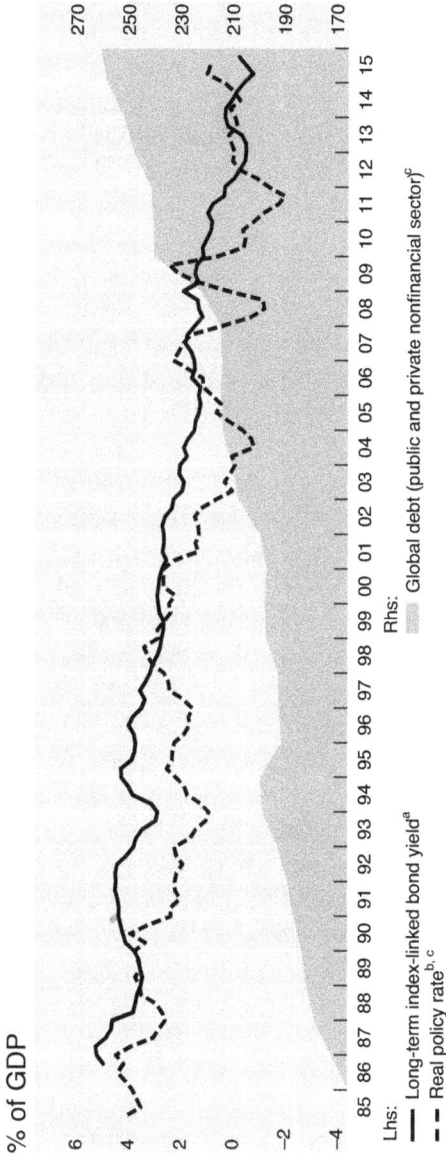

% of GDP

270
250
230
210
190
170

6
4
2
0
-2
-4

85 86 87 88 89 90 91 92 93 94 95 96 97 98 99 00 01 02 03 04 05 06 07 08 09 10 11 12 13 14 15

Lhs:
— Long-term index-linked bond yield[a]
- - - Real policy rate[b,c]

Rhs:
Global debt (public and private nonfinancial sector)[c]

[a]From 1998, simple average of France, the United Kingdom, and the United States; otherwise, only the United Kingdom. [b]Nominal policy rate less consumer price inflation. [c]Aggregate based on weighted averages for G7 economies plus China based on rolling GDP and PPP exchange rates. 2015 figure is based on Q1 or Q2 data.

SOURCES: IMF, *World Economic Outlook*; OECD, *Economic Outlook*; national data; BIS calculations.

and became less tolerant of higher ones, at least without some transitional pain. This process gives rise to a new, insidious form of "time inconsistency," whereby policy steps may appear reasonable when taken in isolation but, as a sequence, lead policy astray.

The bottom line is that, over sufficiently long horizons, low interest rates become to some extent self-validating. Too low rates in the past are one reason—not the only reason—for such low rates today. In other words, policy rates are not simply passively reflecting some deep exogenous forces; they are also helping to shape the economic environment policymakers take as given ("exogenous") when tomorrow becomes today.

Here the international monetary and financial system plays a key role (Borio 2014b, BIS 2015), because successive crises need not occur in the same country, although sometimes they have. Low rates in countries that are fighting a financial bust may induce problems elsewhere. Policymakers in the struggling economies try very hard to stimulate demand but get little traction through domestic channels, for the reasons mentioned before. As a result, exchange rate depreciation becomes the key transmission mechanism. This induces unwelcome exchange rate appreciation in countries that may also be in a bust or at different points in their financial cycle. Appreciation pressure is resisted by keeping interest rates lower than otherwise and/or by intervening in the exchange rate market (Rajan 2014). Thus, easing begets easing.[7]

This helps explain a couple of developments taking place before our very eyes. It is a reason why policy rates appear unusually low for the world as a whole regardless of benchmarks. Figure 7 illustrates this point with the help of a range of Taylor rules (e.g., Hofmann and Bogdanova 2012). And it is also a reason why for quite some time now we have been seeing signs of the build-up of dangerous financial imbalances in countries less affected by the crisis, especially emerging market economies (EMEs) (including very large ones), but also in some advanced economies less affected by the crisis (BIS 2014, 2015). Commodity exporters have been very prominent here, in the

[7]Quite apart from policy responses to spillovers, there are several mechanisms through which the international monetary and financial system can amplify financial booms and busts, including the outsize reach of international currencies and the ebbs and flows of global liquidity. For a fuller discussion, see Borio (2014b) and BIS (2015). For specific aspects, see also Borio and Disyatat (2011); Shin (2012, 2013); Rey (2013); and McCauley, McGuire, and Sushko (2015).

FIGURE 7
UNUSUALLY ACCOMMODATIVE GLOBAL
MONETARY CONDITIONS[a]
(IN PERCENT)

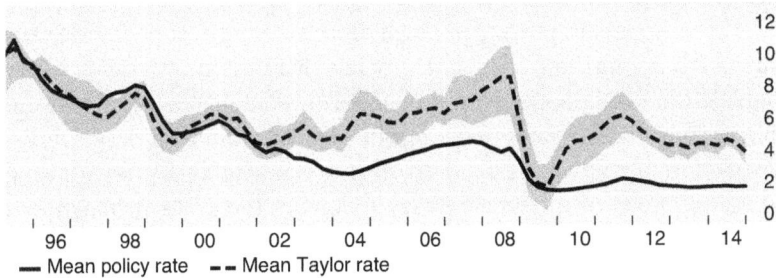

— Mean policy rate -- Mean Taylor rate

NOTES: The Taylor rates are calculated as $i = r^\circ + \pi^\circ + 1.5(\pi-\pi^\circ) + 0.5y$, where π is a measure of inflation, y is a measure of the output gap, π° is the inflation target, and r° is the long-run real interest rate, here proxied by real trend output growth. The graph shows the mean and the range of the Taylor rates of different inflation/output gap combinations, obtained by combining four measures of inflation (headline, core, GDP deflator, and consensus headline forecasts) with four measures of the output gap (obtained using Hodrick-Prescott (HP) filter, segmented linear trend and unobserved components techniques, and IMF estimates). π° is set equal to the official inflation target/objective, and otherwise to the sample average or trend inflation estimated through a standard HP filter. See Hofmann and Bogdanova (2012).

[a]Weighted averages based on 2005 PPP weights. "Global" comprises all economies listed here. Advanced economies: Australia, Canada, Denmark, the euro area, Japan, New Zealand, Norway, Sweden, Switzerland, the United Kingdom, and the United States. Emerging market economies: Argentina, Brazil, Chile, China, Chinese Taipei, Colombia, the Czech Republic, Hong Kong SAR, Hungary, India, Indonesia, Israel, Korea, Malaysia, Mexico, Peru, the Philippines, Poland, Singapore, South Africa, and Thailand.

SOURCES: IMF, *International Financial Statistics* and *World Economic Outlook*; Bloomberg; CEIC; Consensus Economics; Datastream; national data; BIS calculations.

wake of the exceptionally strong commodity price booms. Recently, these financial booms have matured and begun to turn. If serious financial strains did materialize, spillbacks to the rest of the world could spread weakness across the globe: the heft of EMEs has greatly increased over the last couple of decades, from around one third to almost half of world GDP.

Adjusting Monetary Policy Frameworks

This analysis suggests that it would be important to adjust monetary policy frameworks to take financial booms and busts systematically into account (Borio 2014c, BIS 2014, 2015).

This amounts to putting in place more symmetrical policies across financial booms and busts. It means leaning more deliberately against financial booms even if near-term inflation stays low and stable or may be below numerical objectives, and easing less aggressively and, above all, persistently during financial busts, recognizing the limitations of monetary policy following the crisis management phase. Taken together, these adjustments should help reduce the risk of a persistent easing bias that can lead to a progressive loss of policy room for maneuver over time and entrench instability and chronic weakness in the global economy.

Three common objections have been leveled against such adjustments. While they are well founded, I believe none of them is a showstopper.[8] The first is that it is hard to identify financial imbalances as they develop. This is true, but a whole apparatus is now in place to do precisely that in the context of macroprudential frameworks. There is a certain tension, to say the least, in arguing that macroprudential policies should be actively used while highlighting measurement difficulties for monetary policy. Moreover, it is not sufficiently acknowledged that traditional monetary policy benchmarks are also very hard to measure: think of output gaps, nonaccelerating inflation rates of unemployment (NAIRUs), and natural interest rates, just to name a few. This is precisely why the behavior of inflation ends up being the real deciding factor when measuring them—the practice that proved so dangerous pre-crisis. In fact, BIS research has found that financial cycle information—credit and property price growth—can assist in obtaining a better measure of potential output in real time (Figure 8), helping to overcome the deficiencies of traditional approaches (see, e.g., Borio, Disyatat, and Juselius 2013). Our failure to recognize the limitations of traditional monetary yardsticks is probably more a reflection of our familiarity with them than of their inherent properties. Familiarity breeds complacency.

---

[8]For a recent analysis that reviews the literature and reaches more skeptical conclusions about the role of monetary policy, see IMF (2015). See also G30 (2015) for a less skeptical view.

FIGURE 8
U.S. OUTPUT GAPS: EX POST AND REAL-TIME ESTIMATES
(IN PERCENT)

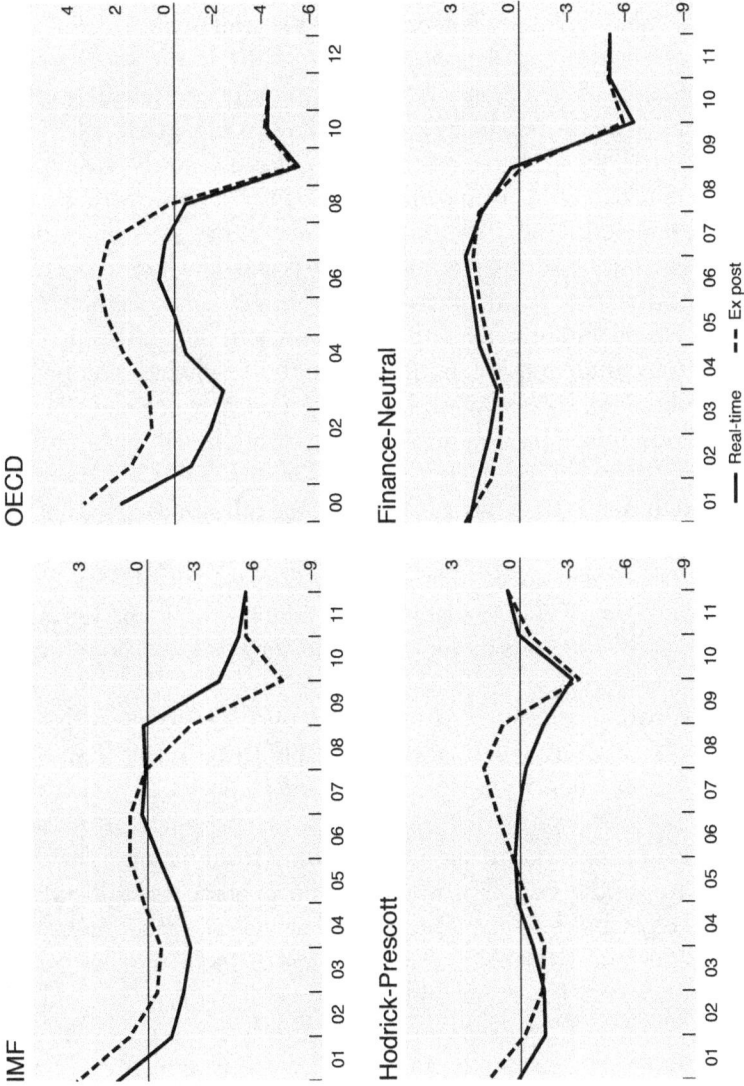

NOTES: For each time t, the "real-time" estimates are based only on the sample up to that point in time. The "ex post" estimates are based on the full sample.
SOURCE: Borio, Disyatat, and Juselius (2013).

The second objection is that it is better to rely on macroprudential policy and leave monetary policy to focus on inflation—a sort of "separation principle." To my mind, this would be too imprudent (Borio 2014d). Even where they have been activated vigorously, macroprudential measures have not prevented the emergence of the usual signs of financial imbalances, such as in EMEs. And as a means of reining in financial booms, as opposed to building resilience, macroprudential tools operate in a similar way to monetary policy: they restrain credit expansion, asset price increases, and risk-taking (e.g., Borio and Zhu 2012, Bruno and Shin 2014). To be sure, they can be more targeted. And they can help relieve pressure on currency appreciation, which may in turn fuel risk-taking where foreign currency borrowing is widespread (Borio, McCauley, and McGuire 2011; Bruno and Shin 2014; Bruno, Shim, and Shin 2015). Even so, there is a certain tension in pressing on the accelerator and brake at the same time, such as when loosening monetary policy while seeking to offset its impact on financial instability through macroprudential measures.

The third objection is that the proposed adjustments are not consistent with inflation objectives. They require too much tolerance for persistent deviations of inflation from targets. This, in turn, could undermine credibility to secure price stability. No doubt, the adjustments pose serious communication challenges: they should not be underestimated.

Still, two responses are possible. For one, it is not clear that central banks have exploited all the flexibility that current frameworks allow. Even when numerical targets are in place, the frameworks often make it explicit that the permitted persistence of deviations depends on factors driving inflation away from targets. The reluctance to use the flexibility available reflects perceived tradeoffs and hence costs and benefits. These could change if, for instance, views about the effectiveness of macroprudential tools and the costs of deflation evolved, possibly under the force of events. Time will tell.

In addition, if mandates are seen as overly constraining the room for maneuver, revisiting them should not be taboo. After all, mandates are a means to an end. That said, the analytical lens through which one perceives how the economy works matters more than mandates. It is easy to see how adding an explicit financial stability objective could sometimes make matters worse. For instance, even if inflation is rising briskly, it could be taken as a reason not to tighten policy in order to avoid short-term damage to a weak banking system: such a response would be myopic. Given where we are, the priority is to use the existing room for maneuver to the full; revisiting mandates should be a last resort.

Conclusion

There are good reasons to question three deeply held beliefs underpinning monetary policy received wisdom. First, defining equilibrium (or natural) rates purely in terms of the equality of actual and potential output and price stability in any given period is too narrow an approach. An equilibrium rate should also be consistent with *sustainable* financial and macroeconomic stability—two sides of the same coin. Here, I highlighted the role of financial booms and busts, or financial cycles.

Second, money (monetary policy) is not neutral over medium- to long-term horizons relevant for policy—that is, 10–20 years or so, if not longer. This is precisely because it contributes to financial booms and busts, which give rise to long-lasting, if not permanent, economic costs. Here I highlighted the neglected impact of resource misallocations on productivity growth.

Finally, deflations are not always costly in terms of output. The evidence indicates that the link comes largely from the Great Depression and, even then, it disappears if one controls for asset price declines. Here I highlighted the costs of declining asset prices, especially property prices, and the distinction between supply-driven and demand-driven deflations.

From this, I drew two conclusions. First, the long-term decline in *real* interest rates since at least the 1990s may well be, in part, a disequilibrium phenomenon, not consistent with lasting financial, macroeconomic, and monetary stability. Here I highlighted the asymmetrical monetary policy response to financial booms and busts, which induces an easing bias over time.

Second, there is a need to adjust monetary policy frameworks to take financial booms and busts systematically into account. This, in turn, would avoid that easing bias and the risk of a debt trap. Here I highlighted that it is imprudent to rely exclusively on macroprudential measures to constrain the build-up of financial imbalances. Macroprudential policy must be part of the answer, but it cannot be the whole answer.

I am, of course, fully aware that questioning deep-seated beliefs is a risky business. I do not pretend to have all the answers. But I do believe it is essential to explore these beliefs critically and to have a proper debate. The stakes for the economic profession and the global economy are simply too high. And, as Mark Twain once famously said: "It ain't what you don't know that gets you into trouble. It's what you know for sure that just ain't so."

References

Atkeson, A., and Kehoe, P. (2004) "Deflation and Depression: Is There an Empirical Link?" *American Economic Review* 94 (2): 99–103.

Ball, L. (2014) "Long-Term Damage from the Great Recession in OECD Countries." *European Journal of Economics and Economic Policies* 11 (2): 149–60.

Bank for International Settlements (BIS) (2014) *84th Annual Report* (June).

_____ (2015) *85th Annual Report* (June).

Basel Committee on Banking Supervision (BCBS) (2010) *An Assessment of the Long-Term Economic Impact of Stronger Capital and Liquidity Requirements* (July).

Bean, C.; Broda, C.; Ito, T.; and Kroszner, R. (2015) *Low for Long? Causes and Consequences of Persistently Low Interest Rates. Geneva Reports on the World Economy* 17. International Center for Monetary and Banking Studies. Geneva: CEPR Press.

Bernanke, B. (2005) "The Global Saving Glut and the U.S. Current Account Deficit." Sandridge Lecture, Richmond, Va., March 10.

Bianchi, F., and Civelli, A. (2013) "Globalization and Inflation: Structural Evidence from a Time-Varying VAR Approach." Economic Research Initiatives at Duke (ERID), Working Paper No. 157 (July).

Bordo, M. D., and Filardo, A. (2005) "Deflation and Monetary Policy in a Historical Perspective: Remembering the Past or Being Condemned to Repeat It?" *Economic Policy* 20 (44): 799–844.

Bordo, M. D., and Redish, A. (2004) "Is Deflation Depressing? Evidence from the Classical Gold Standard." In R. Burdekin and P. Siklos (eds.), *Deflation: Current and Historical Perspectives.* New York: Cambridge University Press.

Borio, C. (2014a) "The Financial Cycle and Macroeconomics: What Have We Learnt?" *Journal of Banking and Finance* 45 (August): 182–98. Also available as BIS Working Paper No. 395 (December 2012).

_____ (2014b) "The International Monetary and Financial System: Its Achilles Heel and What to Do About It." BIS Working Paper No. 456 (August).

_____ (2014c) "Monetary Policy and Financial Stability: What Role in Prevention and Recovery?" *Capitalism and Society* 9 (2), article 1. Also available as BIS Working Paper No. 440 (January 2014).

_____ (2014d) "Macroprudential Frameworks: (Too) Great Expectations?" *Central Banking Journal*, 25th anniversary issue (August). Also available in BIS Speeches.

Borio, C., and Disyatat, P. (2011) "Global Imbalances and the Financial Crisis: Link or No Link?" BIS Working Paper No. 346 (May). Revised and extended version of "Global Imbalances and the Financial Crisis: Reassessing the Role of International Finance." *Asian Economic Policy Review* 5 (2010): 198–216.

_____ (2014) "Low Interest Rates and Secular Stagnation: Is Debt a Missing Link?" VoxEU.org (25 June): www.voxeu.org /article/low-interest-rates-secular-stagnation-and-debt.

Borio, C.; Disyatat, P.; and Juselius, M. (2013) "Rethinking Potential Output: Embedding Information about the Financial Cycle." BIS Working Paper No. 404 (February).

Borio, C., and Filardo, A. (2004) "Looking Back at the International Deflation Record." *North American Journal of Economics and Finance* 15 (3): 287–311. Also available, in extended form, as "Back to the Future? Assessing the Deflation Record." BIS Working Paper No. 152 (March 2004).

_____ (2007) "Globalisation and Inflation: New Cross-Country Evidence on the Global Determinants of Domestic Inflation." BIS Working Paper No. 227 (May).

Borio, C.; Erdem, M.; Filardo, A.; and Hofmann, B. (2015a) "The Costs of Deflations: A Historical Perspective." *BIS Quarterly Review* (March): 31–54.

Borio, C.; Kharroubi, E.; Upper, C.; and Zampolli, F. (2015b) "Labour Reallocation and Productivity Dynamics: Financial Causes, Real Consequences." BIS Working Paper No. 534 (December).

Borio, C.; McCauley, R.; and McGuire, P. (2011) "Global Credit and Domestic Credit Booms." *BIS Quarterly Review* (September): 43–57.

Borio, C.; Vale, B.; and von Peter, G. (2010) "Resolving the Current Financial Crisis: Are We Heeding the Lessons of the Nordics?" *Moneda y Crédito*, No. 230: 7–49. Also available, in extended form, as BIS Working Paper No. 311 (June 2010).

Borio, C., and Zhu, H. (2012) "Capital Regulation, Risk-Taking and Monetary Policy: A Missing Link in the Transmission Mechanism?" *Journal of Financial Stability* 8: 236–51. Also available as BIS Working Paper No. 268 (December 2008).

Bruno, V.; Shim, I.; and Shin, H. S. (2015) "Comparative Assessment of Macroprudential Policies." BIS Working Paper No. 502 (June).

Bruno, V., and Shin, H. S. (2014) "Cross-Border Banking and Global Liquidity." BIS Working Paper No. 458 (September).

Cecchetti, S., and Kharroubi, E. (2015) "Why Does Financial Sector Growth Crowd Out Real Economic Growth?" BIS Working Paper No. 490 (February).

Ciccarelli, M., and Mojon, B. (2010) "Global Inflation." *Review of Economics and Statistics* 92 (3): 453–66.

Drehmann, M.; Borio, C.; and Tsatsaronis, K. (2012) "Characterising the Financial Cycle: Don't Lose Sight of the Medium Term!" BIS Working Paper No. 380 (November).

Drehmann, M., and Juselius, M. (2015) "Leverage Dynamics and the Real Burden of Debt." BIS Working Paper No. 501 (May).

Eichengreen, B., and Mitchener, K. (2003) "The Great Depression as a Credit Boom Gone Wrong." BIS Working Paper No. 137 (September).

Eickmeier, S., and Moll, K. (2009) "The Global Dimension of Inflation: Evidence from Factor-Augmented Phillips Curves." ECB Working Paper No. 1011.

Fisher, I. (1933) "The Debt-Deflation Theory of Great Depressions." *Econometrica* 1 (4): 337–57.

Group of Thirty (G30) (2015) *Fundamentals of Central Banking: Lessons from the Crisis.* Washington: G30 (October).

Hofmann, B., and Bogdanova, B. (2012) "Taylor Rules and Monetary Policy: A Global 'Great Deviation'?" *BIS Quarterly Review* (September): 37–49.

Ihrig, J.; Kamin, S.; Lindner, D.; and Márquez, J. (2010) "Some Simple Tests of the Globalization and Inflation Hypothesis." *International Finance* (December).

International Monetary Fund (IMF) (2015) "Monetary Policy and Financial Stability." *IMF Policy Papers* (September).

Koo, R. (2003) *Balance Sheet Recession: Japan's Struggle with Uncharted Economics and Its Global Implications.* Singapore: John Wiley.

Martínez-García, E., and Wynne, M. (2012) "Global Slack As a Determinant of U.S. Inflation." Federal Reserve Bank of Dallas, Globalization and Monetary Policy Institute Working Paper No. 123.

McCauley R.; McGuire, P.; and Sushko, V. (2015) "Global Dollar Credit: Links to U.S. Monetary Policy and Leverage." *Economic Policy* 30 (82): 189–229. Also available as BIS Working Paper No. 483 (January 2015).

Rajan, R. (2014) "Competitive Monetary Easing: Is It Yesterday Once More?" Remarks at the Brookings Institution, April 10.

_____ (2015) Panel remarks, IMF Conference on "Rethinking Macro Policy III: Progress or Confusion?" Washington, April 15–16.

Reinhart, C., and Reinhart, V. (2010) "After the Fall." NBER Working Paper No. 16334 (September).

Rey, H. (2013) "Dilemma Not Trilemma: The Global Financial Cycle and Monetary Policy Independence." Paper presented at the Federal Reserve Bank of Kansas City Economic Policy Symposium on "Global Dimensions of Unconventional Monetary Policy," Jackson Hole, August 22–24.

Rogoff, K. (2015) "Debt Supercycle, Not Secular Stagnation." VoxEU.org (22 April): www.voxeu.org/article/debt-supercycle-not-secular-stagnation.

Selgin, G. (1988) *The Theory of Free Banking: Money Supply under Competitive Note Issue.* Lanham., Md.: Rowman and Littlefield.

_____ (1997) *Less than Zero: The Case for a Falling Price Level in a Growing Economy.* IEA Hobart Paper No. 132. London: Institute of Economic Affairs.

Shin, H. S. (2012) "Global Banking Glut and Loan Risk Premium." Mundell-Fleming Lecture. *IMF Economic Review* 60 (2): 155–92.

_____ (2013) "The Second Phase of Global Liquidity and Its Impact on Emerging Economies." *Proceedings of the Federal Reserve Bank of San Francisco Asia Economic Policy Conference* (November): 1–10.

Summers, L. (2014) "Reflections on the 'New Secular Stagnation Hypothesis.'" In C. Teulings and R. Baldwin (eds.) *Secular Stagnation: Facts, Causes and Cures.* VoxEU.org eBook, CEPR Press.

3

UNDERSTANDING THE INTERVENTIONIST IMPULSE OF THE MODERN CENTRAL BANK
Jeffrey M. Lacker

The financial crisis of 2007 and 2008 was a watershed event for the Federal Reserve and other central banks. The extraordinary actions they took have been described, alternatively, as a natural extension of monetary policy to extreme circumstances or as a problematic exercise in credit allocation. I have expressed my view elsewhere that much of the Fed's response to the crisis falls in the latter category rather than the former (Lacker 2010). Rather than reargue that case, I want to take this opportunity to reflect on some of the institutional reasons behind the prevailing propensity of many modern central banks to intervene in credit markets.

The Impulse to Reallocate Credit

There is widespread agreement among economists that a vigorous monetary policy response can be necessary at times to prevent a contraction from becoming a deflationary spiral. Financial market turmoil often sparks a flight to monetary assets. In the 19th and 20th centuries, this often took the form of shifts out of deposits and into notes and specie. Under a fractional reserve banking system, this necessitates a deflationary contraction in the overall money supply

Jeffrey M. Lacker is President of the Federal Reserve Bank of Richmond. This article is reprinted from the *Cato Journal*, Vol. 32, No. 2 (Spring/Summer 2012). The views expressed herein are the author's and are not necessarily those of the Federal Reserve System. He thanks John Weinberg for his assistance.

unless offset through clearinghouse or central bank expansion of the note supply. In modern financial panics, banks often seek to hoard reserve balances, which again would be contractionary absent an accommodating increase in the central bank reserve supply. In both cases, the need is for an increase in outstanding central bank monetary *liabilities*.

The Fed's response during the financial crisis was not purely monetary, however. In the first phase—from the fall of 2007 through the summer of 2008—its credit actions were sterilized; lending through the Term Auction Facility and in support of the merger of Bear Stearns and JPMorgan Chase was offset by sales of U.S. Treasury securities from the Fed's portfolio.[1] It wasn't until September 2008 that the supply of excess reserves began to increase significantly. This expansion was accomplished through the acquisition of an expanding set of private assets—loans to banks and other financial institutions and later mortgage-backed securities and debt issued by Fannie Mae and Freddie Mac. While some observers describe this phase of the Fed's response as a standard monetary expansion in the face of a deflationary threat, the Fed's own characterization often emphasized instead the intent to provide direct assistance to dysfunctional segments of the credit markets. Clearly, an equivalent expansion of reserve supply could have been achieved via purchases of U.S. Treasury securities—that is, without credit allocation. Like the Fed, the European Central Bank and other central banks have also pursued credit allocation in response to the crisis.

The impulse to reallocate credit certainly reflects an earnest desire to fix perceived credit market problems that seem within the central bank's power to fix. My sense is that Federal Reserve credit policy was motivated by a sincere belief that central banks have a civic duty to alleviate significant ex post inefficiencies in credit markets. But credit allocation can redirect resources from taxpayers to financial market investors and, over time, can expand moral hazard and distort the allocation of capital. This implies a difficult and contentious cost-benefit calculation. But no matter how the net benefits are assessed, central bank intervention in credit markets will have distributional consequences.

---

[1]Such sterilized actions are equivalent to issuing new U.S. Treasury debt to the public and using the proceeds to fund the lending.

The Threat to Central Bank Independence

Central bank credit allocation is therefore bound to be controversial. Indeed, the actions taken by the Fed over the last few years have generated a level of invective that has not been seen in a very long time. Critics have sought to exploit the resentment of credit market rescues for partisan political advantage. While it is easy to deplore politically motivated attempts to influence Fed policy, we need to recognize the extent to which some measure of antagonism is an understandable consequence of the Fed's own credit policy initiatives.

The inevitable controversy surrounding central bank intervention in credit markets is one reason many observers have long advocated keeping central banks out of the business of credit allocation (see Goodfriend and King 1988, Hetzel 1997, Goodfriend and Lacker 1999, Goodfriend 2001, and Broaddus and Goodfriend 2001). Central bank lending undermines the integrity of the fiscal appropriations process, and while U.S. fiscal policymaking may not inspire much admiration these days, it *is* subject to the checks and balances provided for by the Constitution. Contentious disputes about which credit market segments receive support, and which do not, can entangle the central bank in political conflicts that threaten the independence of monetary policymaking.

The independence that the modern central bank has to control the monetary policy interest rate emerged in stages following the end of World War II. The Treasury-Fed Accord of 1951 freed the Federal Reserve from the wartime obligation to depress the Treasury's borrowing costs. The collapse of the gold standard in the early 1970s and the attendant bouts of inflation led the Fed in 1979 to assert responsibility for low inflation as a long-term objective of monetary policy (Broaddus and Goodfriend 2001: 8). The independent commitment of central banks to low inflation provides a nominal anchor to substitute for the anchor formerly provided by the gold standard.

The substantial measure of independence central banks have been given was a key element in their relative success at sustaining low inflation over the last few decades. In fact, many countries have adopted frameworks that hold their central banks accountable for a price stability goal, while allowing them to set interest rate policy independently in pursuit of their goals. This *instrument independence* has been critical to insulating monetary policymaking from election-related political pressures that can detract from longer-term objectives.

The cornerstone of central bank independence is the ability to control the amount of the monetary liabilities it supplies to the public. But as a by-product, many central banks retain the ability to independently control the composition of their assets as well. For many modern central banks, standard policy in normal times is to restrict asset holdings to their own country's government debt. Some hold gold as well, a vestige of the gold standard. In addition, many make short-term loans to banks, either to meet temporary liquidity needs or as part of clearing and settlement operations, both vestiges of the origin of central banks as nationalized clearinghouses.

The ability of a central bank to intervene in credit markets using the asset side of its balance sheet creates an inevitable tension. The desire of the executive and legislative branches to provide governmental assistance to particular credit market participants can rise dramatically in times of financial market stress. At such times, the power of a central bank to do fiscal policy essentially outside the safeguards of the constitutional process for appropriations makes it an inviting target for other government officials. Central bank lending is often the path of least resistance in a financial crisis. The resulting political entanglements, though, as we have seen, create risks for the independence of monetary policy.

A Time Consistency Problem

At the heart of this tension is a classic time consistency problem. Central bank rescues serve the short-term goal of protecting investors from the pain of unanticipated credit market losses, but they dilute market discipline and distort future risk-taking incentives. Over time, small "one-off" interventions set precedents that encourage greater risk-taking and thus increase the odds of future distress. Policymakers then feel boxed in and obligated to intervene in ever larger ways, perpetuating a vicious cycle of government safety net expansion.

The conundrum facing central banks, then, is that the balance sheet independence that proved crucial in the fight to tame inflation is itself a handicap in the pursuit of financial market stability. The latitude the typical central bank has to intervene in credit markets weakens its ability to discourage expectations of future rescues and by doing so enhance market discipline.

Containing the Interventionist Impulse

Solving this conundrum and containing the impulse to intervene requires one of two approaches. A central bank could seek to build and maintain a reputation for not intervening, in much the way the Fed and other central banks established credibility for a commitment to low inflation in the 1980s. Alternatively, explicit legislative measures could constrain central bank lending. The Dodd-Frank Act took steps in this direction by banning Federal Reserve loans to individual nonbank entities. But Reserve banks retain the power to lend to individual depository institutions and to intervene in particular credit market segments in "unusual and exigent circumstances" through credit programs with "broad-based eligibility."[2] In addition, the Fed can channel credit by purchasing the obligations of government-sponsored enterprises, such as Fannie Mae and Freddie Mac.

Constraining central bank lending powers would appear to conflict with the popular perception that serving as a "lender of last resort" is intrinsic to central banking. But even here, I think our historical doctrines and practices should not escape reconsideration. The notion of the central bank as a lender of last resort derives from an era of commodity money standard, when central bank lending in a crisis was the most effective way to expand currency supply to meet a sudden increase in demand. Indeed, the preamble to the Federal Reserve Act says its purpose is "to furnish an elastic currency," not to furnish an elastic supply of credit. The Fed could easily manage the supply of monetary assets through purchases and sales of U.S. Treasury securities only.[3] While it might sound extreme, I believe that a regime in which the Federal Reserve is restricted to hold only U.S. Treasury securities purchased on the open market is worthy of consideration (see Goodfriend and King 1988, Schwartz 1992, Goodfriend 2001, and Broaddus and Goodfriend 2001).

---

[2] Such programs now require the approval of the Secretary of the Treasury.

[3] The market supply of such securities is likely to be quite ample for some time to come. But even if the supply should shrink, as it did a decade ago, the Treasury could arrange to issue in sufficient quantities to allow the Fed to conduct monetary policy on a Treasuries-only basis. See Broaddus and Goodfriend (2001).

It might seem easy to criticize such a regime by reference to what it would have prevented the Fed from doing in the recent crisis. But that's the wrong frame of reference, I believe—it's an ex post, rather than an ex ante, perspective. Such a regime, if credible, would over time force changes in market practices that would alter the likelihood and magnitude of crises and the behavior of private market arrangements during a crisis. It would strengthen market discipline and incentivize institutions to operate with more capital and less short-term debt funding—changes we are now trying to achieve through regulatory means. The relative costs and benefits of such a regime may be difficult to map out conclusively. But I believe this tradeoff is well worth studying.

Conclusion

My former colleagues Al Broaddus and Marvin Goodfriend (2001: 6) have argued that the design of central bank asset policy is "part of the unfinished business of building a modern, independent Federal Reserve." The 1951 Treasury-Fed Accord gave the Fed independent control of its liabilities, a necessary ingredient in monetary policy independence. But the accompanying power to use the Fed's asset portfolio to intervene in credit markets is a threat to that independence and a threat to financial stability. Sorting out the conundrum of central bank asset policy should be high on the agenda for all those interested in improving the practice of central banking.

References

Broaddus, J. A. Jr., and Goodfriend, M. (2001) "What Assets Should the Federal Reserve Buy?" Federal Reserve Bank of Richmond *Economic Quarterly* 87 (1): 7–22.

Goodfriend, M. (2001) "Why We Need an 'Accord' for Federal Reserve Credit Policy: A Note." Federal Reserve Bank of Richmond *Economic Quarterly* 87 (1): 23–32.

Goodfriend, M., and King, R. G. (1988) "Financial Deregulation, Monetary Policy, and Central Banking." Federal Reserve Bank of Richmond *Economic Review* 74 (3): 3–12.

Goodfriend, M., and Lacker, J. M. (1999) "Limited Commitment and Central Bank Lending." Federal Reserve Bank of Richmond *Economic Quarterly* 85 (4): 1–27.

Hetzel, R. L. (1997) "The Case for a Monetary Rule in a Constitutional Democracy." Federal Reserve Bank of Richmond *Economic Quarterly* 83 (2): 45–65.

Lacker, J. M. (2010) "The Regulatory Response to the Crisis: An Early Assessment." Speech at the Institute for International Economic Policy and the International Monetary Fund Institute, Washington, D.C. (May 26).

Schwartz, A. J. (1992) "The Misuse of the Fed's Discount Window." Federal Reserve Bank of St. Louis *Economic Review* 74 (5): 58–69.

4

THE FED'S FATAL CONCEIT
John A. Allison

I strongly believe that the recent financial crisis, ensuing recession, and slow recovery were primarily caused by government policy. The Federal Reserve made some very bad monetary decisions that created a bubble, i.e., a massive malinvestment. The bubble ended up being focused in the housing market largely because of government affordable housing policies—specifically, the actions of Freddie Mac and Fannie Mae, government-sponsored enterprises that would not exist in a free market. When Freddie and Fannie failed, they owed $5.5 trillion including $2 trillion in affordable housing (subprime) loans. It's true that a number of banks made serious mistakes, and I would have let them fail, but their mistakes were secondary and within the context of government policy.

I've known many people in the Federal Reserve, in monetary policy. They are very smart people. They are highly committed people. However, in my experience, they are guilty of what F. A. Hayek (1989) called "the fatal conceit"—that is, the belief that smart people can do the impossible. I don't care how smart you are or how great your mathematical models are, you cannot coordinate the economic activity of seven billion people on this planet.

The real issue is: What does government policy incentivize real-world human beings to do? I'm going to share with you my own experiences in that regard and also my insights into the actions of other financial company CEOs.

John A. Allison is an Executive in Residence at the Wake Forest School of Business and former chairman and CEO of BB&T Corporation. This article is reprinted from the *Cato Journal*, Vol. 32, No. 2 (Spring/Summer 2012).

The Federal Reserve: A Banker's Perspective

As a banker, I see the Fed as having three primary roles: (1) to control the payments system, (2) act as the number-one regulator, and, of course, (3) conduct monetary policy.

The Payments System

There is no private payments system in the United States. The payments system is controlled by the Fed and, ultimately, the so-called "shadow banking" system has to get back to the payments system. Troubles in the monetary economy, by definition, are caused by the Federal Reserve.

The Fed controls the clearing mechanism for the banks in the United States. The reason it does so is because the Fed subsidizes the banking business, especially small banks and nonbanks, who are inefficient providers. This arrangement has slowed technological advances in the banking industry because the big banks have to wait for the little banks and the nonbanks to be able to implement new technology. Furthermore, it has caused a lot of quality control problems because many nonbanks get a free ride into the payments system. Typically, privacy issues aren't created by banks—they are created by nonbanks using the Fed's operating system. It's a perfect analogy with the post office. You can compare the post office to FedEx and UPS. In fact, if you think the post office is a good thing, you ought to feel really good about the Fed controlling the clearing mechanism. The good news is that the post office is going to go out of business because of e-mail, and the Fed clearing system is going to basically go away largely because of electronic transactions.

Regulation

Regulation is a huge subject. It is also related to monetary policy and sometimes people disconnect the two and forget about the impact of the regulatory role on the Fed's effectiveness. First, the foundation for regulation in the banking industry is FDIC insurance. FDIC insurance is used as the excuse to justify many regulations because the banks are being "protected by the federal government." In my opinion, FDIC insurance is the third contributor to the recent financial crisis, after Fed monetary policy and government affordable housing policy. FDIC insurance destroys market discipline in the banking system. Golden West, Washington Mutual, Indy Mac,

Country Wide, and other large financial institutions that failed, all financed their lending business using FDIC insured deposits. They absolutely could not have done that in the private market. And it became a vicious cycle: as Freddie and Fannie drove down the lending standards in the subprime business, these other private competitors had to be more aggressive, because they had to leverage their high-risk loan portfolio to pay for their high-cost certificates of deposit.

Bert Ely (1994) developed a private insurance model that absolutely would have worked. I believe if that model had been in place, the financial crisis would have been dramatically less than it was. The model was not implemented because of lobbying by large NYC banks and also community banks. If you ran the numbers that Ely was looking at, several of the large banks needed at least double and probably triple their capital or they weren't going to get into the private insurance pool. The Federal Reserve was allowing Citi, et al, to operate with very insufficient capital. Under private insurance standards, Citi, et al, would have significantly increased their capital and would not have failed.

Regulations contributed to the bubble and subprime market in a number of ways. "Fair lending" was supposed to eliminate racial discrimination in the banking business. I joined BB&T in 1971, and by that time there was no racial discrimination because every bank was trying to make money and you wanted to make all the good loans you could make. However, shortly before Bill Clinton got elected in 1992, the Federal Reserve of Boston did a research study that concluded there was a lot of racial discrimination in mortgage lending (Munnell et al. 1992) Turns out the study has been totally discredited (see, e.g., Liebowitz 1993, Zandi 1993). I call it a "childish study"— it only looked at debt to income ratios and didn't consider the reliability of the income, collateral, past payment history, or character type issues. No mature banker would have made a loan based on the meager standards used in the Boston Fed study.

Of course, now the Fed itself has discredited the study. But when Clinton got elected, he was absolutely convinced there was racial discrimination. He had a huge political debt to the African American community that got him elected, and he was really energized about this—both for ethical and political reasons. So basically a dictate came out, and the theory was that the banking examiners had missed the racial discrimination: let's go find banks guilty. And they did that.

I spoke to a number of CEOs who were found "guilty," and they all said, "No, we didn't engage in racial discrimination; however, it was easier just to pay the small fine, change processes, and then put out a press release that we were guilty of discrimination—and that made the politicians/regulators happy."

Well, the regulators came to BB&T and we didn't operate that way. They came to me and said we were guilty of racial discrimination, and I said, "Well, if that's so, that's against our fundamental ethics. Give me the names of the people who are discriminating. I'm going to go fire them now; I'll do it personally." They said, "No, nobody discriminated." "Okay," I said, "How about a system? Do we have a system or process that caused discrimination?" They said, "No, it just happened (magically?)." So I said, "Okay, let's see your evidence." We looked at the evidence and basically found that every loan we made, we should have made, and every loan we turned down, we should have turned down. There was no racial discrimination. Nevertheless, we were still advised to go ahead and admit guilt, because if we admitted it, we would simply pay a small fine and move on. We said, "No," over principle, and the regulators stopped our mergers and acquisitions for months; we had several in process that never materialized. We were ready to go to court, and then a very interesting thing happened that will tell you a lot about the rule of law. The Republicans got elected to control Congress in a negative response to Clinton's policies. Guess what the regulators did? The Republicans were elected on Tuesday, and on Thursday the regulators all went home and we never heard from them again. Fair Lending evolved into "forced" lending to low-income minorities.

Another big factor, psychologically, was the Community Reinvestment Act (CRA). This law was supposed to eliminate "redlining" and also forced banks to get into the low-income home lending business—a business we were not designed to be in. Additionally, CRA was a moral crusade; bankers were ethically supposed to do low-income lending. Now I know there's a lot of greed on Wall Street but when you combine "this is the right thing to do" and "you can make a bunch of money doing it," you create a huge incentive.

One of the myths out there was that the banking industry was deregulated during the Bush administration. Nothing could be further from the truth. We were grossly *misregulated*. There were three major regulatory programs during the Bush administration. The first was the Privacy Act, where we send hundreds of millions of notices to our clients about privacy that no one reads and that was a complete waste of time. The second was Sarbanes-Oxley, which was a redundant system, another tremendous waste of time. And then there was the Patriot Act, which was supposed to catch terrorists. I've talked to many people in government and they all do this dancing act, but the fact is there has never been a single terrorist caught and convicted because of the Patriot Act. The Act cost the banking industry more than $5 billion annually, and I would argue that no one is going to be caught. If you are dumb enough to get caught under the Patriot Act, you are going to get caught anyway. The only significant conviction of the Patriot Act was Eliot Spitzer, the governor of New York, who was convicted of soliciting prostitutes under a law designed to catch terrorists. You should worry about your civil liberties.

The intense focus from the regulators—particularly on Sarbanes-Oxley and the Patriot Act—dramatically misdirected risk management focus in the financial industry. Regulators were threatening to put CEOs in jail and levy large fines on board members, which impacted our behavior radically, and made us put a lot less focus on traditional risk management. I guarantee this happened across the whole industry. The industry was not deregulated, it was massively misregulated.

The cost of regulation is huge. In fact, if you asked me if I would rather eliminate taxes on banks or regulations on banks, it's a no brainer—regulations. BB&T alone has added nearly 1,000 people in the past year to handle regulatory matters. And, of course, what we've done is to reduce production, because we couldn't afford to hire 1,000 people so we shifted people from production into regulation. Moreover, the mental price is high. You can only do so many things and if you are trying to make some regulatory person happy, instead of being productive, creative, and innovative, you become less of a creative and productive person.

With regard to "safety and soundness" regulations, I do not know of a single case where the regulators identified a significant financial problem before the market knew. Now, I know they've gotten involved a lot of times, and when they've gotten involved, they've consistently made the problem worse, not better. I don't view the regulators as actually stopping problems from happening. And why is that? Those who have studied Public Choice theory know that in good times regulators always *underregulate*.

For example, BB&T took over a failed financial institution called Colonial, and we only did it because we had an FDIC guarantee on the credit risk. We had been following Colonial for 15 years. BB&T did a lot of mergers and acquisitions and Colonial fit in our acquisition model. We consciously chose not to buy the company without government assistance. Why was that? First, they were rolling up lots of small weak banks in Florida, and if you roll up a lot of small weak banks, you end up with a big weak bank. Second, they were making many large high-risk real estate loans. Third, we met the CEO, and the CEO was very arrogant. He had an airplane that could probably hold 30 people and he would fly alone from Mobile to Birmingham. We looked at this company, and we said, "These guys are going broke someday. We are not going to buy them." The examiners didn't identify this problem. Why not? First, probably the examiners didn't join the agency until 1995; they had never seen bad times. They didn't understand the business. If they had, what would they have done? Probably nothing. Why is that? This CEO had huge political clout: he was connected to the governor and senators. If the regulators had started problems, he would have gone to the politicians and they would have brought heat on the agency. Why take that chance? So we can look for underregulation in the good times. What about in the bad times?

When things turn negative, regulators typically *overregulate*. This has happened every time we've had a correction in my career: it happened in the early 1980s; it happened in spades in the early 1990s; and it's the worst this time. The regulators inevitably tighten lending standards, including for financial institutions that have good credit histories. They did that at BB&T, tightening our lending standards dramatically. Today BB&T doesn't make loans that we would have made if it were not for the regulatory process, and we put people out of business that we would not have put out of business if it was not for the regulatory process. So on one hand the Federal Reserve is printing money like crazy trying to boost the economy, and on the other hand the banking regulators have tightened up like crazy. Why is that?

If you're a local regulator you don't care what the people in Washington say— the only way you can get in trouble is if your bank gets in trouble. It's a one-sided bet. It's classic Public Choice theory. This time was worse because the leadership of the FDIC was worse, and the attack on community banking from the FDIC was worse than in the early 1980s and early 1990s. I do not think regulatory behavior will change.

Monetary Policy

Over the years I've taken the opportunity to talk to a number of members of the Federal Reserve that are on the Open Market Committee. They're all smart, good human beings, and well-intended. I've talked to Alan Greenspan several times on this issue over the years. I asked them a basic question: "Do you believe in price controls? Do you think the government, for example, can set the proper price for automobiles?" To a person—and with a lot of energy—they said, "Absolutely not, price controls never work—they are destructive." And then I've asked a follow-up question: "When the Federal Reserve sets interest rates isn't that really a price control? Isn't the interest rate perhaps the most important price in the economy?" And not one of them has given me a credible answer. Price controls don't work. The Federal Reserve's attempt to control the price of money does not work. It is hubris to think it does.

The incentives the Fed created by keeping interest rates too low for too long led to the recent financial crisis. It started with Alan Greenspan in the early 2000s. He was the maestro, the hero, and did not want to have bad times on the way out the door. So he created *negative* real interest rates. What that meant is that you could borrow money at less than the inflation rate. That was a big deal in the residential real estate market because residential real estate prices were appreciating very rapidly. There was a huge incentive to expand residential construction and push home sales. Near the end of his term Greenspan started finally raising interest rates, and then Bernanke followed. In a two-year period they raised the Fed funds rate 425 percent. The rate rise was unexpected because Greenspan had been telling the world that the big problem was excessive savings, and that we're going to have deflation. Banks therefore did not expect interest rates to go up and had large losses in their bond portfolios when that happened.

In that process, Bernanke did something incredibly destructive. He inverted the yield curve. Banks make money by borrowing short and lending long. When the yield curve is inverted, short-term rates are higher than long-term rates. Banks margins went negative. Not a great time to be in the banking business when you've already taken losses in your bond portfolios. What did banks do? We're in a funny kind of business: you can make higher returns by taking more risks. Banks went out on the risk spectrum and most of the bad loans were made in this last part of the cycle under the inverted yield curve. By the way, this was one of the longest inversions in history—it was over a year.

Markets *never* invert yield curves. So this was a government policy inversion of yield curves. At the same time Bernanke and the economists at the Federal Reserve were adamant we were not going to have a recession. They didn't predict the recession until after it already happened. Academics talk about perfect information and acting in the long term. Well, in the real world you don't have perfect information and you have to stay in business in the short term to get to the long term, so banks went out on the risk spectrum and made many of the bad loans.

The Greenspan 2000 inflation was particularly destructive. In human history, there are random periods when we suddenly have major advances in our ability to produce for a variety of reasons. In the 1920s, we were having a technological boom (in automobiles, telephones, radio, and electricity). And what should have been happening, what would have happened in a truly private banking system, is that prices would have been *falling* because we were able to produce better goods at lower cost. But the Federal Reserve held prices up to achieve "price stability." The market didn't realize, however, that what was really going on was inflation; it was a bad signal, and people created a bubble in the stock market which then burst, and the Fed piled on (and even Bernanke will admit this) by creating huge liquidity problems—contributing dramatically to the depression. The Fed set the stage for the Great Depression by holding prices up when they should have been falling (see Selgin 2008).

The same thing should have happened in the early 2000s, because of new technology and the rise of China and India in the global economy. For the first time in a long time, billions of people in China and India were more productive, more creative, and more innovative. Our standard of living should have been going up and prices should have been falling. But Greenspan did not want prices to fall.

People in the capital markets and investment business didn't see this hidden inflation, which resulted in lots of bad decisions. Thomas Sargent, an economist at New York University and a Nobel Prize winner, has done a lot of study about inflation expectations and has shown that if people hold "rational expectations," then the Fed's attempt to affect the real economy by inflating the money supply will not work (see, e.g., Sargent 1986). The problem is we couldn't project inflation in this case, because the inflation was hidden. It got even worse because it was the wrong price signal to the Chinese. By holding prices up, and interest rates down, we were telling the Chinese to produce like crazy; driving manufacturing jobs out of the United States, and incentivizing consumption in the United States—remember housing is consumption.

Based on many conversations with bank CEOs and other market participants over the years, I am strongly convinced that private bankers, in a fully competitive market would have created a very different interest rate scenario than the Federal Reserve. We would have never driven interest rates down as low as Greenspan took them and never have raised them as fast, and we never would have inverted the yield curve. Each of us independently, thinking about our own well-being and about profit maximization—and not a bit concerned for the common good—would have competitively created a very different interest rate environment that in hindsight clearly would have eliminated a lot of the problems that we experienced in our economy. Private interest, as Adam Smith said, would have promoted the common good.

I believe that what the Federal Reserve is doing today is very destructive. I think that it's reducing economic productivity, not raising it. And I'll tell you why. Recently, I was in New York talking to a number of private equity firms. And I was saying, "Well, you know, since the interest rates are so low, have you lowered your hurdle return rate for new projects?" They said, "Heck no. We know the Fed has been printing money like crazy. We know interest rates are going up in the future. We don't know whether that means commodities prices are going up first or our sales prices are going up first, so we've kept our hurdle rate of return levels exactly the same." So lower interest rates are not incentivizing real investment. They might be incentivizing some consumption in housing, but they're not incentivizing productive investment.

But there's a deeper issue, and I think this is a really important issue. The Federal Reserve says that they're holding interest rates below market rates. What that means is that they are redistributing wealth from savers to borrowers. That is a very destructive, immoral decision. The arbitrary redistribution of wealth from savers to borrowers, and particularly borrowers that committed lots of bad decisions, is unethical.

What Should We Do?

Like George Selgin (1988) and Larry White (1992), I'm for privatizing the banking system. I'm for getting rid of the Fed. I don't think you should have the Fed and private money/banking because I don't think private money can compete against the government. We tried to compete against Freddie Mac and Fannie Mae and you can't do it. Although we can't get rid of the Fed overnight, I'm quite sure that the free market would choose a private banking system based on a gold standard.[1]

The reason we need to get rid of the Fed is that as long as it exists the temptation for Congress to borrow until we go broke is there. Believing that members of Congress will discipline themselves if they can print money is incredibly naïve.

From 1870 to 1913, the United States did not have a central bank, and yet we had a very successful economy; private banking systems actually have worked. But progress has been limited by the government's monopoly on currency and by regulation.

Markets are about experiments. Now some of the experiments don't work. But the existence of a government agency in any arena destroys the experimentation process and keeps people from learning. Without government impediments, private free markets would have already solved a long time ago the problem of providing sound money.

If you can't get rid of the Fed, then we should at least follow Milton Friedman's (1960) advice of limiting the growth of money to about 3 percent per year. End discretion and adopt a monetary rule, until we can end the Fed.

As a short-term and directionally correct solution for the banking system, I think we ought to raise capital requirements of the banks materially and take away the risk from the public and put it back on the shareholders. But to do that, you have to get rid of FDIC insurance; you have to privatize deposit insurance. And you have to make

---

[1]See White (2011) on why "free banking" and a gold standard would increase monetary and financial stability and would have helped prevent the recent financial crisis.

it illegal for the Fed to bail out insolvent firms. You also have to eliminate 95 percent of the banking regulations; otherwise the banking industry cannot be competitive. As I said, regulations are more expensive than taxes in our industry. Dodd-Frank is a new regulatory cost structure which requires banks to both raise capital and incur radically increased regulatory cost. We end up with a nonviable financial industry. You've got to get rid of regulations if you want banks to maintain more capital.

Conclusion

As interesting as the economic analysis is, I believe that the fundamental fight is over philosophy—over ideas. And I think the Fed reflects that in many ways. How did we get in this mess in a philosophical sense? I think it's a combination of altruism and pragmatism. Everybody has a right to a house. Provided by whom? Everybody has a right to free medical care. Provided by whom? My right to free medical care is my "right" to coerce a doctor to provide me with that medical care or to coerce somebody else to pay that doctor. That is exactly the opposite of the American concept of rights. The American concept of rights is simple: you have the right to what you produce, what you create, but not what somebody else produces, not what somebody else creates. In business, we combine altruism with pragmatism, because you can't really be an altruist and be successful in business. Pragmatism leads to short-term decisionmaking. Negative amortization mortgages, subprime mortgages worked for years and then were a disaster.

Think about the Fed. It is a classic altruistic/pragmatic organization trying to save indebted borrowers and financial institutions that are failing, and it's using pragmatic standards: "Oh we're only doing this because this is an emergency; we won't ever do this again." Classic pragmatism. The problem with being a pragmatist is you can't be rational because rationality requires a long-term perspective. You can't have integrity either, because integrity is acting consistent with principles. Combine altruism with pragmatism and you get something I call the "free lunch mentality." Last presidential election, neither candidate offered any serious solution for Social Security or Medicare even though we have huge deficits, and if they had, they would not have been elected. What's the Fed trying to do? Drive rates down so borrowers can get out of trouble; that's the free lunch mentality. Unfortunately, that mentality leads to a lack of personal responsibility, which is ultimately the death of democracies.

In fact, the central question in our society today that underlies all of these issues, and it relates to sound money is: Do we really believe in personal responsibility or not? It is a fundamental issue. The Founding Fathers talked about the tyranny of the majority. They were talking about the abuse of individual rights, freedom of speech, freedom of religion, but they also realized that when 51 percent of the people figured out they could vote a free lunch from the 49 percent, pretty soon the party's over. Because then 60 percent want a free lunch from 40 percent, then 70 percent want a free lunch from 30 percent, and the 30 percent quit producing.

Interestingly enough, the solution is also philosophical: "life, liberty, and the pursuit of happiness." Each individual's moral right to their own life. Each individual's moral right to the pursuit of their personal happiness. Each individual's moral right to the product of their labor. If they produce a lot, they get a lot, including the right to give it away to whomever they want to, on whatever terms they want to. That moral prerogative demands personal responsibility, because there is no free lunch.

Most people when they hear "life, liberty, and the pursuit of happiness," think about liberty. Liberty is very important because individuals have to be free to pursue happiness. Before Jefferson, before the Enlightenment, everybody existed for somebody else's good: the king, the state, the church. Nobody existed for their own good. What Jefferson said is each of us has a moral right to the pursuit of our personal happiness. We're not guaranteed success in that pursuit, but we have that right. That idea changed the world and created the most successful society—and the most benevolent society in history. When people have the right to freedom of choice, they're naturally nicer to other people and more productive.

If you're going to pursue your happiness, you have to earn self-esteem, and earning self-esteem requires that you live your life with integrity. But there's also another aspect of self-esteem that has social implications. For most people, the primary source of self-esteem is work because you spend a disproportionate amount of time, effort, and energy at work. Something I say to all the employees at BB&T: "It's really important to BB&T that you do your job well. However, it's far, far more important to you. You might fool me about how well you do your job, you might fool your boss about how well you do your job, but you'll never fool you." If you don't do your work the best you can possibly do it, given your level of skill, given your level of knowledge, you will lower your self-esteem. The flip is also true. Do your work the best you can do it, given your level of skill, given your level of knowledge (you cannot do the impossible), and you will raise your self-esteem. And that's more important than getting more money or a promotion because it's about who you are."

There is a major societal issue related to this self-esteem concept. Take an entry level construction worker, a bricklayer. He has a tough life. Reminds me of my granddad. Tough life. But somehow he gets the job done, and he and his wife successfully raise their children. Maybe his granddaughter becomes the CEO of a public company, maybe not. He has a tough, hard life, but he gets something very precious from his work. He gets self-esteem. He gets to be proud of himself. Take that same bricklayer and give him welfare. He's better off financially, but he loses his pride. He loses his self-esteem. You know, there's a lot of focus in our society on security. The Federal Reserve was created to provide security, that is, to reduce "volatility" in the economy. To keep us from making mistakes. Americans care about security, but this is not the land of security. If you want to be secure, stay in Europe. People didn't get on a boat and come to Jamestown to be secure. The United States is the land of opportunity. The opportunity to be great. The opportunity to fail and try again. But most importantly the opportunity of that bricklayer to live life on his own terms. To pursue his personal happiness given his beliefs, his values. That is the American sense of life, and that is what is so precious to protect. The elitists in government, including elitists at the Fed, are a threat to the sense of life that made America great.

References

Ely, B. (1994) "Financial Innovation and Deposit Insurance: The 100 Percent Cross-Guarantee Concept." *Cato Journal* 13 (3): 413–45.

Friedman, M. (1960) *A Program for Monetary Stability.* New York: Fordham University Press.

Hayek, F. A. (1989) *The Fatal Conceit: The Errors of Socialism. The Collected Works of F. A. Hayek*, Vol. 1. Edited by W. W. Bartley III. Chicago: University of Chicago Press.

Liebowitz, S. (1993) "A Study That Deserves No credit." *Wall Street Journal* (1 September): A14.

Munnell, A. H.; Browne, L. E.; McEneaney, J.; and Tootell, G. M. B. (1992) "Mortgage Lending in Boston: Interpreting HMDA Data." Working Paper No. 92–7, Federal Reserve Bank of Boston.

Sargent, T. J. (1986) *Rational Expectations and Inflation*. New York: Harper and Row.

Selgin, G. A. (1988) *The Theory of Free Banking*. Lanham, Md.: Rowman and Littlefield

_____ (2008) "At the Fed, Nothing Succeeds Like Failure." *Cato.org* (22 April).

White, L. H. (1992) *Competition and Currency: Essays on Free Banking and Money*. New York: New York University Press.

_____ (2011) "A Gold Standard with Free Banking Would Have Restrained the Boom and Bust." *Cato Journal* 31 (3): 497–504.

Zandi, M. (1993) "Boston Fed's Bias Study Was Deeply Flawed." *American Banker* (19 August).

5

ALTERNATIVES TO THE FED?

Bennett T. McCallum

I must begin by saying that I have been extremely disappointed—
the word "appalled" may be more accurate—by several developments over the last two years involving the Federal Reserve. It was,
I believe, appropriate that the Fed would respond with expansionary
monetary policy in the face of a major macroeconomic downturn,
which it did. But it did not have to do so by means of operations that
incorporated major excursions into credit policy, as well as monetary
policy, and thereby into the unauthorized exercise of fiscal policy.[1] By
engaging in such operations on a very large scale, the Fed's actions
are almost certain to have detrimental effects on the Fed's independence—and thereby on its resulting ability to focus attention on what
should be its principal objective, namely, price level stability.
Furthermore, the Fed has not been moving quickly—if at all—to
explain and correct this situation.

All in all, the recent experience has had the effect of moving the
Fed away from the type of policy behavior that mainstream academic
analysts have been promoting over the past 15 years—namely, an
activist but rule-based monetary stabilization policy that emphasizes

---

Bennett T. McCallum is Professor of Economics at Carnegie Mellon University.
This article is reprinted from the *Cato Journal*, Vol. 30, No. 3 (Fall 2010). The author
thanks Marvin Goodfriend for helpful comments.
[1]Goodfriend and McCallum (2009) distinguish between pure monetary policy
(changes in base money by central bank purchase or sale of Treasury securities),
pure credit policy (changes in the composition of central bank assets with no change
in base money), and interest-on-reserves policy (with no balance sheet changes).
Since the Fed returns to the Treasury the interest received on the Treasury securities that it holds, it is the case that when the Fed sells Treasuries to fund expansionary credit policy the net results are the same as if the Treasury financed credit
extensions by selling its securities to (i.e., borrowing from) the public.

the avoidance of significant inflation while also avoiding deflation. In saying this, I do recognize that the term "inflation targeting" has been gradually corrupted so as to permit excessive aspects of "fine tuning" relating to output and employment levels, but by and large I believe that the academic literature has been mostly constructive and that much of the commentary tending to discredit it on the basis of recent events has done so mistakenly.

Monetary Policy and Exchange Rates

In previous writings, I have argued that monetary policy and exchange rate policy are linked together so intimately that they should be considered as two sides of the same coin. From that perspective, it seems an unfortunate anachronism that official exchange-rate responsibility is assigned to the Treasury or Finance Ministry in many economies, including the United States, Japan, and—to a small extent—even the European Union. But, in any case, this topic in turn leads us to contemplate other types of monetary regimes— arrangements other than fiat money, managed by a national central bank, in the context of floating exchange rates.

In this regard there are, I believe, three main alternatives that need to be discussed. These are the gold standard, private competitive supply of money, and the Yeager-Greenfield plan for an automatically stabilized unit of account. For all three of these, a major outlet for sympathetic and scholarly discussion has been the *Cato Journal.* For this, the *Cato Journal* deserves much credit, even from readers who are basically supporters of the fiat-floating regime. I will attempt to provide some relevant considerations in the remainder of my presentation.

The Gold Standard

There are many critics of the gold standard among economists who are ardent believers that any monetary arrangement should have price stability as its overriding objective; one might mention Allan Meltzer, Anna Schwartz, and Leland Yeager. One reason for criticism is that while a traditional gold standard tends to protect an economy from major inflations or deflations over a decade or more, it permits a substantial amount of variability at the business-cycle frequency (see, e.g., Bordo 1981). The difficulty that I wish to emphasize here is different, however; it is one stressed in Friedman (1961)—one of his less-famous papers. My own way of thinking about this point begins with the assumption that any gold-standard arrangement today would be one in which the nation's monetary authority (MA) stands ready to exchange gold, at a fixed rate and in both directions, for the principal paper medium of exchange—let us use the term "dollars" and also assume that the medium of exchange (MOE) is the medium of account (MOA).[2] This fixed price is supposed to be maintained indefinitely. But if the MA has the capability of adjusting this price, then there is no *permanent* anchor for the price level even if dollars are at each point of time convertible into gold. The problem is that the population of the United States—like that of other countries—is full of congressmen, businessmen, union leaders, nonprofit organizations, voters, television commentators, and miscellaneous individuals who will be frequently clamoring for the MA to raise or lower the medium-of-exchange price of gold (or whatever is the standard commodity). An increase would then possibly be stimulative but only temporarily and would be followed by price increases for goods in general, that is, by a burst of inflation. Historically, the gold standard provided a reasonable degree of price level stability over long spans of time because the population at large had at that time a semireligious belief that the price of gold should not be varied but should be maintained "forever."[3] But today the same political forces that impinge upon the Fed to be inflationary under our present arrangement would work through this alternative channel under the suggested gold system. Friedman (1961) referred to such a system as a "pseudo gold standard" and pointed out that it amounted in the United States of 1913–1961 to a price-support arrangement for gold producers rather than as a desirable monetary standard.[4]

---

[2] In this regard, I would like to point out that a recent piece by James Grant (2009)—two full pages in the *Wall Street Journal*—in effect adopts the same position (in its final paragraph). This *WSJ* piece has, apparently, been adapted from Grant's highly enjoyable presentation at the Cato Monetary Conference (November 19, 2009).

[3] Timberlake (1989: 317) reports that the London mint price of gold was kept nearly constant from 1665 to 1914.

[4] It should be noted that the present discussion, which focuses on changes over time in the dollar price of gold, does not consider possible variations in the reserve ratio. For an analysis that emphasizes such variations (in a somewhat different model than the one presumed here), see Goodfriend (1988)

Of course, there is the logical possibility of what Friedman called a "real" gold standard, under which actual physical coins or bars of gold would serve as the primary MOE despite the costliness of maintaining such a stock. But as Friedman (1960: 5–7) says, there is a very strong tendency for such a system to evolve into one with "fiduciary elements" and eventually to degenerate into a commodity currency in which the commodity is *paper*—or, today, digital storage capacity. In any event, I have (for simplicity) ruled out this possibility by assumption.

Competing Private Money Suppliers

The second alternative that should be mentioned is the provision of media of exchange by competing private suppliers. The most prominent of writings on this topic is probably the monograph by Hayek (1978), but the most comprehensive review of ideas that I have seen is provided by White (1989). The bulk of his discussion pertains to arrangements under which private issuers of notes and deposits used as MOE are convertible into gold or some other commodity (or bundle). If such convertibility were required by law,[5] there seems to be little reason why a system of this type would not be viable, but there is also no reason why the legal par value would not be subject to the same pressures as those discussed in the previous section. These would be pressures not on individual banks (i.e., private issuers), but on the national monetary authority.

Next, to change the perspective, suppose that there were no legal restrictions on private note-and-deposit suppliers who could then offer purely fiduciary (i.e., inconvertible) currencies. Regarding this case, Friedman (1960: 7) argued:

> Such a currency would involve a negligible use of real resources to produce . . . and would therefore seem to avoid any pressure to undermine it arising from the possibility of saving real resources. This is true for the community as a whole but not for any single issuer of currency. So long as the fiduciary currency has a market value greater than its cost of production—which under favorable conditions can be compressed close to the cost of the paper on which it is printed—

---

[5] I assume that such a requirement would include specification of a minimum gold/paper reserve ratio.

any individual issuer has an incentive to issue additional amounts. A fiduciary currency would thus probably tend through increased issue to degenerate into a commodity currency—into a literal paper standard—there being no stable equilibrium price level short of that at which the money value of currency is no greater than that of the paper it contains.

In the intervening half-century there have been some formal studies of this conjecture, several of which have been summarized by White (1989). The key analytical result seems to be that of Taub (1985), who finds that, because of the dynamic inconsistency involved, such a system could only be sustainable if the issuer were to provide potential users with a contractual commitment to redeemability in some acceptable medium—and this would require, I would add, general belief that the legal system will enforce such contracts. Given recent experience, it may be difficult to generate such belief.

Nevertheless, this last possibility seems worthy of additional consideration. A governmental agency with the sole responsibility of seeing that redeemability contracts are specified and enforced—and without the power to modify par values itself—might provide a type of arrangement that could withstand political pressures for monetary stimulus and also eliminate the possibility of private bank over-issuance.

The Yeager-Greenfield System

The third alternative to be considered is an intriguing but somewhat elusive proposal developed in a number of papers by Leland Yeager (1983, 1985, 1992), plus others that are coauthored with Robert Greenfield (1983, 1989, 1995). The most prominent of these has been Greenfield and Yeager (1983), in which they refer to their proposal as the "BFH" system, as a consequence of its relationship to earlier writings by Fischer Black, Eugene Fama, and Robert Hall. It is my opinion that the system should nevertheless be attributed to Yeager and Greenfield, as they combine various features of the other writers and have championed the resulting product extensively and over a substantial period of time. I will, accordingly, refer to it as the Yeager-Greenfield system.[6]

---

[6] This terminology was also used by Dorn (1989).

The central ingredient of the Yeager-Greenfield proposal is the suggestion that genuine price level stability can be brought about by the appropriate designation of a broad-based consumption bundle as the *unit of account* in a monetary system in which there is little or no role for government involvement. [7] In this system the unit of account (UOA)—the unit in terms of which prices are quoted in most transactions—is based on a commodity bundle defined quite broadly so that movements in the cost of one such composite-commodity bundle closely represent movements in the "general price level." Stabilization of an index number representing the cost of a standard bundle will then amount to general price level stability, and movements in UOA prices of individual commodities will represent movements in the *real* prices of the respective goods; thus fluctuations in output and employment will not be generated by "monetary disequilibria." A second crucial ingredient is the specification of *indirect redeemability* of money—that is, note and deposit claims to standard bundles. The proposal specifies that holders cannot insist on convertibility of notes or deposits into actual, physical standard bundles, but instead only on payment in terms of some agreed-upon "redemption medium" such as gold or securities (Yeager 1992). Accordingly, I would describe the system as one involving a commodity-bundle standard with indirect convertibility—an acronym name might be CBIC. By stabilizing a broad index of prices such a system should provide much more price level stability than a monometallic or bimetallic system; indeed this aspect represents an extended version of Alfred Marshall's (1887) "symmetallism" or Friedman's (1951) "commodity reserve currency"—that is, what one might refer to as "symmetallism on steriods."[8]

---

[7] In Greenfield and Yeager (1983), the emphasis is on a economies in which electronic accounting systems have replaced tangible media of exchange, making them in a sense nonmonetary. The present discussion will ignore that feature, which is somewhat extreme and irrelevant to the points at issue.

[8] In my (1985: 32–38) discussion of Greenfield-Yeager (1983), I was under the mistaken impression that it did not call for any redeemability at all, and consequently I made some incorrect statements. My misreading resulted from statements on their p. 303, lines 15–21; p. 304, lines 10–11; p. 305, lines 37–39; and p. 306, lines 7–11. I did not, incidentally, claim (1985: 34–35) that the Yeager-Greenfield system fails to produce a determinate price level; what I argued (in an admittedly confusing way) was that it *would be* indeterminate if there were no specified link between the standard bundle and the unit of account.

The workings of the Yeager-Greenfield system are, experience suggests, not easy to understand, especially for economists who have not spent years in the study of monetary systems with private money provision. It is therefore interesting to find the following passage in a paper of Yeager's entitled "Toward Forecast-Free Monetary Institutions" in which he is discussing possibilities for central banks such as the Federal Reserve:

> A modified version of Irving Fisher's . . . compensated dollar would further limit any [monetary] authority's discretion, circumvent the problem of lags, and lessen the need for forecasts or even for continuous diagnosis. The authority would be required to maintain two-way convertibility between its money and whatever changeable amount of some redemption medium was actually worth, at current prices, the bundle of goods and services specifying the target price index. (More exactly, the bundle would *define* the dollar.) If the dollar always exchanges against just enough redemption medium (possibly gold, but probably securities) to be worth the bundle, then the dollar is worth the bundle itself. The authority's obligation to redeem its money in this way at the holder's initiative puts teeth into its commitment to a dollar of stable purchasing power [Yeager 1992: 57].

Suppose then that dollars are paper bills and deposits at the MA. Imagine an episode in which the quoted prices of several commodities rise and none fall, so that the dollar price of a standard bundle of goods and services rises above 1.0. Then a dollar will be worth less than a bundle of the standard composition, so private agents will send dollars to the MA for redemption. The MA will redeem them and in the process of doing so will reduce the supply of dollars, thereby adjusting the money supply in the appropriate direction.[9] Since it would be infeasible to store actual bundles of goods and services to match the bundle defined by the chosen price level index, the MA will redeem the dollars by paying (to the dollar-selling agents) securities whose current market value (at current prices) just equals the value of a standard bundle.

---

[9] This statement assumes that "money" refers to the medium of account, which is also the medium of exchange.

In the initial 1983 Greenfield-Yeager article, the dollars were not tangible bills but, instead, electronic bookkeeping entries—an aspect of the presentation that had been featured in papers by Black (1970), Fama (1983), and Hall (1982). But it does not matter, from the perspective of monetary theory, what the physical form is for the evidence that one owns claims that the system is designed to keep very nearly equal in value to the market price of standard bundles. Greenfield and Yeager had a good reason for focusing upon cases in which there was no tangible medium of exchange—namely, so that it would be easier to imagine that the medium of account would differ from any traditional medium of exchange—but that focus is not essential to the logic of their system's monetary design.

It seems clear that the arrangement just described would, if implemented and maintained, keep the value of dollars, in terms of the broad price index adopted, essentially constant. It is also clear, however, that the same problem as that outlined in my discussion of the gold standard would again be present. Then the next issue would again be whether such a system—with competing private money providers instead of a central authority—would be immune to this problem and also the temptation for private suppliers to overissue. The latter difficulty could perhaps be overcome by means of the type of redeemability requirement mentioned at the end of the previous section.[10]

In an earlier discussion of the Yeager-Greenfield system, I considered the possibility that the redemption medium could be Treasury securities (McCallum 2004: 87–89). In that case, since the price of such securities is definitionally related to the interest rate earned by their holders, a MA's policy behavior could be expressed in terms of an interest-rate policy rule, with the rate (and thus the price of securities) adjusted in response to departures of the price level from its target value. One attraction of such a formulation is that it would make possible—at least in principle—quantitative studies of the type used currently by mainstream monetary economists.[11] A second feature is that it would indicate a strong formal similarity between the Yeager-Greenfield system and an interest-rate policy rule, for an

[10] Greenfield and Yeager (1983) suggest that the ordinary enforcement of contracts would suffice.

[11] In practice, however, such studies would be difficult since the relevant time periods would presumably be a few days or hours, rather than the usual quarter-years for which macroeconomic data are available.

inflation-targeting central bank, provided that the latter incorporates a zero inflation rate as its *sole* objective and adjusts its instrument very frequently (e.g., day by day) to achieve that objective.

Conclusion

The results of the foregoing discussion can be summarized briefly. There are two problems associated with a governmentally operated gold standard. The first is that stabilizing the price of gold is not a good substitute for stabilizing a broadly defined price level index. The second is that there are political forces continually at work that tend, whatever the index, to undermine maintenance of the standard. With respect to the first problem, it seems clear that adoption of a much broader index for stabilization is entirely feasible and desirable. For the second the problem is more difficult. It would seem that competing private suppliers of money would not have the same type of temptation to devalue the standard (i.e., inflate) as does a national monetary authority, but a temptation of a different type clearly exists for private suppliers. Some form of regulation might therefore be required, in which case the regulator might be faced with the same temptation to inflate as with a standard monetary authority. The best that can be done, probably, is to adopt institutions that are less subject to temptation than others and that promise to provide stability of a broad price index.

In any event, it is highly unlikely that major movements toward elimination of the Federal Reserve as the dominant monetary authority of the United States will become viable in the foreseeable future. Consequently, it would seem that obtaining a clear mandate for the Federal Reserve to make price stability its overriding objective should be regarded as a leading agenda item. From that perspective, it might be judged that the best practical strategy for the United States at present is to strive to protect the Federal Reserve from the type of politically based reorganization that is currently being considered by Congress,[12] and to campaign for recognition that a central bank/monetary authority should be given a clear lexicographic mandate for

---

[12] Current suggestions are designed to take policy influence away from regional reserve bank presidents, who have been less inflation-prone than Federal Reserve Board members, and to give Congress more influence over the selection of reserve bank presidents (i.e., to increase politicization of monetary policy).

price level stability. I confess, however, that I have little hope that the present U.S. Congress can be persuaded to take such a step.

References

Black, F. (1970) "Banking and Interest Rates in a World without Money." *Journal of Bank Research* 1 (Autumn): 9–20.

Bordo, M. J. (1981) "The Classical Gold Standard: Some Lessons for Today." Federal Reserve Bank of St. Louis *Monthly Review* (May): 2–17.

Dorn, J. A. (1989) "Introduction: Alternatives to Government Fiat Money." *Cato Journal* 9 (Fall): 277–94.

Fama, E. (1983) "Financial Intermediation and Price Level Control." *Journal of Monetary Economics* 12 (July): 7–28.

Friedman, M. (1951) "Commodity Reserve Currency." *Journal of Political Economy* 59: 203–32.

_____ (1960) *A Program for Monetary Stability.* New York: Fordham University Press.

_____ (1961) "Real and Pseudo Gold Standards." *Journal of Law and Economics* 4 (October): 66–79.

Goodfriend, M. (1988) "Central Banking under the Gold Standard." *Carnegie-Rochester Conference Series on Public Policy* 29 (Autumn): 85–124.

Goodfriend, M., and McCallum, B. T. (2009) "Exiting Credit Policy to Preserve Sound Monetary Policy." Carnegie Mellon University (21 October).

Grant, J. (2009) "Requiem for the Dollar." *Wall Street Journal* (5–6 December): W1–W2.

Greenfield, R. L., and Yeager, L. B. (1983) "A Laissez Faire Approach to Monetary Stability." *Journal of Money, Credit, and Banking* 27 (August): 302–15.

Greenfield, R. L.; Woolsey, W. W.; and Yeager, L. B. (1995) "Is Indirect Convertibility Impossible? A Comment on Schnadt and Whittaker." *Journal of Money, Credit, and Banking* 27 (February): 293–97.

Hall, R. E. (1982) "Explorations in the Gold Standard and Related Policies for Stabilizing the Dollar." In R. E. Hall (ed.) *Inflation: Causes and Effects.* Chicago: University of Chicago Press.

Hayek, F. A. (1978) *Denationalization of Money.* 2nd ed. London: Institute of Economic Affairs.

Marshall, A. (1887) "Remedies for Fluctuations of General Prices." *Contemporary Review* 51 (March): 355–75.

McCallum, B. T. (1985) "Bank Regulation, Accounting Systems of Exchange, and the Unit of Account: A Critical Review." *Carnegie-Rochester Conference Series on Public Policy* 23 (November): 13–45.

_____ (2004) "Monetary Policy in Economies with Little or No Money." *Pacific Economic Review* 9 (June): 81–92.

Schnadt, N., and Whittaker, J. (1993) "Inflation-Proof Currency? The Feasibility of Variable Commodity Standards." *Journal of Money, Credit, and Banking* 25 (May): 214–21.

_____ (1995) "Is Direct Convertibility Impossible? A Reply." *Journal of Money, Credit, and Banking* 27 (February): 297–98.

Taub, B. (1985) "Private Fiat Money with Many Suppliers." *Journal of Monetary Economics* 16 (September): 195–208.

Timberlake, R. H. (1989) "The Government's License to Create Money." *Cato Journal* 9 (Fall 1989): 301–21.

White, L. H. (1989) "What Kinds of Monetary Institutions Would a Free Market Deliver?" *Cato Journal* 9 (Fall): 367–91.

Yeager, L. B. (1983) "Stable Money and Free-Market Currencies." *Cato Journal* 3 (Fall): 305–26.

_____ (1985) "Deregulation and Monetary Reform." *American Economic Review Papers and Proceedings* 75 (May): 103–07.

_____ (1992) "Toward Forecast-Free Monetary Institutions." *Cato Journal* 12 (Spring-Summer): 53–73.

Yeager, L. B., and Greenfield, R. L. (1989) "Can Monetary Disequilibrium Be Eliminated? *Cato Journal* 9 (Fall): 405–21.

PART 2

RESTORING A MONETARY CONSTITUTION

6

FROM CONSTITUTIONAL TO FIAT MONEY: THE U.S. EXPERIENCE
Richard H. Timberlake

Over the course of more than two centuries, the United States has had two monetary systems. The first was a gold-silver standard that was framed in its essentials by the U.S. Constitution. In practical terms, it said that any legal tender money created by the federal union or the states or the "people" had to be gold or silver coins, or redeemable in gold or silver coins of specified weight and fineness. Since both gold and silver were constitutional media, the country had a bimetallic standard that ultimately became a monometallic gold standard.[1]

During the period in which the gold standard functioned throughout most of the 19th century until 1914 and with some qualifications until 1930, the purchasing power value of the dollar, as measured by any statistically valid price index, was secularly constant. Occasionally, mild inflations or deflations occurred, and from 1862 to 1879 the federal government instituted a paper-money ("greenback") inflation, but the tendency for the dollar to maintain its exchange value was notable. For all practical purposes, the long-term value of the dollar was constant for more than a century.

Richard H. Timberlake is Professor (Emeritus) of Economics and Finance at the University of Georgia. This article is reprinted from the *Cato Journal*, Vol. 32, No. 2 (Spring/Summer 2012). Readers are referred to Timberlake (2013) for a detailed account of the Supreme Court's monetary decisions.

[1]People could arrange an exchange of goods and services for any medium that was mutually agreeable. However, only gold and silver could be *legal* tender. In the following discussion, for the sake of simplicity, I refer to "the gold standard" as a surrogate term for the bimetallic standard.

In spite of its enviable record for approximating price level stability without human hands-on controls, the gold standard had its critics. Different factions argued for relief from its discipline. Many businessmen chafed at its restrictive effect on monetary availability for industrial expansion, and debtors complained during the occasional bouts of "dear money." Cheap money, plenty of it, and low interest rates became political slogans, but gold endured the strain. For one thing, a standard based on the naturally limited quantities of a metallic commodity was obviously what the Framers of the Constitution had intended, and, second, nothing else seemed constitutional enough to replace it.

The second monetary institution to appear was the Federal Reserve System in 1913, just as the gold standard system looked enduring and stable. Both a gold standard and a central bank determine an economy's stock of money. However, the original Fed was *not* intended to replace the gold standard in that capacity; it was *not* to be a central bank. It was *not* an expression of the federal government's "complete power over the monetary system." The congressional debates and the Federal Reserve Act's concluding sentences confirmed the preeminence of the gold standard and, by implication, constitutional constraints over the monetary system. The final bill stated: "Nothing in this Act . . . shall be considered to repeal the parity provisions contained in an act [Gold Standard Act] approved March 14, 1900."[2] The Fed was to be nothing more than a group of primarily private, super-commercial banks that would help client "member" banks endure short-term liquidity crises. This low-profile image of the original Fed immediately raises the question: If true, how did the Fed subsequently acquire its monetary omnipotence?

Greenback Inflation and the Legal Tender Cases

It all began with the greenbacks that the federal government authorized and issued during the Civil War. Had the notes been tender only for debts payable to and by the government, they would have been legally equivalent to the Treasury notes issued in limited quantities at various times between 1812 and 1860—tender only for government dues and payments, but for that reason generally

---

[2]*Congressional Record*, 63rd Cong., 2nd sess., (5100–06.)

acceptable for most private transactions.[3] Greenbacks, however, had to be accepted by *private* creditors in discharge of *private* debts. This unnecessary flourish overdetermined their acceptability. It was also objectionable to postwar creditors and, therefore, came into the courts for adjudication after the war—first into the state courts and finally to the Supreme Court in 1869, 1870–71, and 1884.[4]

The Court in 1869 had eight members. The chief justice was Salmon P. Chase, who had been secretary of the treasury under Lincoln when Congress passed the Greenback Acts. Lincoln nominated him as chief justice in 1864 and the Senate duly approved him.

While Secretary, Chase had sanctioned the original greenback issue in memos to leading congressmen, agreeing that they were "necessary and proper" in accordance with congressional Republicans' principal argument for justifying their constitutionality. However, in the five years between leaving his Treasury post and the decision on the first legal tender case, *Hepburn v. Griswold* (1869), Chase reversed his opinion. He led the Court debate that by a 5–3 majority found the greenbacks unconstitutional for payment of debts contracted before passage of the first Greenback Act in February 1862 (*Hepburn v. Griswold*, 75 U.S. 603).[5]

The *Hepburn* decision did not sit well with the Grant administration. Because of its war expenditures, the federal government had become the country's chief debtor. Influential politicians in the Grant administration did not want to be politically responsible for what they feared might be redemptions in gold for any of the current

---

[3]The federal government issued Treasury notes several times between 1812 and 1860, in quantities between $3 million and $10 million. Private creditors, of course, could and did accept them. No court case ever tested their constitutionality because they were never *forced* into a private transaction or contract (Timberlake 1993: 71).

[4]Some old-style Treasury notes were issued during the war, along with other government-sponsored currencies—national bank notes and silver currency. However, neither of the latter was legal tender for private debts. Yet, all three currencies were equally acceptable throughout the war and postwar periods. The greenbacks never had a market premium relative to national bank notes or silver, thus emphasizing that the *full* legal tender provision was unnecessary.

[5]The complementary question of constitutionality for debts after the initiation of the greenbacks did not arise. Using the maxim that every debt should be paid in whatever money was current at the time the contract was drawn, the greenbacks should have been legitimate for such later debts.

national debt, which was more than $3 billion. Moreover, as Republicans they objected to a judgment that demeaned the administration's war record (Unger 1964: 75–77).

Presidents Lincoln and Grant had already appointed five of the Court's eight members, three of whom formed the minority that argued and voted in *Hepburn* that the greenbacks were constitutional for all debts unless explicitly provided otherwise in the contract. One of the five majority justices resigned shortly after the case was argued, and one vacancy on the Court already existed, which meant that Grant in 1869 could appoint two new justices. Without much searching, Grant's advisers found two state court justices (both Republicans) who had supported the full legal tender provision of the greenbacks in state cases. Grant nominated these two as associate justices of the Supreme Court in 1869, right after the *Hepburn* decision, and the Republican Senate approved them.[6]

Grant's attorney general then petitioned the Court to retry the legal tender issue with two new cases, *Knox v. Lee* and *Parker v. Davis*. The expanded Court, now weighted by Republicans, decided 5–4 in 1870–71 that the greenbacks were legal tender for all debts public and private, and regardless of when the debts were contracted (79 U.S. 457). In 1884, by which time eight out of the nine justices were Republican appointees, the majority decision in a fourth case, *Juilliard v. Greenman*, confirmed the previous decision, and declared by its 8–1 majority that Congress could authorize full legal tender greenback issues in peacetime as well as in war (*Juilliard v. Greenman, 1884*, 110 U.S. 421).

This infamous decision contended that many European governments had the sovereign power of borrowing money by issuing bills or notes for the money borrowed, and that these notes were full legal tender for private debts. Since this power, the majority argued,

> was universally understood to belong to sovereignty at the time of the framing of the Constitution . . . and the power to make the notes of the government a legal tender in payment of private debts being one of the powers belonging to sovereignty in other civilized nations, and not expressly withheld from Congress by the Constitution; we are irresistibly

---

[6]Grant did not "pack" the Court. He had every right to nominate any two justices he wished. The new justices, however, had their highest responsibility to the Constitution, not to the Grant administration.

impelled to the conclusion that the impressing upon the Treasury notes of the United States the quality of being a legal tender in payment of private debts is an appropriate means, conducive and plainly adapted to the execution of the undoubted powers of Congress, consistent with the letter and spirit of the Constitution, and therefore within the meaning of that instrument, "necessary and proper" for carrying into execution the powers vested by this Constitution in the government of the United States [110 U.S. 449–51].

This passage makes use of a subjunctive syllogism that sounds impressive but proves nothing. It argues that the Framers—and here is the subjunctive syllogism—*would* have known of their own sovereign powers in 1787, and *could* have written a Constitution that *would* have included "the power to make the notes of the government a legal tender in payment of private debt." The decision did not add that the Framers had not acknowledged any such "sovereignty," nor written such a constitution. Rather, the Court majorities in 1871 and 1884 constructed this argument on the presumption that they *knew* what the Framers were thinking and could have done when they wrote the actual Constitution that the Courts in 1871 and 1884 were supposed to interpret as written.

This latter-day reconstruction of the Constitution, no matter how artificially contrived, authorized Congress's complete control over the monetary system. More importantly, it contradicted what had been a universal understanding and belief that only gold and silver coins could be legal tender. Article I, Section 8 states: "Congress shall have Power . . . To coin [gold and silver] Money, regulate the [dollar] Value thereof, and of foreign Coin, and fix the Standard of Weights and Measures." These clauses allowed Congress to specify common values that everyone needed for carrying out day-to-day activities. Now, a Supreme Court had "found" that Congress had complete control over the monetary system, and could make any paper money full legal tender. Would some future Court also "find" that Congress had the power to make 10 inches a foot, and 14 ounces a pound?— as the lone dissenter, Justice Stephen Field, argued in both the 1871 and 1884 decisions (110 U.S. 460–69).

At the time, the legal tender decisions did not have the drama or political significance that was due them. Congress had restored the operational gold standard to serve as the institutional executor of the monetary system; and while the U.S. Treasury had outstanding fiat currencies to manage, the revived gold standard was shepherding the monetary system in its customary fashion. Congress had no reason at this time, and showed no inclination, to implement its newly bestowed power. In fact, it ignored the role the Court decisions had ceded it and emphasized the gold standard's supremacy by passing "The [Gold] Currency Act of 1900" on March 14th of that year.

Passage of the Federal Reserve Act

With little reference to the gold standard or its workings except to re-affirm again its primacy, Congress passed the Federal Reserve Act in 1913. The legal tender decisions were not even mentioned in the congressional debates on the Federal Reserve bill. The new Fed was to be a strictly limited, part-time institution operating within the framework of the gold standard, and a lender of last resort (LOLR) for the commercial banking system (Timberlake 1993: 214–31.)

This model of Federal Reserve operations never happened. Following World War I and the sharp recession of 1920–22, the New York Fed under the guidance of Governor Benjamin Strong initiated a policy of price level stabilization that swept in all the other Federal Reserve banks. Strong excused this policy as temporary. He acknowledged that it was probably unconstitutional, but would only be current until the excess gold in Fed banks had returned to European banks, so that a global reformation of the gold standard could occur (Burgess 1930: 173–97, 317–31; Chandler 1958: 194–206).

The economic data of the time reflect Strong's policy. The more volatile Wholesale Price Index (1926=100), which was at 97 in 1922 when Strong initiated the policy, increased to a high of 104 in 1925, then declined to 95 by the end of 1929. The Consumer Price Index (1935–39=100) increased from 71.6 to 73.3 between 1922 and 1929, an "increase" of 1.7 percent over seven years, or one-quarter of 1 percent per year—not as much as the inflationary bias in the Index. Business and industry boomed during the 1920s. If any of it was malinvestment, Joseph Schumpeter's "creative destruction" took care of that. Measures of the stock of money for this period correlate with the stability of the price level. According to Friedman and Schwartz (1963: 710–13), the M2 money stock (which includes all commercial bank checking accounts, plus currency outside banks, plus time deposits in commercial banks) increased over this seven-year period by 38 percent, or 5.5 percent per year. The prosperity was solid American production in the presence of a stable price level.

Meanwhile, the Fed banks' total earning assets (securities, loans, discounts, and advances to commercial member banks—the items over which the Fed banks have direct control) declined from their inflationary level of $3.13 billion in 1920 to $1.20 billion in 1922. From then until mid-1929, these assets increased by only $0.19 billion, that is, to $1.39 billion. Thus, the net contribution of Fed policy to the monetary expansion of the period was $190 million, or only about $27 million per year, far less than would have occurred if the Fed had allowed the gold standard to function freely without the Fed's accumulation of gold (Timberlake: 1993: 254–73).

Despite the practical success of the New York Fed's stable price level policy, in early 1929 some members of the Fed's Board of Governors repudiated the policy, and, bowing to the passions of the times, embarked on a general anti-speculation crusade to discipline the financial system. This initiative had popular approval because "speculators" and their "greed" are always grist for the moralists' mill.

The new policy, labeled "direct pressure" by its sponsors on the Fed Board, reviewed all commercial bank loan applications for credit from Fed banks to determine whether an applying bank had any taint of stock market dealings. If it did, the bank did not get any credit from "its" Fed bank no matter how much eligible paper it held (Warburton: 1966: 339–40). As needy banks were denied credit assistance, bank failures began in 1930 and continued into 1931 and through 1933, taking out both "speculative" banks and many sound money banks (Friedman and Schwartz: 1963: 299–357). The direct pressure program was an unmitigated disaster. By the time the carnage ended in March 1933, more than 9,000 banks had failed, the banking system was in shambles, and the economy was paralyzed (Timberlake 2007: 325–54).

As the Great Contraction reached its nadir in 1933, Franklin Roosevelt was sworn in as president of the United States. Misunderstanding the real cause of the disaster (the Fed Board and its overzealous anti-speculators), FDR and his administration, along with the Democrats' majority in Congress, began a series of policies designed to end the constraint of the gold standard on Fed-Treasury control of money. By a series of Resolutions and an Act of Congress, the administration through its Treasury Department and congressional majorities called all of the country's monetary gold into

Washington, paying for it the traditional price of $20.67 per ounce. Congress then passed the Gold Reserve Act of 1934, which raised the mint price of gold more than 59 percent. The Treasury then had all the gold melted into 27-pound ingots, stored it three floors deep in the ground, and declared that gold was illegal for use as money— thus violating people's property rights. Previously, a joint resolution of Congress, "Abrogation of the Gold Clauses," passed June 5, 1933, had voided the gold clauses in all private and public bonds, mort-gages, and contracts (White 1935: 712).

The story did not end there, however. Many creditors held debts due them from both private debtors and the U.S. government that contained the now-voided gold clauses, stipulating that the creditor could collect what was due him either in dollars or in a specified quantity of gold. Since the Gold Reserve Act raised the value of gold from $20.67 per ounce to $35 per ounce, the gold value of debts with gold clauses became 69 percent greater. Furthermore, prices had been falling since 1929 and were in almost all cases well below what they had been when the contracts were signed. Therefore, the real gold value of a debt-contract payable in gold had risen because of both declines in prices and the increase in the legal price of gold.

Given these incentives, creditors with gold clauses in their con-tracts tried to exact payment in gold, or its equivalent in dollars, for debts due them from both private debtors and the government. The U.S. Treasury had sold such obligations during and after World War I, and private creditors had used gold clauses ever since then to pro-tect themselves from price level appreciations that would erode the real values of their contracts. Upon refusal of some private corpora-tions, such as the Baltimore and Ohio Railroad, and the U.S. Treasury Department to pay such gold values for their outstanding debts, the creditors brought the cases to the courts. The issue quickly reached the Supreme Court in 1934 and gave rise to an important and controversial set of decisions known as the *Gold Clause Cases* (see Holzer 1980). These cases posed an irresolvable dilemma for the Court. If it decided that Congress's Abrogation of the Gold Clauses in 1933 violated the Constitution's sanctity of contracts and required payment of gold clause debts in gold, it would allow already well-to-do creditors to realize an unanticipated "undeserved enrichment" from the gold-appreciated dollars. If it upheld the Abrogation of the Gold Clauses to prevent creditors from getting unanticipated real gains, it would violate the Fifth Amendment's contracts protection.

A third option would have been to rule that such a "devaluation" far exceeded Congress's power "to coin money and regulate the value thereof," and require Congress to repeal or amend the Gold Reserve Act that had devalued the dollar. This third option, while properly constitutional, was politically impossible, given the mind-set of the administration and Congress.

The opinion of the Court's 5–4 majority stated that the primary and all-important issue " is the power of Congress to establish a monetary system and the necessary implications of that power," and " to invalidate the provisions of existing contracts which interfere with the exercise of its constitutional authority" (294 U.S. 302). Chief Justice Charles Evans Hughes, who read the opinion, reviewed the *Legal Tender Cases* that had allowed Congress the power to make U.S. notes (greenbacks) unqualified legal tender and granted it complete control over the monetary system.

Hughes emphasized Congress's power "To coin money and regulate the value thereof." He held that "the Court in the legal tender cases did not derive from that express grant [of power] alone the full authority of the Congress in relation to the currency. . . [but] in all the related powers conferred upon the Congress [that were] appropriate to achieve 'the great objects for which the government was framed—a national government with sovereign powers'" (294 U.S. 303). Hughes here quoted and used without apology the argument of the infamous 1884 decision discussed above: "The broad and comprehensive national authority over the subjects of revenue, finance and currency is derived from the aggregate of the powers granted to Congress." The Congress is empowered, he quoted further from the *Juilliard* opinion, "'to issue the obligations of the United States in such form, and to impress upon them such qualities as currency for the payment of merchandise and the payment of debts, as accord with the usage of sovereign governments'" (294 U.S. 304).

Nothing in the Constitution implies any such power, nor does any statement suggest a possible inference leading to such a conclusion. The majority opinion in 1935 simply treated these gross distortions of congressional power over money from the *Legal Tender Cases* as if they were quoted from the Constitution itself, and without reexamining the validity of the arguments.

The majority opinion concluded: "We think that it is clearly shown that these [gold] clauses interfere with the exertion of the [monetary] power granted to the Congress"—that is, "monetary powers" nowhere visible in the Constitution but conjured into existence by the Court decisions of 1871 and 1884 (294 U.S. 315–16). Therefore, Congress's Abrogation of the Gold Clauses stood. The creditors could be paid in any U.S. currency that was legal tender, but they had no right to be paid in gold—gold clauses notwithstanding.[7]

The objections of the Court minority, written by Justice McReynolds, began with the flat statement that if the majority's decision were given effect, it would "bring about confiscation of property rights and repudiation of national obligations. . . . [Our] acquiescence in the decisions just announced is impossible; we cannot believe the farseeing framers . . . intended that the expected government should have authority to annihilate its own obligations and destroy the very rights which they were endeavoring to protect. Not only is there no permission for such actions; they are inhibited" (294 U.S. 362).

McReynolds noted that the intention of the gold clause was "to protect against a depreciation of the currency and against the discharge of the obligation by payment of less than that prescribed." He cited the recent gold devaluation of more than 59 percent—the gold dollar went from 25.8 grains to 15.24 grains—and added: "The calculation to determine the damages for failure to pay in gold would not be difficult" (294 U.S. 362–65).[8] Where the majority had openly violated contractual law but maintained economic justice, the minority would uphold contractual law while doing grave economic injustice to the debtor, one of whom, notably, was the U.S. government.

In the minority dissent, McReynolds emphasized:

> There is no challenge here of the power of Congress to adopt such proper "Monetary Policy" as it may deem necessary in order to provide for national obligations and furnish an adequate medium of exchange for public use. The plan under

---

[7]The Court amended its decision in the following way: "We conclude that the Joint Resolution of June 5, 1933, in so far as it attempted to override the obligation created by the bond in suit, went beyond the congressional power." If the dispute was between two private parties (e.g., *Norman v. B&O Railroad*), Congress could nullify the gold clause because it interfered with Congress's monetary powers. However, if the litigation was between a private party and the United States, and because the issue and sale of the bond were integral to U.S. fiscal policy, its terms had to be honored. Therefore, the appellant could collect "damages." However, the Court defined the "damages" in dollar terms, not in gold. Gold already was forbidden as a means of payment.

[8]That is, multiply the dollar value of the debt by 25.8 divided by 15.24, which translates into paying 1.69 times the debt's dollar value.

review in the Legal Tender Cases was declared within the limits of the Constitution, but not without a strong dissent. The conclusions there announced are not now questioned; and any abstract discussion of Congressional power over money would only tend to befog the real issue [294 U.S. 369].

The legal tender currency issued, McReynolds observed further, was a temporary expedient, "until the United States could find it possible to meet their obligations in standard coin. This they accomplished [with Resumption] in 1879."

But why not question those decisions? Did not the "strong dissent" in the *Legal Tender Cases* and the fact that the legal tender issue had two opposing Supreme Court decisions in 1869 and 1871 suggest that maybe something was amiss that should be reexamined?

The minority dissent, however, did not reargue the earlier cases. It also neglected to explain that, despite resumption of gold payments, the greenbacks had become a permanent legal tender, and that their continuing presence implied that Congress had the complete power over the monetary system that all nine members of the Court now accepted. By glossing over the real crux of the matter—the decisions of 1871 and 1884, McReynolds precluded a proper constitutional conclusion.

However, he recognized the implications for future fiscal policy. "If this [abrogation] is permissible," McReynolds warned, "then a gold dollar containing one grain of gold may become the standard, all contract rights fall, and huge profits appear on Treasury books, maybe enough to cancel the public debt" (294 U.S. 372). McReynolds did not refer to Justice Stephen Field's dissent in the *Legal Tender Cases* or to George Bancroft's *Plea for the Constitution* (1886) that had observed the same thing. However, he added, "For the Government to say, we have violated our contract but have escaped the consequences through our own statute, would be monstrous. In matters of contractual obligation, the Government cannot legislate so as to excuse itself" (294 U.S. 379).

Finally, McReynolds discussed the "incalculable financial disaster" that would occur if the U.S. government had to pay for its inflated gold obligations. Although McReynolds held that the estimated cost of paying off government debt at the new gold price "is discredited by manifest exaggeration," he did not produce any estimates of the costs, either for private debts with gold clauses or for the government bonds with gold clauses still outstanding.

The Justices, to repeat, had an impossible puzzle to resolve. If their decision followed the arguments of the dissenting minority, both the government and private debtors would have had to pay off gold clause obligations at $1.69 on the dollar. Bondholders (creditors) would have received a windfall that was completely unexpected and that had nothing to do with their decisions to buy the bonds. At the same time, this payment would have been exactly what the bonds promised—payment in a certain quantity of gold, now worth 69 percent more in dollars. To add fuel to the fire, these same gold clause profiteers were already realizing substantial premiums of various amounts, due to the ongoing decline in the price level that enhanced the buying power of any dollars owed them.[9]

The majority knew that the gold clauses were perfectly legitimate and binding, but they had to find a constitutional path to justify the abrogation law. Since it was agreed that Congress had absolute power over the monetary system, even contracts, the most sacred of constitutional objects, could be nullified when they conflicted with Congress's absolute monetary powers that the earlier Courts had contrived. However, the majority's opinion for government debts with gold clauses denied that the government's "sovereignty" over the monetary system could justify abrogation, because the bonds in dispute had financed critical government fiscal operations. The opinion then made a separate case for "damages" done to owners of gold clause bonds. They found that because of the fall in the price level, gold clause creditors had not suffered any losses, but had experienced "unjustified enrichment." Therefore, Congress's Abrogation of Gold Clauses only required recompense if the creditor could show "damages." Virtually no bond or contract owner suffered any real loss, or could have. It was a time of creditor "heaven" when the real values of all debts appreciated due to the falling price level.

Given the unconstitutional reasoning on both sides of the Court decision, what judgment on the *Gold Clause Cases* might have preserved constitutional integrity and prevented unwarranted "enrichment" of creditors? How could the Court have solved the dilemma? Where should it have started?

---

[9]Prices had stayed constant from 1922 to 1929, and fallen 25.5 percent from 1929 to 1933 (CPI, 1947–49=100).

Constitutional Money

Both the minority and majority opinions referred many times to the *Legal Tender Cases*—*Knox v. Lee* and *Parker v. Davis* in 1871, and *Juilliard v. Greenman* in 1884—to support their common agreement of Congress's total power over money. These decisions, they claimed, were written in stone and sealed by the "divine right of sovereignty." They conveniently ignored the *Hepburn v. Griswold* decision in 1869 that had denied debtors the right to pay off their debts in depreciated greenbacks for debts contracted before greenbacks were authorized. Had the Court dutifully observed that the *Hepburn* case had been reargued and the decision reversed the next year, they would have had both a model for further argument in the *Gold Clause Cases* and a decision that did not rest on the horns of a dilemma. Perhaps Congress did not have the "total power of money creation," so willingly granted to it by the Justices on both sides of the *Gold Clause Cases*. Maybe the Chase Court of 1869 had the right answer on legal tender.

The Supreme Court is the ultimate judicial authority for the determination of disputes over constitutional issues. However, the justices are mortal men and women, subject to the push-and-pull of political pressures and earthly rewards. Being human, they are also imperfect. Given this mundane observation, how might the Court manage itself in order to provide for imperfect decisions? If a Court decision is obviously unconstitutional, regardless of the reason, are the judicial, economic, and political systems destined to live forever under its resulting misjudgment?

The reversal of *Hepburn v. Griswold* by *Knox v. Lee* and *Parker v. Davis* in 1871, and *Juilliard v. Greenman* in 1884 provides the answer. All three decisions on the *Legal Tender Cases* were controversial, and the last two, especially, reflected overt political pressures. Sixty years after the 1871 and 1884 decisions, the Hughes Court in 1934–35 could (and should) have reargued them. By this time the earlier majorities' manifest misinterpretations would have been obvious to anyone and everyone. The Hughes Court could then have struck down the gold devaluation and charged Congress to find other solutions for economic recovery. Such a decision might have provoked a tumultuous political reaction. Nevertheless, in the name of proper constitutional law it should have been done.

Shortly after the *Gold Clause Cases*, Congress passed the Banking Act of 1935, which effectively confirmed Congress's unconstitutional control over the monetary system. During the recent crisis, 2008–12, the Fed has significantly extended the scope of its financial policies. It has no resemblance to the LOLR that Congress approved in 1913. There is no constitutional basis for the form in which it now exists. Since abolishing the Fed seems politically impossible, the next-best remedy would be a congressional mandate—perfectly reasonable since the Fed is a creature of Congress—voiding its monetary discretion, and requiring it to keep the general price level constant at all times and without exception. This rule is not the only one possible. However, the public understands its plausibility, and it is the only practical goal any central bank can achieve.

References

Bancroft, G. (1886) *A Plea for the Constitution of the United States, Wounded in the House of Its Guardians.* New York: Harper.

Burgess. W. R. (ed.) (1930) *Interpretations of Federal Reserve Policy in the Speeches and Writings of Benjamin Strong.* New York: Harper. (Republished by Garland in 1983.)

Chandler, L. V. (1958) *Benjamin Strong, Central Banker.* Washington: Brookings.

Friedman, M., and Schwartz, A. J. (1963) *A Monetary History of the United States, 1867–1960.* Princeton, N.J.: Princeton University Press for the National Bureau of Economic Research.

Holzer, H. M. (1980) *The Gold Clause.* New York: Books in Focus.

Timberlake, R. H. (1993) *Monetary Policy in the United States.* Chicago: University of Chicago Press.

_____ (2007) "Gold Standards and the Real Bills Doctrine in U.S. Monetary Policy," *Independent Review* 11 (3): 325–54.

_____ (2013) *Constitutional Money: A Review of the Supreme Court's Monetary Decisions.* New York: Cambridge University Press.

Unger, I. (1964) *The Greenback Era.* Princeton, N.J.: Princeton University Press.

Warburton, C. (1966) *Depression, Inflation, and Monetary Policy: Selected Papers, 1945–1953.* Baltimore, Md.: Johns Hopkins University Press.

White, H. (1935) *Money and Banking.* Revised and expanded by C. Tippetts and L. Froman. New York: Ginn.

7

REDUCTIONIST REFLECTIONS ON THE MONETARY CONSTITUTION

James M. Buchanan

The Absence of a Monetary Constitution

There exists no monetary constitution, as such, in the United States. What does exist is an institutionally established authority charged with an ill-defined responsibility to "do good," as determined by its own evaluation. We would have no difficulty in classifying an analogously directed military junta in a Latin American setting as nonconstitutional, by which we would mean, quite properly, that it operates in accordance with no predictable rules of behavior. Viewed in this perspective, it becomes difficult, if not impossible, to mount intellectually respectable defenses for continuation of the monetary institutions that are in being. Yet we observe relatively little revolutionary fervor, even among political economists, to challenge the institutionalized status quo.

A shift in regime that would put in place a genuine monetary constitution, one that would incorporate stable and predictable rules of the game, would generate an outward displacement in the value feasibility space for the economy. By reducing the uncertainty involved

---

James M. Buchanan was awarded the Nobel Memorial Prize in Economic Sciences in 1986. He was General Director of the Center for Study of Public Choice at George Mason University. This article is reprinted from the *Cato Journal*, Vol. 9, No. 2 (Fall 1989). The author is indebted to David Fand and Viktor Vanberg for their helpful comments.

in each and every transaction made in nominal monetary values, each potential transactor can share in the newly available increment to value surplus. Failure to introduce a constitutional regime in money, therefore, amounts to a collective refusal to implement a technological improvement that is acknowledged to be mutually beneficial.

Explaining the Persistence of the Status Quo

How do we explain our observed failure to exploit this opportunity to increase our well-being? Small, and possibly influential, groups do exist which secure rents because of the nonpredictability that characterizes the monetary arrangements in existence. Those persons who have invested human capital in acquiring differentially advantageous abilities to foresee and react to the behavioral shifts of those who make decisions for the monetary authorities, of course, would suffer transitional loss from any shift toward an effective monetary regime. But the "Fed-watching" industry, in total, is surely not sufficiently strong to explain the apparent invulnerability of the regime of discretionary authority. We can add in the potential influence of the entrenched bureaucracy of the monetary authority itself, including all levels in the hierarchy. And we still remain with what seems to be an intellectual puzzle in political economy. Why do we, as members of the body politic, put up with institutional arrangements that seem to keep us well within the frontier of potential value? Why do the professional economists, who are presumably competent to analyze alternative institutional structures, seem so reluctant to condemn the existing regime?

The issues here are neither so simple nor so straightforward as I have made them seem to be. Both the propositions advanced and the questions posed above depend on acceptance of a conception of "the economy" that is not shared with many of either my professional peers in economics or my fellow citizens. To put my position dramatically, many economists do not know what they are talking about, and, if economists do not know, how can they expect citizens to cut through massive intellectualized absurdity?

Two Conceptions of the Economy

There are two categorically different conceptions of what an economy or "the economy" is. The first, and that upon which the earlier statements and questions have been based, is the conception of the economy as a *structure* or *order*, described by a set of rules, and within which separate individual actors pursue individually selected objectives, including individually defined economic value. The second conception is one of an economy as an independently existing *organic* unit, to which purpose can be assigned. Macroeconomics, in its very nature, implicitly embodies the second of these conceptions. Macroaggregation (the attempt to measure national product, income, growth, employment) leads almost directly to targeted values or, at least, directions of change in the aggregated variables. By contrast, in the first conception of an economy as an order, the aggregated values *emerge* from the interlinked choices made by individual participants; but these values are not appropriate targets for purposeful manipulation.

Analogies are helpful to illustrate the contrast and comparison between the opposing conceptions. In the first, nonteleological, vision of the economy as an order or structure, the appropriate analogy might be a municipal playground, with tennis courts, swimming pools, swings, sandboxes, basketball courts, and softball diamonds. This playground operates in accordance with rules that allow the separate individual users to pursue their own objectives as they variously utilize the available facilities. In this case, it is clear that users' interests are furthered by the presence of stable and predictable rules concerning usage of the facilities. Discretionary authority on the part of the playground manager to change opening and closing hours, eligibility requirements for using facilities, and rationing schemes for usage would tend to reduce the value of the playground for all potential users. Moreover, if in some initial setting, the manager did, indeed, have such discretion, the imposition of a set of rules would surely be a value-enhancing shift for the regime.

In the second, or teleological vision, the economy, as a unit, becomes analogous to a ship which, if left alone and rudderless, would toss about on a sometimes stormy sea. The replacement of the discretionary authority of the ship's captain by an automaton may seem foolhardy. The very survival of the ship may seem to depend on the skill of the captain and crew who will maneuver the ship safely through possibly troubled waters. Displacement of the captain's discretionary authority by a navigational automaton will, to be sure, generate greater predictability in the direction of the ship's movement, but at the possible expense of navigational disaster in an unpredictable sea.

Neither of the analogies fully captures the attitude of those who hold either the nonteleological or the teleological conceptions of the economy. Those who think of the economy as an order—a structure of rules within which persons separately pursue private purposes—allow for the possible sharing of common purposes among individuals and groups, purposes that may be achieved through collective organization. Those who think of the economy as an organic unit to which macropurpose may be assigned allow for the possible extensive pursuit of private, individually identified goals within the broad limits defined by macromanagement. There remains, nonetheless, a different conceptualization of the economy at the most basic level of comprehension. The economy-as-order is accompanied by the protective state or polity, the function of which is to maintain the rules of the order itself, rather than to steer or direct the economy, as such. The economy-as-organic unit must be accompanied by an activist state or polity, one that is required to macromanage, steer, and direct the economy toward objectively definable goals or purposes.

Dethroning Macroeconomics

Macromanagement through fiscal fine-tuning was the initial heritage of the Keynesian revolution in economic policy, although precursory elements of macropolicy can be located in the central banking theory of the 1920s. The subsequent fall of fiscal policy from favor was due to acknowledged operational flaws rather than to any convergence of economists' attitudes toward the inappropriateness of macromanagement. More or less by default, although aided and abetted by over-enthusiasm on the part of advocates of some variants of monetarism, macromanagement came to be shifted almost exclusively to the monetary authorities. This shift, in itself, remains surprising, especially because it was accompanied by a developing recognition of monumental operational failure in the 1930s.

The discretionary powers of the existing monetary authorities are defended by those who simply cannot conceive that the economy, if constrained appropriately within the "laws and institutions" (so well understood by Adam Smith), can operate to generate maximal value for the persons who participate in the interaction process. There is a difference in mind-set at the most basic level. Many of us see the failure to exploit the opportunity offered by the adoption of a genuine monetary constitution (of almost any description) as equivalent to the explicit refusal to take more rather than less. Therefore, we will not succeed until and unless we effectively excise economic macropurpose from the listing of tasks appropriately assigned to agents of the state. The implications for the status of macroeconomics are clear: so long as macroeconomics remains central to our discipline, we shall not secure reform in our monetary arrangements.

At the same time that we dethrone macroeconomics, with its implied macropurpose for the aggregative economy, from its place in the economists' research program, we must not commit the error of over-extension. In our playground analogy, it seems clear that the discretionary authority of the manager should be restricted by rules. This is not equivalent to saying that the playground would be a more desirable place in the total absence of all rules. A rules-structured, or constitutional, order rather than anarchy is something upon which shared agreement may be reached.

Achieving Price-Level Predictability

Predictability in the value of the monetary unit is *not* a macropurpose of state-directed economic policy. It is, instead, an attribute of the agreed-on rules within which individual actors contract one with another in the complex interaction of voluntary exchanges. In this sense, predictability is not basically different from the security of rights to property, although descriptively such predictability is perhaps closer to enforced standards for ordinary weights and measures. As a commonly desired attribute of the rules or structure, predictability in the value of the monetary unit is within the direct sphere of responsibility of the protective state, in a sense precisely comparable to the provision of security of private rights to property and the enforcement of voluntary contracts.

It is essential to understand the difference between the *emergent* macroproperties of a well-ordered economy and the properties of the structure that are prerequisite to the attainment of the commonly desired emergent properties. With a shift to a constitutional regime that embodies predictability in the value of the monetary unit (predictability that may be generated by any one of several institutional alternatives), all individual contractors share in the relative reduction in transactions costs, thereby releasing resources for employment in various privately valued uses.

A Fundamental Misunderstanding of Economic Process

The macroeconomics of money is complex because the institutions in existence reflect a fundamental misunderstanding of economic process. Our didactic role must be focused on removing this misunderstanding. We waste both our intellectual and our emotional energies by engaging in scientific disputes (no matter how challenging these may be) that find their relevance only because of the flawed understanding and its institutional implications.

8

THE IMPLEMENTATION AND MAINTENANCE OF A MONETARY CONSTITUTION
Peter Bernholz

The Maintenance of Monetary Stability

Long-term monetary stability—an inflation-free monetary system—can be maintained only if politicians and central bankers have no discretionary authority to influence the stock of money. No currency in history has ever maintained its long-term stability without constitutional constraint. History also shows, however, that even the best monetary constitutions cannot be maintained indefinitely. Periods of a century or more of price stability have been experienced only by several countries during the 19th century, and therefore seem to be rare accomplishments. Moreover, major wars have always been the biggest danger for the survival of sound monetary constitutions.

What can be hoped for given these observations? First, apart from avoiding major wars, the rare opportunities for introducing sound monetary constitutions must be seized with courage and determination. Furthermore, to implement and maintain a constitution with characteristics best suited to prevent inflation over the long run, a concrete plan has to be present at the right moment.

Peter Bernholz is Professor Emeritus of Economics at the University of Basel's Center for Economics and Business. This article is abridged from the *Cato Journal* Vol. 6, No. 2 (Fall 1986).

A Concrete Plan for a Monetary Constitution

The following six measures should be included in a plan for a monetary constitution:

1. A constitutional restriction on the power of governments to create budget deficits;
2. A constitutional safeguard that prevents governments and central bankers from influencing the stock of money;
3. A mechanism limiting the stock of money;
4. A requirement that the monetary constitution can be amended only by qualified majorities, say, by two-thirds in both chambers;
5. An obligatory popular referendum to validate all changes of the monetary constitution passed by qualified majorities;
6. No emergency clauses empowering the cabinet to make changes under certain conditions.

The enactment of these measures would narrowly limit discretionary policy, but they are not sufficient to control inflation. The pure gold and silver standards had one clear advantage. The rule of convertibility of bank notes against the precious metal and vice versa, at a fixed parity, could always be tested by everybody and could not be easily reinterpreted by governments, central banks, or supreme courts. The latter condition would not be true for a constitutional rule prescribing, say, an annual monetary growth rate of 2 or 3 percent. First, the public would neither be able to test the rule nor determine if it had actually been followed. Second, it would be difficult to decide which monetary aggregate should grow by which percentage in which period against which base. Here there would be ample room for various interpretations, so that the constitutional rule would be of little value if it were not clearly defined. True, it would not be impossible to define the monetary aggregate, the base, and the relevant period in the constitution. But what would happen if the money aggregate selected became less and less relevant because of financial innovations? Moreover, the observance of the rule could still not be monitored by the public. Who should control the central bank? Another government agency? Or would individual persons have a right to sue the government or the central bank for violating the rule?

Stabilizing a weighted price index would lead to similar problems. The prices and thus the index could be manipulated by the government. And if the weights and commodities of the basket were fixed in the constitution they might lose their relevance over time, because of substitution and other factors.

A Simple Monetary Arrangement

Given these difficulties, there seems to be good reason to favor a simple monetary arrangement such as the pure gold standard. To return to a gold standard, however, would require greater flexibility than prevailed before World War I to prevent the higher variance of real variables. Moreover, during World War I no European country with notes issued by the government or a central bank monopoly maintained the gold standard. This was true even for neutral countries. Only Albania, which had neither government notes nor a central bank, stayed on the gold standard (League of Nations 1946: 93). Albania is perhaps not a good example, but it seems that only a removal of the monetary system from the sphere of the state may be sufficient to maintain a stable monetary constitution under adverse conditions.

My own tentative proposal to solve these problems would be to abolish the central bank, institute a pure gold standard, and allow free banking. The monetary constitution would only postulate that each creditor had the right to demand payment from each debtor in gold at the fixed parity. Any violation of this rule would be severely punished by private and/or public law. Moreover, the constitution would grant the right of any bank fulfilling certain conditions—including unlimited liability of its shareholders—to issue bank notes and to create any type of claim preferred. Finally, any government owned or controlled banks would be outlawed by the constitution.

These are radical proposals. But the Scottish free banking system combined with the gold standard seems to have worked quite well without a central bank as a lender of last resort (White 1984). And the Swiss system seems not to have experienced too many problems before the founding of the national bank in 1907. But the most important feature of the proposal would be the complete removal of government influence from the monetary system and the opening up of the path of innovation in the field of money.

References

League of Nations (1946) *The Course and Control of Inflation: A Review of the Monetary Experience after World War I*. Paris: League of Nations.

White, L. H. (1984) *Free Banking in Britain: Theory, Experience and Debate, 1800–1845*. New York: Cambridge University Press.

PART 3

RULES VERSUS DISCRETION

9
COMMITMENT, RULES, AND DISCRETION
Charles I. Plosser

The debate regarding rules versus discretion in the conduct of monetary policy is an old one dating back at least to Henry Simons (1936). His famous paper in the *Journal of Political Economy*, entitled "Rules versus Authorities in Monetary Policy" is a classic. Simons's view stressed the importance of establishing the "rules of the game" as opposed to the "delegation of legislative powers," that granted "authorities" to central banks. Today we would characterize authorities as discretionary powers in contrast to rules. He rightly struggled with these concepts and their implications for a free society in the classical liberal sense. His conclusion was that establishing rules of the game was clearly preferable and the lesser of two evils when it came to monetary policy.

The modern version of the debate surrounding rules versus discretion is best captured in the work of Finn Kydland and Edward Prescott (1977), again in the *Journal of Political Economy* and titled "Rules Rather than Discretion: The Inconsistency of Optimal Plans." They showed that a regime that precommits policymakers to behave in a particular way is preferable to a regime that allows policymakers pure discretion—that is, to choose a policy independently at each point in time.

The idea is very counterintuitive to most people and particularly unappealing to many policymakers. After all, the policymaker could choose the same set of actions under discretion as he could

Charles I. Plosser is the former President and CEO of the Federal Reserve Bank of Philadelphia. This article is reprinted from the *Cato Journal*, Vol. 36, No. 2 (Spring/Summer 2016).

under commitment. So it would seem that a discretionary policy can certainly be no worse than a policy that entails precommitment. Therefore, the argument goes, there is value in retaining "flexibility," or as some monetary policymakers I know used to say, "optionality," so that decisions can respond "appropriately" to current events. Thanks to Kydland and Prescott and others, we now know that this argument is flawed. The fatal flaw in this conventional wisdom stems from its failure to recognize the important role played by expectations of future policy in economic decisions made today.

Expectations, Commitment, and Discretion

Expectations of the future play a crucial role in all sorts of decisions. This is particularly evident in financial markets, where investment decisions and the valuation of securities depend importantly on assessments of future economic outcomes. But it is equally true for individuals buying a home or a car, and for businesses considering capital expenditures.

Before going further, it is useful to be a bit more precise and define what I mean by "commitment" and "discretion." Commitment essentially means that policymakers deliver on past promises about future actions. Discretion, on the other hand, means the policymaker is not bound by previous actions or plans and thus is free to make an independent decision every period.

Discretion means the policymaker may find it preferable to change his or her mind, or re-optimize, and do something other than what was promised. The temptation to renege on previous promises or plans is what economists refer to as the time-inconsistency problem, and it has surprisingly troublesome consequences. In particular, it can mean that outcomes under a discretionary regime are likely to be worse than those under a regime where the policymaker is constrained to follow through on previous commitments.

To illustrate the issue, consider the case of patent protection. Research and development (R&D) by the private sector is an important source of innovation in our economy. From new drugs to computers, research has led to new products that have enhanced our health and productivity. Thus, investment in research generates important returns that contribute to the improvements in living standards both here and around the world.

To encourage such investment, governments often seek to ensure that private returns to innovation are sufficient to elicit the socially optimal amount of investment in new ideas. In practice, governments often give temporary monopoly rights to companies and individuals, in the form of a patent, as a means of assuring that the private inventor can earn a sufficient rate of return on what may be a very costly and risky research endeavor. In one sense this is assuring property rights to new inventions.

Suppose, however, that after the discovery, the discretionary policymaker decides to make the new product's design freely available to all. The result would be more competition and lower prices, making society better off. The policymaker thus reoptimizes to do the best thing at the time and reneges on past promises. We all know the problem of such a discretionary strategy—while achieving short-term benefits, it is likely to have devastating effects on future investments in research and inventive activity. Thus, removing the discretion of the policymaker to revoke the patent protection raises overall welfare. The expectations of future policies and behaviors have important implications for decisions today and, thus, future welfare.

Commitment, or the lack thereof, also has important implications for monetary policy. Just as firms' R&D decisions are affected by their expectations about the future of patent protection, many economic decisions are affected by their expectations about the future course or path of monetary policy. The stance of monetary policy is, after all, not simply the current level of the policy instrument, but includes its expected path over time. As a result, the central bank faces a time-inconsistency problem. That is, it will be tempted to pursue policies that deliver temporary economic benefits that may be inconsistent with longer-term goals. Realizing that the central bank will have the latitude, or discretion, to give in to this temptation, people will make decisions today that drive the economy to a suboptimal outcome.

Thus, in a wide range of cases, a policy governed by commitment dominates one of discretion. The challenge is: How do we get commitment? Are there institutional arrangements that would make it easier for policymakers to honor their commitments?

Looking back, societies have employed various means to try to pre-commit to a policy path and thereby produce better outcomes. None are perfect. Indeed, in a democratic society it is impossible to obtain full commitment. Legislation is one mechanism for supporting commitment. But, of course, laws can and do change. Nonetheless, it can be difficult and costly to do so. So laws can and do enhance the credibility of a commitment as in Simons's rules of the game.

Institutional Design

More generally, institutional design can be a useful means to enhance commitment. Creating institutions that align the incentives of the policymaker to behave in a more rule-like or committed manner also can be helpful.

For example, at Cato's 2013 monetary conference, I gave a paper entitled, "A Limited Central Bank," which appeared in the *Cato Journal* (Plosser 2014). I argued that there were other ways to strengthen commitment and limit discretionary behaviors in a central bank. I suggested that designing an institution with a more limited purpose and fewer authorities can improve the ability of policymakers to both commit to future behaviors and be held accountable for the outcomes. In particular, I suggested designing the central bank with a more narrow mandate as a way to focus the activities of the policymakers. The narrow mandate also improves transparency and enables the public to hold the policymakers accountable. Broad and expansive mandates that are accompanied by broad authorities and powers invite discretion and shifting priorities. Along these lines, I also argued for limiting the range of assets that the central bank can purchase and thus the markets in which it is allowed to directly intervene. This also can help limit the scope for discretion and better align the authorities with the more narrow mandate.

A monetary regime that is based on the gold standard provides a form of commitment. In principle, there is very little room for discretionary monetary policy under a gold standard. Indeed, a metallic standard of some form has served as a form of standard and commitment on and off for centuries. Although, in the end, the system was far from perfect. Economic forces and the incentive of governments, politicians, to be discretionary, especially during wars, eventually led to the abandonment of the discipline of the gold standard. Nevertheless, it does illustrate that the importance of commitment is not a new one and how difficult it can be to sustain.

Many countries have adopted fixed exchange rate regimes as means to attain credibility and ensure commitment. Certainly, the

Bretton Woods system that eventually replaced the gold standard after World War II was a commitment device, although it, too, eventually broke down.

Some countries have chosen to peg their exchange rate to the dollar as a means of restricting the ability of their central bank to create inflation. Doing so, however, simply puts monetary policy in the hands of another country.

Other approaches to strengthen credibility and commitment include rule-based strategies. Rules are a means of limiting discretionary behavior by constraining policy choices. For example, Milton Friedman, who was highly critical of discretionary monetary policy-making, suggested adopting a rule that required constant growth of the money supply—the so-called k-percent rule (Friedman 1960).

More recently, rules have been developed that specify a feedback mechanism from, say, inflation and an output gap measure, for setting the funds rate. The most well-known version of such a rule is the one proposed by John Taylor. There are a number of variations of such feedback rules that have been proposed and investigated for their robustness properties. That is, do they perform well in different models? The general result is these simple rules often produce good results in a wide variety of models, which is quite encouraging. This is an important development because it means that complete agreement on a model is not necessary to adopt a rule that enhances credibility and is likely to work well over time, even as models are improved.

Rules also improve communication and reduce instability caused by surprise discretionary actions by the central bank. A rule, in essence, provides a reaction function that helps the public and markets understand how monetary policy will react to incoming data. It thus provides the right kind of forward guidance and reduces uncertainty and surprises when it comes to monetary policy. This then contributes to a more stable and efficient economy. Had the Fed been operating under a transparent, well-understood rule prior to the crisis, the efforts at forward guidance in the face of the zero lower bound might have proved to be more helpful rather than mostly confusing.

Many central banks around the world have adopted inflation targeting frameworks as a means to strengthen credibility and commitment. Under inflation targeting, the central bank announces a numerical target or target range for a specific inflation measure and commits to keeping inflation in that range over a specified period. The Fed finally joined most of the other major central banks around the world in quantifying an inflation target in January 2012 after nearly two decades of debating the issue. Inflation targets are a step in the right direction, but are not very specific about the monetary policy strategy that will lead to that outcome. Thus, they allow a wide range of discretionary actions.

Monetary Policy Strategies

So where do we go from here. My discussion highlights the fact that full commitment is hard to attain in practice. Moreover, policymakers are very reluctant to give up discretion. The attempt by the Federal Open Market Committee (FOMC) to make statements about the future path of policy recognizes the importance of expectations and a desire to influence them. But at the same time, the Committee tried to retain complete discretion to change its policy as circumstances change. But the Committee did not, and still does not, provide much guidance as to how that would be done. This tension between rules and commitment versus the desire to be discretionary has loomed large over the past several years and created significant challenges in communication and clarity of a monetary policy strategy.

However, that does not mean that progress cannot be made. There are people inside the Fed who value the importance of a more systematic approach to policy even if there is no agreement on the precise form that such a strategy might take. A more systematic strategy would make monetary policy more predictable, it would make communication easier, and it would improve transparency. In doing so, it would make the Fed more accountable.

Paul Volcker once said to me that Montagu Norman, the long-time Governor of the Bank of England (1920–44), once told him that a basic prescription for all central bankers should be, "Never explain and never apologize." While I don't know whether the quote or its attribution is accurate, I do know that the message is one that captures the attitude and practice of central bankers through much of the 20th century.

But as we know, times have changed. Transparency has replaced secrecy, and openness and communication have replaced mystery. While there are those who long for the mystique and thrilling days of yesteryear and wish for a little more mystery and a little less openness, I don't think the clock can be turned back—nor should it be.

Indeed, I give a lot of credit to the Fed for its efforts to become more open and transparent, but I think the desire to maintain absolute discretion has seriously interfered with that agenda. It is very difficult to communicate clearly a monetary policy strategy, or to use forward guidance as part of that strategy, when the fundamental approach to policy is discretion. I would go so far as to argue that discretion is not a strategy but the absence of a strategy.

So how might the FOMC move to a more systematic way of articulating given that they are not yet ready to adopt a single rule? I think there is a path forward that is really quite simple, and, although far from perfect, puts monetary policy and the Fed on a better trajectory.

To move an entire institution from one that values discretion over commitment is challenging. One strategy is legislation. As I mentioned, I have proposed one such approach that creates a more narrow central bank with limited objectives and limited powers or authorities. In such a framework, I believe that a more systematic or rule-like approach to monetary policy is more likely to flourish. I believe the design of the institution is important, because it helps shape the incentives and activities of the policymakers.

Another legislative approach is to mandate a rule or policy strategy that policymakers must pursue. This approach, too, has its merits and is closely aligned with proposed legislation in the House. The disadvantage, from my perspective, of this legislation is that it gets Congress deeply involved in the technical aspects of monetary policy and invites greater politicization of monetary policy choices. I am not convinced at this point that as a society it would be the best way to proceed. I would prefer an approach that focuses on the limits of the institution's goals and objectives and its authorities rather than on micromanaging the tactical arrangements and policy prescriptions. More generally, I am concerned that any legislative approach in the current environment would lead to compromises that are likely to lead to less independence and greater politicization of the Fed and monetary policy. I do not think this is wise.

My suggestion, which requires no legislative action, and the risks it entails, is for the Fed to take the initiative and implement a shift toward a more systematic monetary policy strategy. It has the authority to do so if it chooses.

The approach is quite simple, is mostly in place, and one I have stressed before. As I mentioned, there are many within the Fed that understand and value the importance of a more systematic implementation of policy. This is evidenced by the fact that the staff regularly calculates the implications of various robust rules and reports on them to the FOMC. The basic model used by the Fed, affectionately known as FRB/US, incorporates and relies, to a great extent, on rule-like behavior for monetary policy. This work provides a good starting point to move forward.

The FOMC could begin to reshape its policy communication in a way that emphasizes the usefulness of these various rules in the formulation of policy. Publishing the outcomes and implications of the various rules on a timely basis as part of a quarterly monetary policy report would be an important step forward. More useful would be for the Committee to discuss its policy choices in the context of such guideposts provided by the rules. At times, these rules may give a wide range of options. If so, that leaves some latitude for the Committee to exercise judgment and discretion as to the best policy choice. But such an approach would require, almost demand, the Committee explain why its decision differs from the guideposts. This practice would improve the communication and transparency of the monetary policy strategy at work.

I believe that this approach could accomplish several desirable objectives. First, it would force the Committee to directly confront the implication of the rules and to justify its policy choices should it choose to significantly deviate from the guideposts. Second, such a process would change the nature of the discussion by the Committee in important ways and place the rules and their implications front and center. So while this suggestion does not impose a single rule on the FOMC, it does help discipline the discussion and thought processes in ways that are likely to help promote a more systematic approach to policy.

Conclusion

There is a strong case to be made that a monetary policy regime that demonstrates a high degree of commitment would lead to better economic outcomes. However, perfect commitment by policymakers is almost impossible to achieve in a democratic society. Rule-based policy is one useful mechanism to enhance the credibility of commitment, but it is not perfect. The Fed could improve commitment and communication through a more transparent public discussion of robust rules rather than simply rejecting any role for rules in its approach to decision making. Indeed, policymakers should and could take a more proactive approach. Doing so would be a step in the right direction, head off, perhaps, even worse legislation, and enhance communication and the public's understanding of its monetary policy strategy.

References

Friedman, M. (1960) *A Program for Monetary Stability*. New York: Fordham University Press.

Kydland, F. E., and Prescott, E. C. (1977) "Rules Rather than Discretion: The Inconsistency of Optimal Plans." *Journal of Political Economy* 85 (3): 473–92.

Plosser, C. I. (2014) "A Limited Central Bank." *Cato Journal* 34 (2): 201–11.

Simons, H. C. (1936) "Rules versus Authorities in Monetary Policy." *Journal of Political Economy* 44 (1): 1–30.

10

REAL AND PSEUDO MONETARY RULES
George Selgin

Milton Friedman is perhaps the best-known exponent of monetary rules. He also wrote a well-known paper entitled "Real and Pseudo Gold Standards" (Friedman 1961). I wish here to pay twofold homage to Friedman by insisting on a distinction between real and pseudo monetary rules. Just as Friedman (1961: 67) maintained that, though they may "have many surface features in common," real and pseudo gold standards "are at bottom fundamentally different," I shall argue that despite their superficial resemblance, real and pseudo monetary rules are fundamentally different—both in their operation and their consequences. Indeed, I shall argue that what Friedman called a "pseudo gold standard" is really an instance of a pseudo monetary rule, while what he calls a "real gold standard" is an instance of a real monetary rule.

Real Monetary Rules

A monetary rule, as typically defined, encompasses two very different sets of possibilities. For example, Froyen and Guender (2012: 101) define a monetary rule as "a prescribed guide for the conduct of monetary policy." That broad definition includes both what I consider rules in the strict sense of the term—what I shall call "real monetary rules"—and rules in a much looser sense, which I consider to be "pseudo monetary rules."

George Selgin is a Senior Fellow and Director of the Center for Monetary and Financial Alternatives at the Cato Institute. He is also Professor Emeritus of Economics at the University of Georgia. This article is reprinted from the *Cato Journal*, Vol. 36, No. 2 (Spring/Summer 2016).

To understand the difference between a real and a pseudo monetary rule, as well as my reason for insisting on these terms, one must briefly review the traditional arguments for monetary rules. The essence of these arguments is succinctly stated by Leitzel (2003: 50), who notes that while "discretion allows decisions to respond more closely to actual conditions . . . in the hands of a fallible or corrupt decision maker, a greater reliance on judgment may not be such a good idea."

Jacob Viner (1962: 246) gives a more detailed summary:

> On purely a priori grounds . . . it can be said for an unambiguous rule, *provided it is enforceable and enforced*, that it is a complete protection within the immediate area of its subject matter against arbitrary, malicious, stupid, clumsy, or other manipulation of that subject matter by an 'authority.' It can be said *for a rule rigid through time, if it works and is counted on to work*, that it provides absolute certainy and predictability, with respect to the behavior prescribed by the rule [emphasis added].

A once popular and still occasionally heard objection to monetary rules is that discretion-wielding authority can almost always do better, since the authority can always reproduce the outcome of the rule yet can also respond to circumstances that the rule doesn't provide for. As Turnovsky (1977: 331) puts it, except when a rule happens to coincide with an optimal response, "a judiciously chosen discretionary policy will always be superior." In other words, a discretionary policy need never do worse than a rule, and it might do better.

Such arguments entirely miss the point. There are, first of all, several reasons why discretionary policy may in practice not be "judiciously chosen," in Turnovsky's sense of being an optimal response to the current state of the economy. The first, which O'Driscoll (2016) elaborates on in his contribution to this volume, is that the authorities may lack the knowledge required to employ discretion "judiciously." The essential point was best expressed by Friedman (1960: 93):

> We seldom in fact know which way the economic wind is blowing until several months after the event, yet to be

effective, we need to know which way the wind is going to be blowing when the measures we take now will be effective, itself a variable date that may be a half year or a year or two years from now. Leaning today against next year's wind is hardly an easy task in the present state of meteorology.

Friedman is of course referring to "long and variable lags." His argument hinges on the fact that monetary authorities, being incapable of anticipating such lags with any degree of precision, can be guilty of errors of commission more serious than the errors of omission to which a well-chosen rule might commit them. The more recent findings of behavioral economics tend to reinforce the knowledge-based case for rules. Adam Gurri (2013) sums up those findings pithily: "The fact is that the matter of human beings using their discretion repeatedly in circumstances of high uncertainty has already been settled—they are terrible at it."

The insights of behavioral economists refer only to what one might call the "best-case scenario"—namely, the "well-intentioned, wise, and skillful exercise of discretionary authority," as Viner (1962: 247) put it. The case for rules offered by public-choice theorists, in contrast, views discretionary behavior as a worst-case setting (see Buchanan and Brennan 2008), in which the "natural proclivities" of politicians and bureaucrats predominate—including their tendency to make decisions based on a "narrowly defined self-interest" that "run[s] counter to the basic desires of the citizenry" (Brown 1982: 39).

A final, and especially subtle, argument for a monetary rule is that it can serve to avoid the suboptimal, "time-inconsistent" equilibria to which discretionary monetary regimes are prone. For example, suppose that a zero inflation regime is considered optimal, but that, where such a regime is in place and expected to remain so, a discretionary central banker would be tempted to take advantage of the fact by increasing the money stock so as to *temporarily* boost employment and output. The fact that the monetary authority will be tempted to do so means the public will anticipate inflation; thus, inflation surprises won't have any real impact. Consequently, the discretionary equilibrium is suboptimal. By tying the authority's hands, a zero inflation monetary rule can achieve an optimal outcome that could not be achieved otherwise (White 1999: 204–5).

It seems obvious that a genuine or real monetary rule must be capable of accomplishing the things that monetary rules are supposed to accomplish. Yet, it is no less obvious that most "prescribed guides for the conduct of monetary policy" fail to meet that requirement. As Jacob Viner (1962: 247) observed, "A rule doubtfully or irregularly enforced, and a rule subject at any time to revision, may involve less certainty and predictability than a control operated by a discretionary authority which follows a known set of principles." Such a rule may also involve more sheer error, causing more rather than less economic instability.

It follows that a real monetary rule, as opposed to a mere guide for policy, must be both strict and robust. By "strict" I mean that it must be rigorously enforced so that the public is convinced there will be no deviations from the rule. As Mullineaux (1985: 14) notes, "The monetary authority . . . *must* do what the rule says and not something else." By "robust" I mean that the rule must be capable of perpetuating itself, by not giving either politicians or the public reason to regret its strict enforcement and to call either for its revision or its abandonment in favor of discretion.

Pseudo Monetary Rules

A pseudo monetary rule is one that is either not well enforced or not expected to last. Although real monetary rules have existed in the past, such rules are almost unknown today. In contrast, pseudo monetary rules are perhaps even more common than avowed monetary discretion.

To distinguish real from pseudo monetary rules, one must recognize the difference between a rule that is merely *implemented* and one that is *enforced*. Kenneth Rogoff (1986: 1) identifies three "institutional devices for implementing monetary policy rules"—namely, a constitutional amendment, an independent monetary authority, and an arrangement in which reputational considerations encourage abiding by the rule. In fact, of these three devices, only the first is capable of providing for anything like the strict enforcement that a real monetary rule requires. The other devices, in contrast, can serve only as the basis for pseudo monetary rules, for none offers any reliable assurance that a "prescribed guide for the conduct of monetary policy" will actually be heeded.[1]

As I have noted, the distinction between a real and a pseudo monetary rule matters, because a pseudo monetary rule—that is, a monetary policy "guide" that can easily be evaded, or that is likely to invite calls for revision if strictly enforced—lacks the advantages of a real rule. As Leitzel (2003: 51) has observed, "Evasion of the rule (or, relatedly, the possibility of varying the enforcement of the rule) lessens the distinctions between the alternatives. . . . When those who are governed by the rules have the power to enforce or amend or avoid the rules, resistance [to the temptation to take advantage of this] cannot be purchased cheaply." A pseudo rule is as likely as discretion to turn monetary policy into a plaything of politics: the main difference being that lobbying efforts, instead of being directed toward the authorities themselves, are directed toward the rulemakers.

Although the "Fed Oversight Reform and Modernization Act" (H.R. 3189, U.S. Congress 2015) is widely understood to call for the implementation of a genuine monetary rule, and it has been denounced for that reason by its critics, it would, if passed, establish a very weak sort of pseudo monetary rule. The Act calls for the Federal Open Market Committee (FOMC) to adopt a "directive policy rule," but allows the FOMC to specify in advance circumstances under which it might amend that rule.

The Act also includes a "changing market conditions" clause, allowing the FOMC to abandon its directive policy rule if it determines that the rule "cannot or should not be achieved due to changing market conditions." In that case, the FOMC would have to submit a report explaining its decision, together with an

---

[1]Rogoff (1986: 1) writes: "The main problem with passing a constitutional amendment to govern monetary policy is the lack of flexibility in dealing with unforeseen events. In principle, of course, a law can be made fully state-contingent. But it is unrealistic to think that the designers of a law will have the imagination to plan for every type of shock and the analytical brilliance to guess how to deal with shocks which have seldom or never been experienced." This is true. However, the problem is not a particular "institutional device for implementing" a monetary policy rule; it is the very concept of a monetary rule itself in the strict sense of the term. Indeed, it is an instance of what Friedman (1962: 239) characterized as "the stereotypical" complaint about rules. The answer, of course, is that it is at least as "unrealistic" to expect discretion to be used in an "analytically brilliant" rather than a short-sighted or otherwise irresponsible way.

appropriately updated directive policy rule, to the comptroller general within 48 hours of its decision; and the comptroller general would, in turn, be required to "conduct an audit and issue a report determining whether such updated version and the Federal Open Market Committee are in compliance with this section." A determination of noncompliance would oblige the Fed chair to testify and explain why the monetary authority is not in compliance with the policy directive. Moreover, the committees in question could call for a more comprehensive GAO audit of the Fed. Nevertheless, the Act does not provide for enforcement of the directive policy rule. Hence, the Fed Oversight Reform and Modernization Act of 2015 is a perfect example of a pseudo rule made almost indistinguishable from discretion by the fact that "those who are governed by the rules have the power to enforce or amend or avoid the rules."

Yet a pseudo rule, as long as it remains in effect, retains the more obvious shortcoming of a genuine rule relative to discretion, to wit: the lack of flexibility. That is, it continues to be a source of errors of omission that might, in principle, be avoided under a judicious and perfectly informed discretionary regime. Instead of being a middle-ground between a real rule and complete discretion, a pseudo monetary rule can end up being worse than either.

Consider, for example, the case in which a definite value for a particular foreign exchange rate serves as a monetary authority's "prescribed guide for the conduct of monetary policy," where the authority enjoys complete autonomy to implement the guide as it sees fit, subject only to potential reputational repercussions of failing to do so. Such a pegged exchange rate regime is an example of a pseudo monetary rule. It is distinct from a fixed exchange rate regime, such as a currency-board system, in which a rigid exchange rate is constitutionally prescribed and enforced. Because it lacks any strict enforcement mechanism, a pegged exchange rate regime is less than fully credible, and it is consequently vulnerable to speculative attacks. Consequently, such a regime may end up combining the disadvantages of monetary policy inflexibility with those of exchange-rate uncertainty and associated risk premia (Schuler 2007).

Enforcement by Contract

A monetary rule can be enforced either by means of contracts binding upon monetary authorities, or by means of automatic arrangements that dispense with such authorities altogether. I'll refer to these alternatives as enforcement by contract and enforcement by design.

Enforcement by contract involves subjecting monetary authorities to loss when they fail to comply with a monetary rule. The loss might consist of outright penalties, of reduced compensation, of loss of ownership equity, or of dismissal. This sort of enforcement is often considered in discussions of means for enforcing monetary rules. Yet it is a solution practically unknown in contemporary monetary arrangements.

The one contemporary arrangement that comes closest to involving a monetary rule enforced by contract is New Zealand's Policy Targets Agreement (PTA). The PTA supposedly "represents a contract between the Minister of Finance/Treasurer and the Governor of the Reserve Bank, and it forms a central element of the Bank's mandate and accountability" whose "specific objective is maintaining CPI inflation within the specified target band" (Reserve Bank of New Zealand, n.d.). However, a look at the actual details concerning this contractual arrangement makes it clear that it does not actually provide for strict enforcement of New Zealand's CPI target. New Zealand's monetary arrangement is, in other words, yet another instance of a pseudo rather than a real monetary rule.

According to section 49 of the Reserve Bank of New Zealand (RBNZ) Act of 1989, which established the current New Zealand arrangement, "The Governor-General may, by Order in Council, on the advice of the Minister, remove the Governor from office," and "the Minister may tender advice" provided the governor-general is "satisfied" that one of several conditions has been met, one of which is "that the performance of the Governor in ensuring that the Bank achieves the policy targets fixed under section 9 or section 12(7)(b) has been inadequate" (New Zealand Parliament 1989).

In fact, although the targets were violated on several occasions during the 1990s, no action was taken. And although inflation declined after New Zealand switched to inflation targeting, it isn't clear that the RBNZ Act, and the PTA in particular, had much to do with it. According to Sherwin (2010: 264), "Governments that were willing to commit themselves to far-reaching reforms across all sectors of the economy were never likely to be tolerant of continuing high inflation, or to shrink from the hard decisions needed to contain inflation, regardless of the precise policy regime in place."

While the strict contractual enforcement of official monetary rules is practically unknown today, such enforcement operated effectively in the past, when rule violations led to loss of shareholder wealth. I have in mind the means by which issuers of paper money were compelled to abide by metallic standards.

Although the fact is sometimes overlooked today, in the past, most banks of issue were wholly private institutions, and as such were bound by the same sort of contractual obligations to which deposit-granting banks are subject today. In particular, they were required by law to redeem their demandable liabilities in specific amounts of "outside" money or legal tender, and were held to be in default if they failed to do so.

Gary Santoni (1984: 12–13) offers the Bank of England as a case in point. That Bank, he notes, "was a privately owned for-profit central bank from its inception in 1694 until the early 1930s." Furthermore, the Bank's obligation to redeem its notes in a fixed quantity of gold was a matter of private contract rather than one of government policy. These arrangements created "a unique incentive structure" that effectively "related the wealth of the Bank's owners inversely to the rate of inflation":

> If bank notes were issued in such quantities as to cause their market price in terms of gold to fall below the price promised by the Bank, people would arbitrage the difference by trading gold for notes in the market at the low price and exchanging notes for gold at the Bank for the higher price. In the process wealth would be transferred away from the stockholders to those engaging in the arbitrage. The guarantee was believable because customers knew that stockholders would lose wealth if the Bank over issued its notes relative to the supply of goods in general and gold in particular [Santoni 1984: 18].

Santoni goes on to show how the British government's decision to authorize the Bank to suspend gold payments in 1797—and to assume effective control of the supply of paper money for the duration of the Napoleonic Wars and beyond—changed the structure of constraints dramatically, eventually resulting in both higher inflation and lower share values. In general, the conversion of banks of issue from private firms to public or semipublic monetary authorities had the effect of undermining the strict enforcement of convertibility rules, transforming former real gold standards everywhere into pseudo gold standards that ended up being no more credible than the more recent pegged exchange rate regime discussed previously (Selgin 2015a).

While the historical gold standard depended on a combination of profit incentives in the gold mining industry and strict convertibility of paper money into gold, Hayek (1978) envisions a system in which unrestricted competition among both private and public issuers of inconvertible (or fiat) paper money are compelled by considerations of profit and loss to regulate their currencies so as to stabilize their purchasing power, lest their failure to do so should cause them to lose market share to rival issuers. Although intriguing, Hayek's scenario is entirely hypothetical. Moreover, as Lawrence White (1999: 227–39) and others have shown, it is far from clear that profit considerations alone would always suffice to rule out the possibility that an issuer might prefer the one-time gain from hyperinflating to the long-run profits to be had by supplying a currency of stable purchasing power.

Robust Contract-Enforced Monetary Rules

Besides being strictly enforced, a real monetary rule must also be "robust." That is, it must be chosen so that its strict enforcement is not likely to be a cause of such regret as might lead to its frequent revision or abandonment.

A strictly enforced monetary rule might become a cause for regret for either of two reasons. Most obviously, the rule might be one whose strict enforcement occasionally leads to economic distress that a different rule, or monetary discretion, might easily have avoided. Somewhat less obviously, the rule's strict enforcement might result in frequent punishment or dismissal of monetary authorities who have in fact acted in good faith, using the best available information.

I shall say relatively little concerning the relative merits of alternative rules with respect to the first of these potential causes of regret, as the topic is already the subject of a vast literature, and one that includes some of the other contributions to this volume. Instead, my concern is mainly with the other possible cause of regret that a robust rule ought to avoid. What sort of rules can we reasonably expect a central banker to abide by, assuming that he or she is subject to sanctions when the rule is violated? The question is crucial because no amount of sanctions can suffice to guarantee strict adherence to a rule that even the most competent central banker cannot avoid breaking.

If one is to answer the question, it is useful to distinguish three sorts of macroeconomic variables: (1) variables that the central bank controls more-or-less directly; (2) variables whose long-run values it can control only indirectly and, therefore, imperfectly; and (3) variables over which it exercises no long-run influence. Call these variables "instruments," "nominal control variables," and "real variables," respectively.

A robust monetary rule, in the sense of one that is bound to be adhered to provided it is enforced with sufficient stringency, must, in the first place, refer to an objective or target variable the long-run value of which is subject to the central bank's control. That means a rule concerning either an instrument, such as B (the monetary base) or i (the nominal federal funds rate), or a nominal control variable, such as M (any monetary aggregate), P (some measure of the price level), or Py (a measure of nominal income or spending), rather than a real variable like real output, the unemployment rate, or the velocity of money.

But among rules involving nominal target variables, some are more robust, because they are subject to less "control error," than others. The most robust rules, subject to the least control error, involve targets that depend on the fewest weasel variables, where a "weasel variable" is any real variable that can influence the short-run behavior of the target variable.

Consider, for example, three different monetary rules, each calling upon a central bank to stick to a prescribed growth rate for B, M, and P, respectively. The most robust rule is the one that involves the fewest weasel variables—that is, the one that offers a central banker the fewest opportunities to weasel out of trouble if the rule is violated. To see which of the three rules meet that requirement, consider the equation of exchange:

(1) $MV = Py$.

Let $M = mB$, where m is the base-money multiplier, a real variable that depends on the banking system reserve ratio and the public's preferred ratio of currency to deposits. Taking natural logarithms gives

(2) $\ln m + \ln B + \ln V = \ln P + \ln y$.

If, using (2), we write the target variable for each of the three rules as a function of B, the instrument over which the central bank has complete control, we get

(3) $\ln B = \ln B$,

(4) $\ln M = \ln m + \ln B$, and

(5) $\ln P = \ln m + \ln B + \ln V - \ln y$.

Evidently, of the three rules, the one calling for a fixed growth rate for the monetary base is the most robust, as there can be no legitimate reason for a central banker to fail to adhere to it—and hence no way for him or her to weasel out of trouble if the rule is, in fact, violated. A money-stock growth target, in contrast, appears to involve one weasel variable—the base-money multiplier—but actually involves several, as the multiplier is itself a function of several real variables. An inflation-rate rule, finally, involves the same weasel variables as a money-stock rule, and two more besides—namely, the velocity of money and real output—making it the least robust of the three.

Consider again, for the sake of concreteness, New Zealand's PTA, and forget for the moment the many ifs, mights, and mays, that call to question the likelihood of its ever really being enforced. According to the agreement,

> On occasions when the annual rate of inflation is outside the medium-term target range, or when such occasions are projected, the Bank shall explain . . . why such outcomes have occurred, or are projected to occur, and what measures it has taken, or proposes to take, to ensure that inflation outcomes remain consistent with the medium-term target.

Now suppose that the Reserve Bank governor, having allowed New Zealand's inflation rate to exceed the prescribed range, is called upon to offer such explanations, on the understanding that he will be dismissed unless the explanations are fully compelling. It is easy to imagine the governor blaming the error on the Bank's having overestimated New Zealand's real rate of economic growth, or its having underestimated the rate of growth of velocity, or the money multiplier. Moreover, it is easy to see how such mistakes may be entirely innocent, so that dismissing the governor would achieve very little, though it would almost certainly increase the pressure to revise the rule. Accepting the excuses, on the other hand, would risk undermining the rule's credibility.[2]

---

[2] A nominal GDP rule is also less easy for a central banker to weasel out from than a price-level rule, because it does not call on policymakers to anticipate and accommodate changes in output. That is, unlike a strict inflation target, it doesn't require that the central bank be capable of accurately forecasting supply innovations or "shocks." The contrary suggestion that a nominal GDP rule, because it involves targeting Py, requires the central bank to control both P and y, and is therefore harder to enforce than a price-level rule, is based on a crude misunderstanding. A central bank that controls or targets Py actually has an easier, not a harder, task to perform than one that attempts to target P.

Milton Friedman (1962: 242) presumably had similar considerations in mind in claiming that a price-level rule "is the wrong kind of rule because the objectives it specifies are ones that the monetary authorities do not have the clear and direct power to achieve by their own actions." However, a constant monetary growth rule, which was Friedman's preferred rule at the time, though better, is itself subject to the same criticism. As Leitzel (2003: 52) notes, "[T]he monetary authorities cannot control the growth rate of a monetary aggregate precisely"; hence, rigorous enforcement of such a rule "would itself be a questionable practice." Such considerations, together with the collapse of what had previously been regarded as a relatively stable "money demand function" over the course of the 1970s, ultimately led Friedman to favor a monetary base rule—that is, a rule involving no weasel variables.

The disadvantage of a base rule is of course that, although its strict enforcement may never be a cause of regret stemming from the necessity of punishing well-meaning and competent central bankers, it would almost certainly be a recipe for regret concerning avoidable economic distress. For it is all too easy to imagine occasions in which a strictly enforced base rule would prove inconsistent with a relatively stable level of overall spending, and, hence, with the avoidance of macroeconomic disturbances.

Certain rules can, however, avoid both sorts of regret, making them particularly robust. An example is the monetary rule proposed by McCallum (1987), a simplified version of which might be written as

$$(6)\ B_t = k + \lambda\,(X^\circ - X_{t-1}),$$

where $X\,(= \ln P + \ln y)$ is the nominal GDP (NGDP) growth rate, X° is the target rate, and k is the base growth rate estimated to be consistent with achieving the long-run NGDP growth rate target. Because it calls for a particular pattern of adjustments to the monetary base, McCallum's rule, like Friedman's monetary base growth rule, is one that the monetary authorities cannot possibly violate unintentionally. But instead of calling for the base to grow at a constant rate, McCallum's rule calls upon the authorities to adjust the base in response to perceived changes in nominal spending (Py), with the ultimate objective of maintaining a stable level or growth rate of such spending—a goal much more likely to avoid macroeconomic disorder. In the case of such a "feedback rule," the authority is subject to sanctions, not for failing to achieve the desired spending target—the feedback rule itself, if properly designed, sees to that—but for failing to adjust the monetary base according to the prescribed feedback rule.

My discussion of robust monetary rules will recall for many the debate some years ago concerning target versus instrument rules for monetary policy. In that debate, a monetary instrument was defined just as I have defined it, that is, as "a variable the central bank administers or controls so closely that control error can be ignored" (Froyen and Guender 2012: 101). However, participants in that debate (for example, Svensson 2005) understood a "robust rule" to be one that minimized some postulated policy loss function. That definition conforms to mine only to the extent that it favors rules limiting the incidence of potentially avoidable (and therefore regrettable) economic distress. The targets versus instruments literature ignored entirely the second potential sort of regret—that stemming from having to punish innocent central bankers. Consequently, and not surprisingly, that literature concluded that target rules were more robust than instrument rules, including instrument rules involving feedback from some ultimately desired target.

Enforcement by Design

A monetary rule can be said to be enforced by design, rather than by contract, when the monetary system itself automatically implements the rule, without need for an authority that might fail to comply with it, and therefore without any need for sanctions. Enforcement by design eliminates the possibility of either unintentional rule violations or intentional ones resulting from political pressure and like influences. As Leitzel (2003: 50) notes, "A fixed rule that is implemented automatically, like a machine, eliminates this incentive for politicking. Machines are notoriously difficult to persuade, being immune to the blandishments of reason, love, or money." Because a monetary rule enforced by design does not rely on sanctions, such a rule is necessarily robust to the extent that there is no question of its not being properly enforced. Such a rule may however be a cause of avoidable distress that could put its sustainability in doubt, thereby undermining its credibility.

Officially dollarized monetary systems are the only prominent examples today of monetary arrangements involving rules enforced by design. By employing a foreign nation's paper currency as their own circulating means of payment, often without establishing any monetary authority of their own, dollarized nations effectively commit themselves to the equivalent of a fixed exchange rate rule, while depriving themselves of any immediate means for modifying or abandoning the rule. Such arrangements are examples of what Schuler (2007) regards as genuinely fixed (as opposed to less-credibly "pegged") exchange rate regimes. According to my own terminology, they supply a foundation for real rather than pseudo monetary rules.

Orthodox currency boards—arrangements in which a domestic monetary authority issues a distinct domestic currency that is both freely convertible on demand into a "host" foreign currency and fully backed by host foreign currency reserves—also serve to fix rather than merely peg the domestic–host currency exchange rate (Hanke 2002). Because a currency board holds 100 percent foreign-currency reserves, it can never be forced to suspend, and is therefore neither as vulnerable to speculative runs nor as likely to be confronted by them as a conventional pegged-rate system. The persons in charge of the currency board may also lack any power to alter its fixed-rate commitment, which might be embodied in the board's enabling legislation or even in the national constitution. For these reasons, we might also consider a currency board as an instance of a real monetary rule enforced by design. In any event, it comes much closer to such a rule than an ordinary, central bank based exchange rate commitment, which is no more than a pseudo rule.

Dollarization and currency boards are designed to implement currency convertibility rules. But it is also possible to conceive of monetary arrangements designed to automatically enforce other sorts of rules. A hypothetical possibility of this sort was proposed years ago by Milton Friedman, when he (perhaps somewhat facetiously) suggested replacing the FOMC with a computer programmer so as to regulate the New York Fed's open-market operations in a manner guaranteed to keep the money stock growing at a prespecified rate. Importantly, the success of such a scheme rests no less on the elimination of the FOMC—or any other body capable of either reprogramming the computer or overriding its instructions—than on the adequacy of the computer program itself.

Although Bitcoin as yet doesn't quite qualify as money—that is, as a generally accepted medium of exchange—a monetary regime using Bitcoin's blockchain technology, whether based on Bitcoin or some other cybercurrency, would represent a variation on Friedman's computer-controlled open-market purchases, and one having the decisive advantage of relying on an open-source software that is highly tamper resistant. In the case of Bitcoin, the software is programmed so that the supply of bitcoins increases at a diminishing rate, eventually leveling-off as the limit of 21 million bitcoins is approached. Because such a quantity rule hardly seems calculated to avoid long-run economic distress stemming from growth and fluctuations in the real demand for money balances, its long-run sustainability as the basis of an actual, national, or international monetary regime, would be quite doubtful. A modified program using the same blockchain technology might, however, provide for more flexible and macroeconomically friendly patterns of money stock adjustment (Selgin 2015b).

An interesting proposal for a monetary rule enforced by design is Scott Sumner's plan for a "market-driven" NGDP targeting regime. According to Sumner (2013: 4), his plan involves "setting up a nominal GDP futures market and then adjusting the monetary base to stabilize nominal GDP futures prices. The market, not central banks, would set the level of the monetary base and short-term interest rates under this sort of policy regime."

To arrive at his market-driven arrangement, Sumner would first establish a contract-based NGDP targeting scheme, in which FOMC members' salaries are tied to the accuracy of their NGDP forecasts (Sumner 2013: 11), with hawks being punished and doves rewarded if NGDP increases too slowly; and doves being punished and hawks rewarded if it rises too quickly. Next, Sumner imagines that FOMC members "vote" by actually taking either long or short positions in NGDP futures contracts, with the Fed offering to buy or sell unlimited quantities of NGDP futures contracts at a fixed price of $1.0365 per contract (reflecting a 3.65 percent NGDP growth target), while at the same time "linking" its open-market security purchases to NGDP futures market transactions. Finally, he would allow anyone to participate in the NGDP futures market and to thereby influence the Fed's open-market operations.

But while Sumner's proposal, assuming it would work as he suggests, would in a sense make monetary policy and NGDP targeting automatic, it is not clear that it would do so in the crucial sense of ruling out departures from, or even the complete abandonment of, the proposed rule. For suppose that the Federal Reserve chose to cease buying and selling futures contracts, or to buy and sell them at a different value. Or suppose it modified or severed the "link" connecting its NGDP futures market transactions from its open-market purchases and sales. Are such steps altogether impossible under the proposed system? If so, why? And if not, what is to prevent them from being taken? What, if any, sanctions would be applied, and to whom? If the answer is none, the NGDP futures targeting arrangement, despite its presumed "automaticity," is, in fact, another instance of a pseudo rather than a real monetary rule.[3]

Conclusion: A Matter of Degree

In distinguishing between real and pseudo monetary rules, I do not wish to be understood to suggest that these alternatives are separated by a hard and fast line. On the contrary, the line is a very fine one, the difference ultimately being one, not in kind, but in degree to which adherence to a rule is regarded as unbreakable. In fact, there is no such thing as an absolutely unbreakable monetary rule, for monetary arrangements are human creations and there is nothing human beings can create that they cannot also destroy.

Yet, however fine the line between the two may be, the distinction between real and pseudo monetary rules seems to me necessary and important. For unless that distinction is made, the difference between monetary rules and monetary discretion becomes hopelessly blurred, and there can be no reasonable accounting for the relative advantages and shortcomings of the two alternatives.

---

[3]Some years ago, Sumner (2009) wrote of his proposal in a manner expressly suggesting that it its long-run viability rested, not on either sanctions or other devices serving to guarantee its perpetuation, but solely on the likelihood that it would avoid macroeconomic distress. "Even if the program stabilized 12-month forward NGDP expectations, it might not stabilize longer term NGDP expectations if the public expected the Fed to abandon the policy at some point in the future. However, I don't see this as a major drawback, as I believe stabilizing 12-month forward NGDP expectations would keep nominal wage rates well behaved, and . . . I regard aggregate nominal wage instability as the key factor behind macroeconomic instability."

References

Brown, P. J. (1982) "Constitution or Competition? Alternative Views on Monetary Reform." *Literature of Liberty* 5 (3): 7–52.

Buchanan, J. M, and Brennan, G. (2008) *The Reason of Rules: Constitutional Political Economy*. New York: Cambridge University Press.

Friedman, M. (1960) *A Program for Monetary Stability*. New York: Fordham University Press.

_____ (1961) "Real and Pseudo Gold Standards." *Journal of Law and Economics* 4 (October): 66–79.

_____ (1962) "Should There Be an Independent Monetary Authority?" In L. B. Yeager (ed.), *In Search of a Monetary Constitution*, 219–43. Cambridge, Mass.: Harvard University Press.

Froyen, R. T., and Guender, A. V. (2012) "Instrument versus Target Rules As Specifications of Optimal Monetary Policy." *International Finance* 15 (1): 99–123.

Gurri, A. (2013) "Rules vs Discretion Revisited: The Insularity of Economists." *The Ümlaut* (30 September).

Hanke, S. H. (2002) "Currency Boards." *Annals of the American Academy of Political and Social Science* 579 (1): 87–105.

Hayek, F. A. (1978) *The Denationalisation of Money*, 2nd ed. London: Institute of Economic Affairs.

Leitzel, J. (2003) *The Political Economy of Rule Evasion and Policy Reform*. London: Routledge.

McCallum, B. (1987) "The Case for Rules in the Conduct of Monetary Policy: A Concrete Example." Federal Reserve Bank of Richmond *Economic Review* (September/October): 10–18.

Mullineaux, D. J. (1985) "Monetary Rules and Contracts: Why Theory Loses to Practice." Federal Reserve Bank of Philadelphia *Business Review* (March/April): 13–19.

New Zealand Parliament (1989) "Reserve Bank of New Zealand Act." Public Act No. 157.

O'Driscoll, G. P. Jr. (2016) "Monetary Policy: The Knowledge Problem." *Cato Journal* 36 (2) (Spring/Summer): 337–52.

Reserve Bank of New Zealand (n.d.) "The Evolution of Policy Targets Agreements." Available at www.rbnz.govt.nz/monetary-policy/about-monetary-policy/independent-review-of-the-operation-of-monetary-policy-2/the-evolution-of-policy-targets-agreements.

Rogoff, K. (1986) "Social Institutions for Overcoming Monetary Policy Credibility Problems." Paper presented at the American Economic Association Meetings, New Orleans (December).

Santoni, G. (1984) "A Private Central Bank: Some Olde English Lessons." Federal Reserve Bank of St. Louis *Review* 66 (April): 12–22.

Schuler, K. (2007) "The Problem with Pegged Exchange Rates." *Kyklos* 52 (1): 83–102.

Selgin, G. (2015a) "Law, Legislation, and the Gold Standard." *Cato Journal* 35 (2) (Spring/Summer): 251–72.

_____ (2015b) "Synthetic Commodity Money." *Journal of Financial Stability* 17 (April): 92–99.

Sherwin, M. (2010) "Inflation Targeting: The New Zealand Experience." Ottawa: Bank of Canada.

Sumner, S. (2009) "Spot the Flaw in Nominal Index Futures Targeting." *TheMoneyIllusion* (9 May): www.themoneyillusion.com/?p=1184.

_____ (2013) "A Market-Driven Nominal GDP Targeting Regime." Arlington, Va.: Mercatus Center, George Mason University.

Svensson, L. E. O. (2005) "Targeting versus Instrument Rules for Monetary Policy: What Is Wrong with McCallum and Nelson." Federal Reserve Bank of St. Louis *Review* 87: 613–25.

Turnovsky S. (1977) *Macroeconomic Analysis and Stabilization Policy.* Cambridge, U.K.: Cambridge University Press.

Viner, J. (1962) "The Necessary and the Desirable Range of Discretion to Be Allowed to a Monetary Authority." In L. B. Yeager (ed.), *In Search of a Monetary Constitution*, 244–74. Cambridge, Mass.: Harvard University Press.

White, L. H. (1999) *The Theory of Monetary Institutions.* Oxford, U.K.: Blackwell.

11
LEGISLATING A RULE FOR MONETARY POLICY
John B. Taylor

In these remarks I discuss a proposal to legislate a rule for monetary policy. The proposal modernizes laws first passed in the late
1970s, but largely discarded in 2000.

A number of years ago I proposed a simple rule as a guideline for
monetary policy.[1] I made no suggestion then that the rule should be
written into law, or even that it be used to monitor policy, or hold
central banks accountable. The objective was to help central bankers
make their interest rate decisions in a less discretionary and more
rule-like manner, and thereby achieve the goal of price stability and
economic stability. The rule incorporated what we learned from
research on optimal design of monetary rules in the years before.

In the years since then we have learned much more. We learned
that such simple rules are robust to widely different views about how
monetary policy works (see Taylor and Williams 2011). We learned
that such rules are frequently used by financial market analysts in
their assessment of policy and by policymakers in their own deliber-
ations (see Asso, Kahn, and Leeson 2007). We learned that when policy is close to such rules, economic performance is good: inflation is
low, expansions are long, unemployment is low, and recessions are

---

John B. Taylor is Mary and Robert Raymond Professor of Economics at
Stanford University and George P. Shultz Senior Fellow in Economics at Stanford's
Hoover Institution.
This article is reprinted from the *Cato Journal*, Vol. 31, No. 3
(Fall 2011).

[1]See Taylor (1993) and also the *Economic Report of the President* (1990: 85)
where the idea of such a systemic policy was described in less technical and less
quantitative language.

short, shallow, and infrequent; but when policy is short-term focused and deviates from such rules, economic performance is poor (see Meltzer 2009).

Why legislate a policy rule now? Because monetary policy has recently become more discretionary, more short-term focused, much less rule-like than it was in the 1980s and 1990s, and economic performance has deteriorated. A legislated rule can reverse the short-term focus of policy and restore credibility in sound monetary principles consistent with long-term price stability and strong economic growth.

Signs of a shift toward more discretion appeared as far back as 2002–04, when the policy interest rate was held below settings that worked well during the 1980s and 1990s. But policymakers have doubled down on discretion since then. When the bursting housing bubble led to tensions in the financial markets in 2007, policymakers used the central bank's balance sheet to finance an ad hoc and chaotic series of bailouts which led to the panic in the fall of 2008. After helping to arrest the panic, they then further expanded the balance sheet in order to finance massive purchases of mortgage-backed and Treasury securities (the first tranche of so-called quantitative easing, or QE1). And now they have embarked on yet another program of large-scale purchases (QE2), which increases risks about inflation down the road or further disruptions when the balance sheet is scaled back. A legislated rule would increase certainty that the size of the balance sheet will be reduced in a timely and predictable manner and thereby reduce this risk.

My research shows that these discretionary actions were, on balance, harmful. But even if one disagrees, the actions should raise concerns about a monetary system in which a great deal of power is vested in an organization with little accountability and without checks and balances. The purchase of mortgage-backed securities explicitly shifts funds to one sector and away from others, an action which should be approved by Congress. Putting taxpayer funds at risk is a credit subsidy, which should be appropriated by Congress. Some of the discretionary actions are inconsistent with the intent of the Constitution because they take monetary policy into fiscal or credit allocation areas and thereby circumvent the appropriations process. The recent QE2 action irritated many countries around the world, and may have impacted U.S. foreign policy by affecting the ability of the United States to negotiate positions at the recent G20 meeting.

In sum, these recent discretionary actions, combined with the success of a more strategic rule-like policy in the decades before, raise the question of legislating rules for monetary policy.

While passing such legislation necessarily involves the president and the Congress of the United States, it does not mean that the president or Congress should insert themselves in the operational decisionmaking process of the Federal Reserve. Indeed, legislation in the 1970s, which I will summarize here, was constructive in bringing about longer-term reforms at the Federal Reserve, as described positively in a retrospective by Ben Bernanke (2008: 177): "The Congress has also long been aware of the importance of Federal Reserve transparency and accountability. In particular, a series of resolutions and laws passed in the 1970s set clear policy objectives for the Federal Reserve and required it to provide regular reports and testimony to the Congress."[2]

The objective, as Milton Friedman (1962: 51) said many years ago, is to find a way of "legislating rules for the conduct of monetary policy that will have the effect of enabling the public to exercise control over monetary policy through its political authorities, while at the same time it will prevent monetary policy from being subject to the day-by-day whim of political authorities."

Brief Review of Legislation

Though modern monetary rules focus on the interest rate, much can be learned from the history of legislation relating to the monetary aggregates. Such legislation includes House Concurrent Resolution 133 of 1975, the Federal Reserve Reform Act of 1977, the Full Employment and Balanced Growth Act of 1978, and the American Homeownership and Economic Opportunity Act of 2000.

House Congressional Resolution 133 was adopted on March 24, 1975, just as the recession of 1973–75 was reaching its trough. Early versions of the resolution called on the Fed to increase the money supply and reduce interest rates, which was certainly not consistent with the Congress staying out of the day-to-day operations of the Fed. But after extensive discussions with the Fed, including testimony by Arthur Burns, the final version focused on requirements to report

[2]Bernanke first made these remarks at the Cato Institute's 25th Annual Monetary Conference, November 14, 2007.

and testify about the growth of monetary and credit aggregates. In particular the Resolution said that "the Board of Governors shall consult with Congress at semi-annual hearings . . . about the Board of Governors' and the Federal Open Market Committee's objectives and plans with respect to the ranges of growth or diminution of monetary and credit aggregates in the upcoming twelve months."

William Poole (1976), in one of the first economic assessments of the Resolution, was critical of how it was implemented, pointing to the problem of base drift. But the requirements to report and testify started a trend toward transparency and accountability which continued into the 1980s and 1990s.

Much of the money growth reporting language in Resolution 133 was incorporated into the Federal Reserve Reform Act of 1977. This reform act also added a new sentence (in Section 2A) on purpose and long-run goals, stating that: "The Board of Governors of the Federal Reserve System and the Federal Open Market Committee shall maintain long-run growth of the monetary and credit aggregates commensurate with the economy's long-run potential to increase production, so as to promote effectively the goals of maximum employment, stable prices, and moderate long-term interest rates." This sentence has remained in the Federal Reserve Act ever since, and now constitutes the entirety of Section 2A.

The Full Employment and Balanced Growth Act of 1978 modified the reporting requirements of the Federal Reserve Act. It still focused on "the ranges of growth or diminution of the money and credit aggregates," but it called for a report and testimony in February and July of each year. The money growth ranges for the current calendar year would be given in the February report and testimony, and the ranges for the following calendar year in the July report and testimony, which gave a slightly longer-term focus.

Some ambiguity remained, however, about whether the Fed should be held accountable for deviations from these ranges. As amended in 1978 the Federal Reserve Act stated: "Nothing in this Act shall be interpreted to require that the objectives and plans with respect to the ranges of growth or diminution of the monetary and credit aggregates disclosed in the reports submitted under this section be achieved if the Board of Governors and the Federal Open Market Committee determine that they cannot or should not be achieved because of changing conditions: *Provided*, that in the subsequent consultations with, and reports to, the aforesaid Committees of the Congress pursuant to this section, the Board of Governors shall include an explanation of the reasons for any revisions to or deviations from such objectives and plans."

The required reporting on the monetary and credit aggregates was completely eliminated in the American Homeownership and Economic Opportunity Act of 2000, which struck everything after the statement of purpose sentence of Section 2A, and added a new Section 2B on testimony and reports to the Congress. These reports were to contain "a discussion of the conduct of monetary policy and economic developments and prospects for the future, taking into account past and prospective developments in employment, unemployment, production, investment, real income, productivity, exchange rates, international trade and payments, and prices." Thus, reporting about the ranges for growth of the monetary aggregates was eliminated.

Along with these changes in reporting requirements came an end to the Fed's establishing ranges for the monetary aggregates. The Monetary Policy Report of July 20, 2000, explained in a footnote that "At its June [2000] meeting, the FOMC did not establish ranges for growth of money and debt in 2000 and 2001. The legal requirement to establish and to announce such ranges had expired, and owing to uncertainties about the behavior of the velocities of debt and money, these ranges for many years have not provided useful benchmarks for the conduct of monetary policy." Later, in its Monetary Policy Report of February 15, 2006, the Fed announced that it would no longer even publish data on M3 because such publication "was judged to be no longer generating sufficient benefit in the analysis of the economy or of the financial sector to justify the costs of publication."

Four things can be taken away from this short review. First, the legislation only required *reporting* of the ranges of the monetary aggregates, not that they be set in any particular way, certainly nothing close to a rule such as keeping the growth rate of money constant over time and equal to some specific percent. The Fed had full discretion to choose both the aggregates and the ranges. Second, the ranges were not really used as a measure of accountability. Though the proviso language required some justification for deviations, the reduced reliability of the aggregates as instruments of monetary policy and the increasing focus on the interest rate instrument in the 1980s and 1990s rendered accounting for deviations meaningless. Third, the reporting requirements changed over time. Most importantly, when the monetary aggregates became less reliable, the requirements for reporting about them were eliminated. Fourth, when the ranges for the monetary aggregates were finally removed from the legislation in 2000, nothing comparable about the interest rate instrument was put in their place. A legislative void was created concerning reporting requirements and accountability. You could say that the reporting-accountability baby was thrown out with the monetary aggregate bathwater.

Proposed Legislative Changes

The most straightforward way to legislate a rule for monetary policy would be to fill this void by reinstating reporting requirements and accountability requirements that were removed from the Federal Reserve Act by the American Homeownership and Opportunity Act of 2000. But rather than focus on "ranges of growth or diminution of the money and credit aggregates," it would focus directly on the rule-like response of the federal funds rate.

The proposed legislation—call it the Federal Reserve Policy Rule Act—would first repeal the parts of the American Homeownership and Opportunity Act of 2000 pertaining to monetary policy, which are in Title X, Section 1003. It would then use much of the language in the reporting and accountability sections of Federal Reserve Act as it existed just prior to the passage of the 2000 Act, but modernized to incorporate policy decisions about the interest rate.

Reporting Requirements

The reporting section of the legislation would thus state that "The Board of Governors of the Federal Reserve System shall transmit to the Congress no later than February 20 and July 20 of each year a written report setting forth (1) the strategy, or rule, of the Board and the FOMC for the systematic adjustment of the federal funds rate in response to changes in inflation and in the real economy during the current year and future years, along with any additional systematic adjustments needed to achieve the price stability objective, (2) the procedure for adjusting the supply of bank reserves to bring about the desired federal funds rate, recognizing that the rate is determined by the supply and demand for reserves in the money market." Because of the large current size of the Fed's balance sheet, a transitional exit rule to reduce bank reserves in a predictable way would also need to be established and reported.[3]

Accountability Requirements

The accountability parts of the new law would also build on the Federal Reserve Act prior to 2000 and say that "Nothing in this Act shall be interpreted to require that the plans with respect to the systematic quantitative adjustment of the federal funds rate disclosed in the reports submitted under this section be achieved if the Board of Governors and the Federal Open Market Committee determine that they cannot or should not be achieved because of changing conditions: *Provided*, that in the subsequent consultations with, and reports to, the Committees of the Congress pursuant to this section, the Board of Governors shall include an explanation of the reasons for any revisions to or deviations from the rule for the systematic quantitative adjustments of the federal funds rate."[4]

This accountability language could be strengthened by not permitting any deviations from the rule, but that does not seem reasonable. As explained in Levin and Taylor (2010), "On occasion, of course, policymakers might find compelling reasons to modify, adjust, or depart from the prescriptions of any simple rule, but in those circumstances, transparency and credibility might well call for clear communication about the rationale for that policy strategy." In my view, the requirement to explain deviations as soon as they were apparent, or at the next scheduled hearing would be conducive to better policy. There are many examples now of economists examining deviations from policy rules, though usually long after the fact. It may be more difficult in real time, but it is certainly feasible.

This proposal would limit the Fed's discretion by requiring that it establish and report on a policy rule for the federal funds rate. For example, if the Fed decides to use the Taylor Rule,[5] it would meet reporting requirement number (1) of the proposed law by reporting that its systematic interest rate adjustment is 1.5 percent for each percent change in inflation and 0.5 percent for each percent

[3]For a specific example of such an exit rule, see Taylor (2010).
[4]The italics were in the Federal Reserve Act
[5]This rule says that the interest rate should be set to equal one-and-a-half times the inflation rate plus one-half times the GDP gap plus one. The GDP gap is the percentage difference between real GDP and potential GDP (see Taylor 1993).

difference between real GDP and potential GDP; then a fixed adjustment of +1 would be needed to achieve an inflation goal of 2 percent.

The proposal does not require that the Fed choose any particular rule for the interest rate, only that it establish some rule and report what the rule is. For example, the Board of Governors and the FOMC could decide that their strategy does not entail any response to changes in real GDP and that they will only respond to inflation as measured by a commodity price index. If the Fed's experience dealing with the mandate to establish and report growth rates for the monetary aggregates in the late 1970s and 1980s is any guide, the mere effort to establish such a strategy will be constructive. But if the Fed deviates from its chosen strategy, the Board of Governors must provide a written explanation and answer questions at a congressional hearing. So while the proposal limits discretion, it does not eliminate discretion. It provides a degree of control by the political authorities without interfering in the day-to-day operations of monetary policy.

Conclusion

I have tried in these remarks to show why it is important for price stability and economic growth to restore a more strategic rule-like monetary policy with less short-term oriented discretionary actions. By reviewing U.S. legislative history since the late 1970s, I have shown that it possible to legislate a rule for monetary policy such as the one that worked well in the 1980s and 1990s, and I have written some illustrative legislative language. Such legislation would also bolster the independence of the Federal Reserve by increasing accountability and reducing the tendency to take discretionary actions which venture into fiscal or credit allocation policy.

There are of course alternative ways to limit discretion, some of which are not mutually exclusive with the proposals here, such as removing or modifying the "maximum employment" term in Section 2A, which, as I described earlier, has been carried over from outmoded views about the relation between unemployment and inflation. But in the current circumstances, it is important to get started. By building on experience and the legislative history of the Federal Reserve Act as it pertains to reporting and accountability for the instruments of policy, the legislative change proposed here is a reasonable and practical place to begin.

References

Asso, F.; Kahn, G.; and Leeson, R. (2007) "The Taylor Rule and the Transformation of Monetary Policy." Federal Reserve Bank of Kansas City, RWP 07–11.

Bernanke, Ben S. (2008) "The Fed's Road toward Greater Transparency." *Cato Journal* 28 (2): 175–86.

Economic Report of the President (1990) Washington: U.S. Government Printing Office.

Friedman, M. (1962) *Capitalism and Freedom.* Chicago: University of Chicago Press.

Levin, A. T., and Taylor, J. B. (2010) "Falling Behind the Curve: A Positive Analysis of Stop-Start Monetary Policies and the Great Inflation." NBER Working Paper No. 15630.

Meltzer, A. H. (2009) *A History of the Federal Reserve*, vol. 2. Chicago: University of Chicago Press.

Poole, W. (1976) "Interpreting the Fed's Monetary Targets." *Brookings Papers on Economic Activity* 1976 (1): 247–59.

Taylor, J. B. (1993) "Discretion versus Policy Rules in Practice." *Carnegie Rochester Conference Series on Public Policy* 39: 195–214.

_____ (2010) "An Exit Rule for Monetary Policy." Testimony before the Committee on Financial Services, U.S. House of Representatives (25 March).

Taylor, J. B., and Williams, J. C. (2011) "Simple and Robust Rules for Monetary Policy." In B. Friedman and M. Woodford (eds.) *Handbook of Monetary Economics*, vol. 3, 829–59. Amsterdam: North-Holland, Elsevier.

12

NOMINAL GDP TARGETING: A SIMPLE RULE TO IMPROVE FED PERFORMANCE

Scott B. Sumner

The history of central banking is a story of one failure after another. This record does not mean that our actual monetary regimes have been the worst of all possible regimes—far from it. But it does mean that we can improve policy by learning from experience. Every proposed reform is a response to a previous failure, an implicit display of lessons learned.

A big part of this story has been the search for a robust monetary system that could produce good outcomes under a wide variety of conditions, without having to rely on a central bank run by a benevolent and omniscient philosopher king. It is a search for a monetary rule that can provide the appropriate amount of liquidity to the economy, under widely differing conditions. In this article, I argue that the optimal monetary rule is a nominal GDP (NGDP) target, or something closely related. To understand the advantages of this approach, it helps to see how the theory and practice of central banking have changed over time—that is, to see what went wrong with some previous monetary regimes, and how past reformers responded to those failures.

Scott B. Sumner is the Ralph G. Hawtrey Chair of Monetary Policy and Director of the Program on Monetary Policy at the Mercatus Center, George Mason University. He is also Professor of Economics at Bentley University. This article is reprinted from the *Cato Journal*, Vol. 34, No. 2 (Spring/Summer 2014). An earlier version of the article appeared as a Mercatus Center Working Paper at George Mason University. The author thanks the Mercatus Center for financial support on that project.

The Gold Standard

It is not hard to see why gold and silver were used as money for much of human history. They are scarce, easy to make into coins, and hold their value over time. Even today one finds many advocates of returning to the gold standard, especially among libertarians. At the same time most academic economists, both Keynesian and monetarist, have insisted we can do better by reforming existing fiat standards.

It is easy to understand this debate if we start with the identity that the (real) value of money is the inverse of the price level. Of course, in nominal terms a dollar is always worth a dollar, but in real terms the value or purchasing power of a dollar falls in half each time the cost of living doubles. During the period since we left the gold standard in 1933 the price level has gone up nearly 18-fold; a dollar today has less purchasing power than six cents back in 1933. That sort of currency depreciation is almost impossible under a gold standard regime; indeed the cost of living in 1933 wasn't much different from what it was in the late 1700s. This long-run stability of the price level is the most powerful argument in favor of the gold standard.

The argument against gold is also based on changes in the value of money, albeit in this case short-term changes. Since the price level is inversely related to the value of money, changes in the supply or demand for gold caused the price level to fluctuate in the short run when gold was used as money. Although the long-run trend in prices under a gold standard is roughly flat, the historical gold standard was marred by periods of inflation and deflation.[1]

Most people agree on that basic set of facts, but then things get more contentious. Critics of the gold standard like Ben Bernanke point to periods of deflation such as 1893–96, 1920–21, and 1929–33, which were associated with falling output and rising unemployment. This is partly because wages are sticky in the short run (see Bernanke and Carey 1996; Christiano, Eichenbaum, and Evans 2005). Supporters point out that the U.S. economy grew robustly

---

[1]The price level effects of changes in stock supply or stock demand for (monetary or nonmonetary) gold are mostly reversed in the long run, as changes in the relative price of gold lead miners to increase or decrease the flow supply of gold. Although changes in the flow supply or flow demand for gold can have a lasting effect on the price level (and purchasing power of gold), Lawrence H. White (1999a) showed that the net effects of such changes were quite small historically.

during the last third of the 19th century, despite frequent deflation and a flawed banking system that was susceptible to periodic crises. They note wages and prices adjusted swiftly to the 1921 deflation, allowing a quick recovery. Countries with more stable banking systems, such as Canada, did even better. The big bone of contention is whether the Great Depression should be blamed on the gold standard or meddlesome government policies (see Cole and Ohanian 2004). My own research suggests the answer is "both" (see Silver and Sumner 1995).

I do see some weaknesses in the arguments put forth by advocates of the gold standard. It is true that some of the worst outcomes were accompanied by unfortunate government intervention, particularly during the 1930s (see Cassel 1936 and Hawtrey 1947). However it is worth pointing out that governments also intervened during the classical gold standard in the period before World War I.

Advocates of gold often base their arguments for gold on the assumption that it's dangerous to give the government control over money. They claim it is much easier and more tempting for governments to debase fiat money, as compared to gold coins. That's true, but it doesn't mean that a gold standard prevents meddlesome governments from creating instability in the short run, as in the 1930s. For instance, during the interwar years major countries such as the United States and France often failed to adjust their money supplies to reflect changes in the monetary gold stock.

Here is how I see the debate today. Advocates of gold correctly claim that a gold standard will tend to preserve the value of money over long periods of time, and will sharply reduce the ability of governments to extract wealth from savers. Critics are right that a real-world gold standard is likely to deliver unacceptably large short-term fluctuations in the price level. I think they are also correct in assuming that wages are much stickier than they were during the gold standard's heyday, and that the sort of deflation that led to just a brief surge in unemployment during 1921 (when wages quickly adjusted downwards) might now lead to unacceptably high and persistent unemployment rates.[2] A classical gold standard could probably do considerably better than the sort of regime we had between the world wars. However, if we could count on the authorities to accept

---

[2]In contrast to 1920–21 when wages fell sharply, the severe recession of 2007–09 merely led to a slowdown in the rate of growth in nominal wages.

the discipline of such a standard, why not make them adhere to a monetary rule to stabilize inflation or the growth of NGDP?

Obviously this debate could go on to look at all sorts of political models of policymaking. Instead, I will focus on purely technical issues and sketch out what I think are the pros and cons of various fiat money regimes, and leave for others the public choice issues of whether such regimes are politically feasible. However, I will return to politics at the end, when I argue that NGDP targeting would help avoid many extremely counterproductive government interventions in nonmonetary aspects of the economy. There are good reasons why many economists with libertarian leanings, including Friedrich Hayek, have embraced some version of this policy target (see Selgin 1995 and White 2008).[3]

Money Supply Targeting and the Taylor Rule

In the United States, gold was phased out in two steps: (1) domestically we left the gold standard in 1933, and (2) internationally the last links were broken in the late 1960s and early 1970s. What followed was a period of very high inflation, which led to renewed interest in finding some sort of anchor for the price level. Between 1979 and 1982, Paul Volcker was seen as leading a "monetarist experiment" trying to control inflation by reining in the money stock.

Contrary to the belief of many economists, the Fed never really adopted the sort of rigorous money supply rule that had been advocated by Milton Friedman (1968) and other monetarists. Even during the early 1980s there was significant variation in the money supply growth rate. The problem is that monetary velocity—that is, the ratio of nominal GDP to the money stock—also seemed volatile, especially in the wake of the so-called monetarist experiment. That is not to say that Volcker's experiment was a complete failure; he did break the back of double-digit inflation, and by doing so proved that monetary policy rather than fiscal policy (which was expansionary under President Reagan) was the key determinant of inflation.

Like central bankers everywhere, Fed policymakers greatly prefer to target interest rates, not the money supply. So once inflation

---

[3]The late William Niskanen, former chairman of the Cato Institute, was a strong proponent of a final demand rule. His preferred target was domestic final sales (see Niskanen 2001).

was brought down to relatively low levels, they went back to targeting the federal funds rate. But memories of the Great Inflation of 1966–81 led many economists to look for a policy rule that would prevent a recurrence of high inflation. John Taylor proposed a rule for adjusting the fed funds target in such a way as to keep inflation near 2 percent and output as close to potential as possible, reflecting the Fed's dual mandate. The key insight was that as inflation rose above target, nominal interest rates had to be raised by more than one for one with inflation, assuring that even real interest rates were higher than before.

It is hard to overstate the importance of the Taylor Rule. In America, Paul Volcker and Alan Greenspan were feted as heroes who had adeptly steered the economy into the Great Moderation, the period of relative stability between 1983 and 2007. In fact, there was no miracle. All of the foreign central banks that operated under somethig like the Taylor Rule also achieved success in bringing inflation down to low and stable levels. It may be politically difficult to bring down the rate of inflation, especially when contracts have been negotiated on the assumption that high inflation would continue. But once this is done, it turns out to be very easy to prevent a recurrence of high inflation. Just promise to raise nominal interest rates by more than any increase in the inflation rate, until you are back on target.

Obviously something went wrong after 2007 (or maybe even before).[4] If the Great Moderation had continued, there would be little reason to abandon the Taylor Rule. But before we consider alternatives, let's discuss what did *not* go wrong with that rule; high inflation did not return. Over the past five years the CPI (even including food and energy prices) has risen at the slowest rates since the mid-1950s, barely over 1 percent per annum.[5] Instead, the problem since 2007 has been a severe recession and accompanying financial distress.

---

[4]David Beckworth (2012) argues that excessive NGDP growth contributed to the housing bubble of 2003–06.

[5]Some skeptics argue that the CPI understates the true rate of inflation. In fact, there is no possibility of objectively measuring the rate of inflation when (highly subjective) estimates of the quality of goods are changing at a rapid pace. It should be noted, however, that even purely private attempts at estimating inflation (such as the MIT "billon prices project") show very low rates over the past four years.

Robert Hetzel (2009, 2012) makes a distinction between the "market disorder view" and the "monetary disorder view." Although the market disorder view is the conventional wisdom, the fact that NGDP fell during 2009 at the fastest rate since the 1930s suggests that monetary policy failure was at the center of the crisis. Like Hetzel, I do not believe that financial distress alone can explain the crisis of 2008 and its aftermath (Sumner 2011). Instead, I see an almost perfect storm of bad luck and bad policy. Interestingly, some of the most popular culprits do not seem to be the real problem. For instance, many critics think that the Fed's dual mandate (price stability and high employment) is itself a problem. In the past I shared this view, believing like others that the mandate was hopelessly vague, and that the Fed could hit only one policy target at a time. Indeed the failures of the 1970s might themselves have been partly due to the Fed trying to hit an employment target that had become unachievable due to growing structural problems with the economy.

Yet, it is hard to see how the dual mandate can be to blame for our recent difficulties. Yes, it would have been better had Congress instead insisted on an explicit NGDP growth target, with level targeting. Under level targeting the central bank promises to make up for any near-term overshoots or shortfalls of the policy target. But it is not realistic to expect mere politicians to be able to devise a sophisticated monetary policy rule. It makes more sense to view the mandate as Congress simply asking the Fed to do the best it can at producing good outcomes in those two areas, while leaving the Fed to figure out how. If it seems I am being too generous to Congress, keep in mind that this interpretation is clearly consistent with the Taylor Rule, a policy that seemed pretty successful for roughly a quarter century.[6]

Others might argue that this approach is too generous to the Fed, implicitly assuming that they will adopt the optimal policy rule. I'd make a slightly more modest claim: the Fed will adopt the sort of policy that the consensus of the macroeconomists view as best practices. If you follow Fed policy over time, including those that failed, they almost invariably reflected the consensus views of mainstream academic macroeconomists. Change that thinking, and you can impact Fed monetary policy. For instance, on September 12th, 2012, the

---

[6]Admittedly, it was an unconscious decision by the Fed in the early part of that period, as the Taylor Rule was not discussed until the 1990s.

Fed undertook some policy initiatives that were influenced by Michael Woodford (2003), probably the most important and influential contemporary monetary economist.[7]

In truth, I think the Taylor Rule is flawed, but I do not see the dual mandate as being the heart of the problem. It is important to distinguish between policy *goals* and a policy *target*. There is no reason why the Fed cannot have multiple policy goals. Indeed, since nominal shocks can have real effects in the short run, it makes sense to have goals related to both inflation and some measure of real economic activity. At the same time, the Fed can target only one variable at a time. The Taylor Rule took a weighted average of inflation and output gaps (deviations from estimates of the natural rate of output), and formed a single target from that composite. NGDP is a single target that can also satisfy the dual mandate, since NGDP growth is the sum of inflation and real growth, where growth obviously depends on the state of employment. In most theoretical models, a target linked to a weighted average of inflation and employment will better address the Fed's dual mandate. In practice, however, it would be far easier to get widespread agreement on an NGDP target, which does not require the Fed to estimate "economic slack" or the "natural rate of unemployment."

If the dual mandate itself hasn't been a problem, then why did monetary policy seem to fail so dramatically after 2007? I see three intertwined problems that together pushed monetary policy far off course. First, the Fed failed to "target the forecast"—that is, policymakers relied too much on past trends rather than forecasts of where the economy was headed. Second, the Fed depended too heavily on interest rate targeting as the instrument of monetary policy. Finally, the Fed failed to engage in level targeting—that is, it did not make up for under- or overshooting of the target path. Instead, the Fed let bygones be bygones and set a new and lower growth target after it severely undershot its inflation and employment objectives in 2009.

A good example of the Fed's failure to target the forecast occurred in the September 2008 FOMC meeting, which occurred right after

---

[7]The Fed undertook an open-ended quantitative easing program, where the amount of assets purchased depends on progress toward the policy goals. The Fed also announced that it would maintain an easy money policy for some period after the economy has recovered, which represents an incremental move toward level targeting.

Lehman Brothers failed. The Fed decided not to cut interest rates, keeping the fed funds target at 2 percent, where it had been since April. It cited equal risks of inflation and recession. It is easy to understand the recession worries because the United States had been in a recession since December 2007, but what about inflation? On the day of the meeting, the five-year TIPS spread (a market indicator of inflation forecasts) had fallen to only 1.23 percent, well below the Fed's inflation target. If those indicators called for easing, why did the Fed stand pat? It turns out that inflation over the previous 12 months had been well above the Fed's 2 percent target. The Fed was responding to past data, not forecasts. It was like trying to steer a car while looking only in the rearview mirror.

Lars Svensson (2003) has argued that central banks should target the forecast—that is, set policy such that the central bank's forecast for the economy is exactly equal to the policy goal. For instance, if a central bank has a 2 percent inflation target, it should set the fed funds rate and monetary base at a level expected to produce 2 percent inflation. This is such common sense that many noneconomists are shocked to learn that real-world central banks do not behave this way. Instead, they resemble a ship's captain who says that while he hopes to reach the port of New York, and has been heading that way, given the current setting of the helm, along with forecasted wind and currents, he expects to end up in Boston. The attitude is perhaps somewhat understandable when interest rates are stuck at zero, but the Fed wasn't even targeting the forecast in the second half of 2008, when rates were still above zero.

In mid-December 2008 the fed funds target reached a level of zero to 0.25 percent, effectively ruling out further reductions. In theory, this should not have been a problem. There's a long academic literature discussing alternative operating procedures. Indeed, Ben Bernanke (1999) wrote articles discussing what the Bank of Japan should have been doing but was failing to do, when rates in Japan hit zero in the late 1990s. In practice, however, the Fed became very timid and failed to aggressively pursue a policy of monetary stimulus. Bernanke called for help from the Treasury. Under normal circumstances that should not have been necessary, because monetary policy is usually more effective in boosting aggregate demand than fiscal policy. Also, pure monetary policy does not boost the deficit and, therefore, does not impose the burden of higher future (distortionary) taxes.

It is not clear why the Fed did not attempt its own more aggressive stimulus. Bernanke expressed vague worries about unspecified "risks and costs" of taking such an aggressive stand. But he was not burdened by similar worries when he encouraged the Bank of Japan to be more aggressive in the early 2000s (see Bernanke 2003).

At one time I believed that the first two problems mentioned earlier were the most crucial ones. Those weaknesses made the policy somewhat slow to adjust to market conditions. But I have since come to conclude that the third problem—the Fed's failure to engage in level targeting—is actually the most important. Level targeting is a very powerful tool both for limiting central bank discretion and for establishing policy credibility. It essentially forces a central bank to do what it says it is trying to do.

Consider the case of Japan, which has experienced mild deflation since the mid-1990s. Because its deflation rate has been quite modest, often below 1 percent, the Bank of Japan can claim that it has merely fallen a bit shy of its goal of achieving price stability. The BOJ has been rather vague about what its goal of price stability actually means, but most observers have taken it to mean something close to a target of zero inflation—or just above zero. Quite recently the Japanese government expressly called upon the BOJ to aim for a rate of 2 percent. With level targeting the central bank commits itself to making up for past inflation shortfalls or overshoots. Thus, if the BOJ had been targeting Japan's GDP deflator, which has actually fallen by more than 15 percent since the mid-1990s, it would have been forced long ago to generate enough inflation to make up for previous shortfalls, so as to have left the deflator not much different now than it was back then. With level targeting, deflation could not have gone on for very long, partly because after a short bout of deflation, expectations of future inflation would have risen enough to reduce real interest rates and boost the price level. Market expectations would thus have helped to stabilize Japan's price level. Nominal GDP level targeting in the United States along a 5 percent trend growth rate prior to 2008 would similarly have helped to greatly reduce the severity of the Great Recession.

The Case for Nominal GDP Targeting

All the aforementioned problems could be fixed without going to NGDP targeting. We could have the Fed target the price level, along a level path or a slightly rising trend line. We could commit to return to the trend line if Fed policy under- or overshot in the short run. We could target the forecast, set policy at a level expected to succeed. We could switch from an interest rate instrument to a policy instrument that is not subject to the zero rate bound—the monetary base, or the price of CPI futures contracts. So why consider NGDP targeting instead?

There are several reasons for doing so, both theoretical and practical. I shall review them in a moment. But first let's start by clearing up a couple things. First, nominal GDP targeting is not a way to boost growth in the economy, or to generate a higher inflation rate. If the long-run trend rate of growth in the economy is 3 percent, then a nominal GDP growth target of 5 percent will deliver the same long-run rates of inflation as a 2 percent inflation target. A nominal GDP target is consistent with any preferred rate of inflation or deflation. Friedrich Hayek, for instance, occasionally argued that monetary policy should aim at a stable level of nominal income (Hayek [1935] 1967), which would have meant having a rate of deflation equal to the long-term growth rate of real GDP (see White 1999b, 2008).

Second, a nominal GDP targeting regime responds to demand shocks (or changes in velocity) in exactly the same way as an inflation targeting regime. In both cases the money supply adjusts to fully offset any sudden change in velocity.

If nominal GDP targeting accommodates shifts in money demand, and produces the same long-run rate of inflation as inflation targeting, then how does it differ? It differs in how it responds to productivity (supply) shocks. Suppose that an oil embargo in the Middle East reduces our oil imports by 10 percent while boosting the price of oil by 60 percent. If the Fed targeted inflation, policymakers would have to tighten money enough to deflate all nonoil prices in order to keep the overall CPI on target. Nominal wages, however, are sticky or slow to adjust, so a sudden fall in the price of domestically produced goods would sharply increase unemployment.

Of course, the Fed might prevent particular supply shocks, like shocks to oil and food output, from having such an adverse consequence by using a "core" price level index that excludes food and energy prices. In practice, this would not be a perfect solution, because energy is a component in the production of many final goods whose prices are included in even the core CPI. But productivity shocks can occur in any sector of an economy. For instance, the computer revolution drove productivity higher at an unusually rapid pace during the late 1990s. Because nominal wages are sticky in the short run, this initially led to much higher profits, higher levels of capital investment, and very low rates of unemployment. Of course, all these trends reversed in the early 2000s. Had the Fed had been targeting NGDP instead of inflation, policy would have been tighter during the high-tech boom, and perhaps also during the housing boom of 2004–06.[8]

One way to think about NGDP targeting and the business cycle is to consider how such targeting would affect labor markets. NGDP is the total nominal income in the economy.[9] The ratio of nominal wages to NGDP can be thought of as the share of NGDP earned for each hour's work. Now assume that nominal hourly wages are sticky. What happens if NGDP suddenly falls? There are two possibilities: (1) employment might be unaffected, in which case nonwage income (capital income) would absorb the entire shock; and (2) with less income to go around, and the same wage per hour, there would be fewer hours worked and more unemployment.

In practice, both profits and employment tend to decline when NGDP falls, but in the short run the biggest burden falls on workers, as unemployment is highly (and negatively) correlated with NGDP relative to trend. The year 2009 saw both the biggest fall in NGDP since the 1930s and the largest increase in unemployment since the 1930s. That is not a coincidence.

Elsewhere I have argued that the optimal monetary policy would stabilize aggregate hourly nominal wage growth (Sumner 1995). This policy would help keep labor markets in equilibrium and employment close to its natural rate. But there are all sorts of practical problems in measuring aggregate wage rates, and it is unlikely that a wage target would be politically feasible. NGDP targeting can be thought of as the next best thing. A stable path of NGDP growth would tend to stabilize employment more effectively than an inflation target, because employers' ability to meet their wage bills depends more on NGDP growth than on the rate of inflation. During periods such as

[8]George Selgin (1995) and David Beckworth (2008) explain of how NGDP targeting delivers better results when there are productivity changes.
[9]Technically NGDP is gross income, but the rates of change in gross income are highly correlated with changes in net national income.

late 2007 and early 2008, when prices rose rapidly despite slow NGDP growth, wages also grew slowly. So NGDP targeting is the better way to keep aggregate nominal wages close to equilibrium, helping to stabilize employment.

A second advantage to NGDP targeting is that it limits asset market instability. Asset bubbles tend to form when NGDP growth is higher than average. That's not to say that NGDP targeting would entirely eliminate asset bubbles. After all, the recent tech and housing bubbles occurred during periods when NGDP growth was only modestly above its trend. The big advantage here of NGDP targeting shows up on the downside. Financial market crises are highly correlated with falling NGDP, and are almost certainly made worse by it. The most famous example of this occurred in 1929–33, when U.S. nominal income was cut in half. Some economists believe that the Great Depression was triggered by a financial crisis (e.g., Hall 2010). Yet, the first financial crisis occurred more than a year into the Depression, and was probably caused by the collapse in spending that was already in progress.

In the late 1990s and early 2000s a severe decline in NGDP caused a financial crisis in Argentina. Then, in 2008–09, falling NGDP in the United States and Europe caused a relatively modest financial crisis to become much larger. For instance, IMF estimates of the total losses to the U.S. banking system from the current crisis nearly tripled between April 2008 and April 2009, as NGDP growth expectations plunged sharply. What started as a localized subprime mortgage crisis spread to other types of mortgages in other regions of the country and also to commercial and industrial debt. In Europe sovereign debt even became engulfed in the crisis. None of this should be at all surprising. The decline in NGDP was the largest since the 1930s, and it is out of their nominal earnings that people, businesses, and governments acquire the funds for repaying their debts.

Many have argued that inflation targeting is the best way to avoid unexpected and "unfair" transfers of wealth between creditors and borrowers. However, Selgin (1997) has shown that is true only if the economy's productivity is not also changing, and that in general a nominal GDP target, or a closely related "productivity norm," would lead to less disappointment among debtors and credits. The basic idea is that changes in productivity alter living standards, in turn changing people's willingness and ability to borrow and lend.

An expected improvement in productivity, for example, will make creditors seek higher returns on their loans, while also making it possible for borrowers to afford higher rates. However, an unexpected improvement will cause lenders to wish they had charged a higher rate. Under inflation targeting that sort of disappointment is not avoided. In contrast, under NGDP targeting the positive productivity shock is offset by an opposite—and equally unexpected—change in the inflation rate, keeping ex post real rates closer to where they would have been if both lenders and borrowers had been equipped with perfect foresight.

Now consider a specific case where nominal interest rates are 5 percent and people expect 5 percent nominal GDP growth composed of 2 percent inflation and 3 percent real growth, and (to give an example the opposite of the one already considered) there is an unexpected negative supply shock that boosts inflation to 5 percent while forcing real GDP growth down to 0 percent. In this case, lenders end up earning a zero real rate of return. But that only makes them suffer along with everyone else. With zero real GDP growth, there is no extra real income to share between lenders and borrowers. Under NGDP targeting, lenders know that each dollar they receive in the future will represent a given percentage of society's total nominal income, while borrowers know they can always pay what is owed. However, if inflation were being targeted at 2 percent, nominal GDP growth would shrink, making it difficult if not impossible for many borrowers to pay off their debts.

Pragmatic Arguments for Nominal GDP Targeting

As compelling as I think the theoretical advantages of nominal GDP targeting are, I have come to believe that there are even more powerful pragmatic arguments for it that mostly revolve around some overlooked practical shortcomings of inflation targeting.

Ben Bernanke has long advocated inflation targeting. But even he must be surprised and disappointed with how poorly it worked during the recent crisis. Three practical issues contributed to this poor outcome. First, real-world measures of inflation are highly subjective and sometimes very inaccurate (see Alchian and Klein 1973). Second, it is difficult to target inflation in a symmetrical fashion, partly because the public does not understand inflation targeting. Finally, inflation targeting encourages policymakers to think in terms of monetary policy affecting inflation and fiscal policy affecting real growth—a perception that is both inaccurate and potentially counterproductive.

Recall that inflation targeting is about more than just inflation. Advocates like Bernanke see it as a tool for stabilizing aggregate demand, and hence reducing the severity of the business cycle. This is certainly understandable, as demand shocks tend to cause fluctuations in both inflation and output. So a policy that avoids them should also stabilize output.

I have already discussed one problem with this view—namely, the economy might get hit by supply shocks, as when oil prices soared during the 2008 recession. Some of that can be avoided by looking at the core inflation rate. But even the core inflation rate was surprisingly sticky, or slow to fall during 2008–09, even after oil prices plunged. This made it harder for the Fed to aggressively stimulate the economy. It is not hard to figure out what went wrong with demand-side models that predicted inflation would fall sharply during a severe slump; in fact, according to the Bureau of Labor Statistics (BLS), housing prices did not fall. On the contrary, housing prices rose between mid-2008 and mid-2009, despite one of the greatest housing market crashes in all of world history. And they didn't just rise in nominal terms; they rose in relative terms, that is, faster than the overall core CPI. If we take the longer view, we find that house prices rose about 8 percent between 2006 and 2012 (according to the BLS) whereas the famous Case-Shiller house price index shows them falling by nearly 35 percent. That is quite a serious discrepancy, especially given that housing is 39 percent of the core CPI.

Many people might argue that the BLS number is better in the sense that it measures the rental equivalent of housing costs, whereas Case-Shiller shows the sales price, which most consumers don't see in any given year. But the real question is: "Better for what purpose?" People like Ben Bernanke don't favor inflation targeting because they hope to keep consumers happy; they favor it because they hope to stabilize the economy. That means avoiding unemployment as much as possible. The level of employment in the housing construction industry is almost certainly more closely related to the price of new homes then the rental equivalent of apartments in buildings constructed 30 years ago. If you had to predict the crash in housing construction after 2006, which measure would work better—an 8 percent increase in housing prices or a 35 percent decrease?

There are of course errors in the measurement of both inflation and NGDP growth. But there's an important extent to which NGDP is a more objectively measured concept. The revenue earned by a computer company (which is a part of NGDP) is a fairly objective concept, whereas the price increase over time in personal computers (which is a part of the CPI) is a highly subjective concept that involves judgments about quality differences in highly dissimilar products.

Although the core CPI did not decline as quickly as expected during 2009 (due to high housing prices) core inflation did eventually fall to 0.6 percent in the late summer of 2010. That decline caused the Fed to push for higher inflation via quantitative easing, which meant buying bonds to increase the monetary base. In principle, this program should have been completely uncontroversial because inflation was well below the Fed's 2 percent target. Instead, the Fed ran into a firestorm of controversy. The public was outraged to hear news reports that the Fed was trying to raise their cost of living at a time when many people were suffering from the recession.

It is pretty obvious that the public and the Fed were operating under completely different mental frameworks. When Bernanke called for "higher inflation" he meant a higher level of aggregate demand, which economic theory suggests should raise both the inflation rate and, in the short run, the real incomes of Americans. In contrast, when average Americans hear the term "higher inflation," they think in terms of higher food and energy prices (due to a reduction in aggregate supply), which reduces their real incomes. The Fed understood that more spending would mean more inflation but hoped it would also result in greater employment and output.

The Fed does not directly increase inflation by creating more money; rather the Fed raises total spending or aggregate demand. Whether that increase leads to inflation depends on the growth of real output. It is very strange to call the goal of such a policy "higher inflation," because the inflation is essentially a side-effect of the increased aggregate demand—the desired effect of which is greater employment and real growth. Nevertheless, Fed officials routinely talk as if the side-effect were the thing that really mattered. No wonder the public is confused.

According to some news reports, the Fed was taken aback by the intense criticism of QE2, and that this had made them more cautious about doing further stimulus. The dual mandate, which the Fed interprets as calling for about 2 percent inflation, would seem to have called for (and still calls for) a more expansionary monetary policy. Yet the Fed has held back, despite high unemployment and an inflation rate that has averaged only a bit above 1 percent since mid-2008, when the recession first became severe. It would have been both more accurate and less provocative for the Fed to have said in 2010 that the goal of QE2 was to boost American's nominal incomes, not their cost of living.

Confusion over the nature of inflation targeting creates another political problem: it leads to the perception that central banks control inflation, and the fiscal authorities control real GDP growth. Our textbooks treat monetary and fiscal policy similarly, as two tools for controlling spending. Yet one almost never sees any discussion of fiscal policy from an inflation-targeting perspective. If inflation is above target, the press almost always focuses on what the central bank needs to do. When there is an output shortfall, on the other hand, it's much more likely that people will call for fiscal stimulus. Yet there is absolutely nothing in economic theory that would justify this imagined asymmetry, at least from the perspective of demand side-initiatives like higher government spending.

One example of this confusion occurred in Britain during the recent recession. The pace of recovery there had been especially disappointing. Yet between 2010 and 2012 inflation ran well over the Bank of England's 2 percent target. Admittedly the Bank understood this to be due in part to transitional factors, such as a higher VAT rate and increased oil prices, so it was prepared to tolerate inflation that was modestly above its target. The political pressure caused by the high inflation nevertheless made it unwilling to further boost NGDP growth, which was far below trend. At the same time, the perception that the British recovery was lagging led to further calls for fiscal stimulus, despite Britain's high deficit and debt ratios. But fiscal stimulus cannot boost spending if the monetary authorities are targeting inflation. It's like the legislature stepping on the gas pedal at the same time that the central bank presses on the brake.

The point is that fiscal and monetary policy both work by influencing aggregate demand. If the central bank targets inflation at 2 percent, any fiscal policy that succeeds in increasing aggregate demand, will also tend to boost inflation, causing the central bank to tighten so as to keep inflation near its target. It's been known for decades that the fiscal multiplier is zero when the central bank targets inflation. But because people have become used to thinking that monetary policy determines the rate of inflation, while fiscal policy determines real growth, they have overlooked this. If central banks instead targeted spending, the futility of fiscal stimulus would be more evident. If, for example, the Bank of England was committed to a 4 percent nominal GDP growth target, and everyone knew it, the government would not be able to argue that by spending more it could make the economy grow faster. Since it obviously couldn't even boost the growth rate of nominal GDP, how could it possibly cause real GDP to go up?

The preceding analysis points to still another advantage of NGDP targeting: such targeting would make it easier for the public to appreciate the need for sound supply-side policies. If the fiscal authorities understood that the central bank was going to allow only 4 percent NGDP growth, then they would know that the only way to boost real growth would be with supply-side policies, even in the short run. Tax reform that lowered MTRs would tend to increase aggregate supply, and hence improve the inflation/output growth split in NGDP growth.

Conversely, bad economic policies would be more difficult to justify. When NGDP is allowed to fall sharply, as when inflation is kept stable despite an adverse supply shock, unemployment tends to rise. This makes it harder to insist on market-oriented policies, which typically call for "creative destruction," with unemployment in parts of the economy tolerated for the sake of allowing for more expansion elsewhere. When spending collapses generally, however, people will ask "Where do the workers go who have lost their jobs?" It's not an easy question to answer. Nor is it therefore so easy to argue against bailouts and other measures aimed at keeping even those firms or industries that ought to fail from actually failing. In contrast, with NGDP targeting there is never a general collapse of spending, regardless of what's happened to productivity generally or to any particular industry or firm. Therefore with such targeting, bailouts like the recent ones of GM and Chrysler would have been much harder to justify. Since they would not boost NGDP, any extra spending on cars made by these two companies would be fully offset by less spending on other American-made products. NGDP targeting would help to restore policymaking to a "classical" framework, where decisions to benefit special interest groups would always have relatively visible opportunity costs.

It would also be much easier to avoid bailouts of big banks, because proponents of "too big to fail" could no longer claim that failing to bail out banks would push us into a recession. Indeed with NGDP growing at a steady rate it is much less likely that we would have the sort of contagion of financial failures that could produce a systemic crisis.

And finally, NGDP targeting would help to depoliticize monetary policy. The current ill-defined dual mandate allows each side of the political divide to latch onto its preferred policy indicator and argue that money is either too easy or too tight. Indeed this polarization has been especially pronounced during the Great Recession. NGDP targeting would provide for much greater transparency as to whether policy was overshooting the target, or falling short.

Can We Trust the Fed to Target Any Variable?

Many libertarians are skeptical of the Federal Reserve, and instead favor a more laissez-faire regime, such as free banking. The issues involved here go well beyond the scope of this article. However, I believe there are several ways to reduce the discretion of central banks under an NGDP targeting regime.

One, which I have already mentioned, is the importance of level targeting. Think of level targeting as a way of "keeping them honest." From the 1960s to the 1980s inflation almost always exceeded the Fed's policy goal. Whenever the Fed missed they promised to try to do better. But those promises lacked credibility, because the Fed was targeting growth rates, not levels, and so never felt obligated to actually make up for its mistakes. The public became skeptical, and rightly so. At the other extreme, the Bank of Japan (BOJ) has repeatedly fallen short of its inflation targets, has also kept promising to do better, and has also lost the Japanese public's confidence.

In contrast, if a central bank fell short of its price *level* target by 1 percent every single year, it would lower the inflation *rate* only during that first year. For instance, suppose the BOJ had a price level target of 100. In the first year it falls 1 percent short due to a flaw in its targeting method, ending up at 99. For it to allow the price level to drop to 98 the next year would mean being short 2 percent at the end of the second year—a failure to honor its commitment. However, if each additional year the BOJ falls 1 percent short of the policy goal, then the CPI will stay at 99, which means that policymakers will actually reach their goal for stable prices in every single year except the first. The public can adjust to any *level* of prices; what causes problems is *unanticipated changes*. The same rationale would apply to level targeting of NGDP.

In previous articles, I have also discussed how central bank discretion could be removed by a policy of targeting NGDP futures prices (Sumner 1989, 2006). The basic idea is to set the monetary base at a level where NGDP growth is expected to be right on target. Each time someone buys an NGDP futures contract from the central bank, their purchase signals worry that NGDP growth is too high, obliging the Fed to restrain money growth. Each sale of NGDP futures contracts to the Fed signals concern of a slowdown, and leads the Fed to inject more base money into the economy. Failure to do so would expose the Fed to potentially unlimited losses.

In essence, the market, not the central bank, would be setting the monetary base and the level of interest rates. Indeed the Fed's only role in this sort of regime would be to set the target path for nominal GDP. The Fed would essentially be defining the medium of account (i.e., during 2014 the dollar might be defined as one seventeen trillionth of expected 2014 U.S. nominal output.) Once the Fed is that far removed from the process, it is relatively easy to move on to free banking.

Conclusion

Many libertarian economists are acutely sensitive to the very real dangers of excessive inflation. But I believe some have a blind spot for shortfalls in nominal spending, which are arguably even more damaging. The United States had a relatively efficient small government policy regime under Presidents Harding and Coolidge. It was far from perfect, but as soon as the Depression began policy became more interventionist—and (with the exception of the dollar devaluation of 1933–34) almost completely counterproductive.

An almost identical sequence of events took place in Argentina during the late 1990s and early 2000s. Argentina grew quite rapidly from 1990 to 1997, partly thanks to neoliberal policy reforms. But Argentine monetary policy became contractionary in the late 1990s and early 2000s, causing a significant decline in nominal GDP. Finally, a new and more left-wing government took command, devalued the currency, and pursued a statist policy agenda. The new regime blamed Argentina's troubles not on tight money, but on its former free market policies, just as FDR had done 70 years earlier. The fall in NGDP also worsened a fiscal crisis. This led the Argentine government to swing to the opposite extreme—printing money to pay its bills. The result was high and rising inflation. The government blamed "capitalists" and put on wage and price controls. More recently, the sharp decline in NGDP in the eurozone has led to calls for "fiscal union." This might slightly ameliorate the current crisis, but the resulting increase in moral hazard would be storing up much more severe problems down the road.

Nominal GDP targeting provides the best environment for free market policies to flourish. It removes one of the most powerful excuses for statist policies, the claim that they will somehow create jobs. In the current policy environment, where NGDP growth has fallen far below trend, there is an unfortunate tendency for some on the right to view NGDP targeting at a sort of left-wing proposal, aimed at inflation. In fact, from Hayek in the 1930s, to people like McCallum (1985), Hall and Mankiw (1994), and Selgin (1995) in the 1980s and 1990s, to the so-called market monetarists of today, nominal GDP targeting of some sort has long had strong appeal among economists sympathetic to free markets and low inflation.[10] We need to look beyond the current crisis, and to think long and hard about what sort of pragmatic monetary regime will best serve the economy in the decades to come.

---

[10]Lars Christensen (2011, 2012) coined the term "market monetarist," and has been a forceful advocate of combining NGDP targeting with a more laissez-faire approach to banking. As far as I know Bill Woolsey (1992) was the first to connect futures targeting with free banking. The number of market monetarists in the blogosphere is growing rapidly, and includes David Beckworth, Lars Christensen, David Glasner, Josh Hendrickson, Marcus Nunes, Nick Rowe, Evan Soltas, Yichuan Wang, and Bill Woolsey.

References

Alchian, A. A., and Klein, B. (1973) "On a Correct Measure of Inflation." *Journal of Money, Credit and Banking* 5 (1): 173–91.

Beckworth, D. (2008) "Aggregate Supply-Driven Deflation and Its Implications for Macroeconomic Stability." *Cato Journal* 28 (3): 363–84.

_____ (2012) "Bungling Booms: How the Fed's Mishandling of the Productivity Boom Helped Pave the Way for the Housing Boom." In D. Beckworth (ed.) *Boom and Bust Banking: The Causes and Cures of the Great Recession*. San Francisco: Independent Institute.

Bernanke, B. S., and Carey, K. (1996) "Nominal Wage Stickiness and Aggregate Supply in the Great Depression." *Quarterly Journal of Economics* 111 (3): 853–83.

Bernanke, B. S. (1999) "Japanese Monetary Policy: A Case of Self-Induced Paralysis?" Manuscript: Princeton University.

_____ (2003) "Some Thoughts on Monetary Policy in Japan." Speech given to the Japan Society of Monetary Economics (31 May). Available at www.federalreserve.gov/boarddocs/speeches/2003/20030531/default.htm.

Cassel, G. (1936) *The Downfall of the Gold Standard*. London: Oxford University Press.

Christensen, L. (2011) "Scott Sumner and the Case against Currency Monopoly . . . or How to Privatize the Fed." Blog post at *The Market Monetarist* (23 October): http://marketmonetarist.com/2011/10/23/scott-sumner-and-the-case-against-currency-monopoly-or-how-to-privatize-the-fed.

_____ (2012) "NGDP Level Targeting: The True Free Market Alternative." Blog post at *The Market Monetarist* (19 July): http://marketmonetarist.com/2012/07/19/the-ngdp-level-targeting-the-true-free-market-alternative-we-try-again.

Christiano, L. J.; Eichenbaum, M.; and Evans, C. L. (2005) "Nominal Rigidities and the Dynamic Effects of a Shock to Monetary Policy." *Journal of Political Economy* 113 (1): 1–45.

Cole, H. L., and Ohanian, L. E. (2004) "New Deal Policies and the Persistence of the Great Depression: A General Equilibrium Analysis." *Journal of Political Economy* 112 (4): 779–816.

Friedman, M. (1968) "The Role of Monetary Policy." *American Economic Review* 58 (1): 1–17.

Hall, R. (2010) "Why Does the Economy Fall to Pieces after a Financial Crash?" *Journal of Economic Perspectives* 24 (4): 3–20.

Hall, R., and Mankiw, N. G. (1994) "Nominal Income Targeting." In N. G. Mankiw (ed.) *Monetary Policy*, 71–94. Chicago: University of Chicago Press for the NBER.

Hawtrey, R. G. (1947) *The Gold Standard in Theory and Practice*. London: Longmans, Green and Co.

Hayek, F. A. ([1935] 1967) *Prices and Production*. 2nd ed. Reprint. New York: Augustus M. Kelley.

Hetzel, R. L. (2009) "Monetary Policy in the 2008–2009 Recession." Federal Reserve Bank of Richmond, *Economic Quarterly* 95 (2): 201–33.

_____ (2012) *The Great Recession: Market Failure or Policy Failure?* Cambridge: Cambridge University Press.

International Monetary Fund (2008–10) *Global Financial Stability Report*. Various issues. Washington: IMF.

McCallum, B. T. (1985) "On Consequences and Criticisms of Monetary Targeting." *Journal of Money, Credit, and Banking* 17 (4): 570–97.

Niskanen, W. A. (2001) "A Test of the Demand Rule." *Cato Journal* 21 (2): 205–09.

Selgin, G. (1995) "The 'Productivity Norm' vs. Zero Inflation in the History of Economic Thought." *History of Political Economy* 27 (4): 705–35.

_____ (1997) *Less than Zero: The Case for a Falling Price Level in a Growing Economy*. Hobart Paper No. 132. London: Institute of Economic Affairs.

Silver, S., and Sumner, S. (1995) "Nominal and Real Wage Cyclicality during the Interwar Period." *Southern Economic Journal* 61 (3): 588–601.

Sumner, S. (1989) "Using Futures Instrument Prices to Target Nominal Income." *Bulletin of Economic Research* 41 (2): 157–62.

_____ (1995) "Using Monetary Policy to Target a Nominal Wage Index." *Journal of Economics and Business* 47 (2): 205–15.

_____ (2006) "Let a Thousand Models Bloom: The Advantages of Making the FOMC a Truly 'Open Market'." *B.E. Journal of Macroeconomics* 6 (1): 1–27.

_____ (2011) "Re-Targeting the Fed." *National Affairs*. No. 9 (Fall).

Svensson, L. E. O. (2003) "What Is Wrong with Taylor Rules? Using Judgment in Monetary Policy through Targeting Rules." *Journal of Economic Literature* 41 (2): 426–77.

White L. H. (1999a) *The Theory of Monetary Institutions*. Oxford: Blackwell.

_____ (1999b) "Hayek's Monetary Theory and Policy: A Critical Reconstruction." *Journal of Money, Credit and Banking* 31 (1): 109–20.

_____ (2008) "Did Hayek and Robbins Deepen the Great Depression?" *Journal of Money, Credit and Banking* 40 (4): 751–68.

Woodford, M. (2003) *Interest and Prices*. Princeton, N.J.: Princeton University Press.

Woolsey, W. W. (1992) "The Search for Macroeconomic Stability: Comment on Sumner." *Cato Journal* 12 (2): 475–85.

13

TOWARD FORECAST-FREE
MONETARY INSTITUTIONS
Leland B. Yeager

The beginning of wisdom . . . is to know that the future is
unknowable. . . . Recognizing the inscrutability of the future
requires . . . humility and intellectual self-discipline. It
requires the candid recognition that human history is a dis-
continuous process, rather than the neat projection of established trends. . . . But the occasional awareness of our
limitations is quickly elbowed aside by our all too human
eagerness to define, right now, the shape of things to come.

—Irving Kristol[1]

[O]ur future is not determined by mathematical curves but
by our own intelligence and will. But if this is so, the whole
so-called science of business-forecasting inevitably becomes
very much discredited. What the economist can do is to
examine present facts and proposed lines of action, and to
show how they are likely to influence the development of economic life. But he can never make a prediction of our future
independent of our own actions. And we should never lose
sight of the fact that the future is influenced by coming events

Leland B. Yeager is Professor Emeritus of Economics at the University of
Virginia and Auburn University. This article is reprinted from the *Cato Journal*,
Vol. 12, No. 1 (Spring/Summer 1992).
[1]Irving Kristol, quoted from *Fortune*, February 1969, by Fiedler (1990: 130).

about which we know nothing, and the prediction of which in any case does not belong to economic science.

—Gustav Cassel[2]

If you must forecast, forecast often!

—Anonymous[3]

The Passion for Forecasts

A passion for forecasts carries to an extreme the "passion for news" diagnosed, with amusing exaggeration, by Jacques Ellul (1967: 53–63). News entertains. Being *au courant* serves one's sense of prestige. Unconcerned with enduring principles and connections, losing any sense of continuity, the ordinary citizen excites himself only over the latest events. Reflection would involve the news of the day before yesterday rather than just of this morning. To avoid drowning in the flood of news, he must forget. "[T]he more superficial, unimportant, and spectacular the information, the more people will be interested in it. . . . public opinion revolves only around problems of the immediate present" (Ellul 1967: 55). Someone living in the news demands immediate solutions, perhaps sensing that tomorrow he will have forgotten the problem exciting him today.

Gordon Williams's brief radio broadcasts, supposedly on economics, illustrate these passions. They have nothing to do with economic principles—unless one so counts the notion that spending (other than on imports) is good and more is better. Williams is preoccupied with the latest officially released economic number and even with forecasters' guesses about a number scheduled for release that morning. His and other broadcasts often say not that the stock market closed yesterday at 2572.8 (or whatever) on the Dow but that the market will open this morning at that figure. Speaking that way

---

[2]Cassel ([1927–28] 1951: 332–33).
[3]The second of "three central laws of forecasting" cited by Fiedler (1990: 141). Many years ago I heard or saw this maxim attributed to either Marcus Nadler or Jules Blackman, professors at New York University.

seems more up-to-the-minute and future-oriented than reporting what is, after all, a numerical detail of recent history.

The passion for news and forecasts shows up in media discussions of whether inflation is dead and whether the Federal Reserve should turn its attention to "fighting" something else. This attitude gives policy a short-run bias. The typical commentator seems to lack understanding of or concern for unintended policy consequences working themselves out only over time in unforeseeable ways.

Foretelling the Future versus Scientific Prediction

Accurate economic forecasts (beyond short-run extrapolations, anyway) are hardly possible apart from forecasts of all human affairs. So-called economic behavior depends on innumerable factors, including noneconomic ones and including people's theory-conditioned and subjective reactions to their experiences. Almost by definition, history is the unfolding of unique events and combinations of events. Minor causes can have major consequences, as the recently fashionable mathematics of "chaos" should have impressed on economists. If only Queen Victoria had been a man—if only one microscopic detail had been different at her conception in August 1818—the crowns of Great Britain and Hanover would have remained linked, and subsequent history might well have unfolded quite differently from the tragic way it did.

Because history is unique, foretelling the future is fundamentally different from the if-this-then-that predictions of natural science. A chemist can predict the result of placing zinc in hydrochloric acid, but he cannot foretell how much zinc and how much acid will generate how much hydrogen in a particular year. Similarly, it is unreasonable to expect an economist to foretell a country's balance of payments or inflation rate or interest rates in the unique historical circumstances of a few years later. Astronomers can foretell events within our solar system because known bodies move subject to known forces, with outside disturbances essentially absent. An economic system, in contrast, responds to all sorts of changing outside influences.

Econometric research can take advantage of the unplanned experiments cast up by history to shed some light on whatever dependable relations may hold among some economic magnitudes. Research of this sort is not the same thing as foretelling the future and hardly justifies adopting policies that presuppose it.

Degrees of Dependence on Forecasting

But even if forecasts are unreliable, what alternative do we have to making them? Must not decisions of all sorts rest on judgments about the future? Isn't budgeting indispensable, even though largely an exercise in forecasting? Well, yes, but a distinction holds. Forecasts are more crucial to some arrangements and policies than to others. The mistake is to depend on them needlessly. It is sensible to avoid, when we can, making ourselves dependent on trying to do what we cannot do well.

Forecast-dependent policies require foretelling prices, output growth or recession, unemployment, interest rates, balances of payments, or whatever, and then, if these outcomes are judged unsatisfactory, trying to make them turn out differently. In making so much depend on the subjective judgments of the authorities, such policies make the economic environment less predictable; for they set private decisionmakers to guessing what the authorities will do. Financial journalists plausibly relate many episodes of volatility in the stock, bond, and foreign-exchange markets to uncertainties and changing conjectures about monetary policy. Injecting avoidable uncertainties about policy tends to waste the scarce human capacity to cope with the change and uncertainty that is inescapable.

A contrasting type of policy relies, instead, on something more akin to scientific if-this-then-that prediction: It involves examining the likely operating properties of alternative sets of institutions and choosing the set judged to have the most attractive properties on the whole. It holds down the scope of frequent large centralized decisions, whose effects are harder to cope with than the gradually occurring cumulative effects of innumerable decentralized private decisions.[4]

All planning necessarily looks to the future. But just as the logic of a market economy recommends decentralized planning, so it recommends "competition in prediction" as "an integral part of competition in the wider sense. . . . [T]he many different views of the future held by independent operators cannot . . . be aggregated into a 'common

[4]In not-yet-published papers, Roger Koppl sets fourth the "big-players argument" concerning the disruptiveness of large-scale decisions and market interventions. (See Koppl 2002—Ed.)

view.' . . . [D]ecentralization of the forecasting function [is] one of the advantages of the market economy over the centrally-directed economy. . . . [It is] natural and desirable that the economy should work to a plurality of views, rather than to a single view of [the] future" (Lutz 1969: 149–50; quoted in Nutter 1983: 118).

Trying to impose conformity on the market's multitude of forecasts risks compounding errors. If, for instance, a central authority substitutes its own single five-year forecast of oil supply and demand for the variety of forecasts that individual decisionmakers would otherwise derive from their own observations and foresight, unnecessary wastes will occur. The very spread in mistakes distributed among independent forecasts, involving overlapping margins of error, would bring differential adjustments in expectations and behavior that would diminish average forecasting error over time (Nutter 1983: 118–19).

The Example of a Price-Level Rule

Targeting on a price index exemplifies a relatively forecast-free and discretion-free policy (although other reforms might excel it in these respects). An unambiguous rule relieves the monetary authority of constantly reconsidering what weights to give to fighting inflation, resisting recession, promoting employment, stimulating growth, improving the balance of payments, making credit easy, aiding government finance, appeasing politicians, and pursuing other desired results. One clear objective is less difficult to attain when its possible rivals are out of the way, and the authority's performance becomes easier to monitor. Private expectations can crystallize around price stability, which further facilitates the authority's task.

Criticisms, like the proposal itself, are old and familiar. Imbalance between money's supply and demand shows up in the target price index only with a lag. Further lags between index movements and policy responses and their impact might make those responses perverse and destabilizing when they took belated effect. But this difficulty would presumably plague a policy of sharp shifts, not a steady policy. Steadiness is easier in pursuing a single goal than multiple goals with changing weights. Like a good driver, the authority might make frequent small corrections instead of belated sharp swerves. Through continual diagnosis of price-level pressures—distinct from ambitious forecasting—the authority would try to avoid blundering off course. The authority might stay alert to incipient inflation or deflation signaled by industrial-production figures, exchange rates, interest rates and their term structure, and sensitive commodity prices determined in auction markets (Johnson 1988). These indicators should remain just that and not become rivals of the price-level target.

Watching sensitive commodity prices does not presuppose that they move dependably in parallel with the consumer price index; they do not. In the long run the two sets of prices drift apart under real as opposed to monetary influences. In the short run commodity prices are more volatile and respond more quickly to monetary disturbances (Boughton 1989, Marquis and Cunningham 1990). The latter contrast recommends commodity prices as a tool for diagnosing disequilibria that, left uncorrected, would in time inflate or deflate consumer prices and, in the deflationary case, would also temporarily shrink real activity.

A modified version of Irving Fisher's (1920) compensated dollar would further limit any authority's discretion, circumvent the problem of lags, and lessen the need for forecasts or even for continuous diagnosis. The authority would be required to maintain two-way convertibility between its money and whatever changeable amount of some redemption medium was actually worth, at current prices, the bundle of goods and services specifying the target price index. (More exactly, the bundle would *define* the dollar.) If the dollar always exchanges against just enough redemption medium (possibly gold, but probably securities) to be worth the bundle, then the dollar is worth the bundle itself. The authority's obligation to redeem its money in this way at the holders' initiative puts teeth into its commitment to a dollar of stable purchasing power. Private arbitrageurs and speculators, understanding the system, would reinforce this stability. This solution to the question of *how* to implement a stable-price-level rule admittedly seems too simple to be genuine; but if so, I await seeing its flaw identified.[5]

[5]Admittedly one might imagine a "paradox of indirect convertibility" plaguing a system in which money is redeemable not directly in the goods or goods defining the dollar but only indirectly in some convenient medium of equivalent value. Knut Wicksell expressed such a worry in 1919. W.W. Woosley and I believe that we have refuted misconceptions on this topic, along with clarifying genuine difficulties, in our article of 1992.

Objections to Stabilization

Objections to stable money mentioned so far are really objections to more or less tacitly assumed *methods of implementing* the policy. Some modern "Austrian" economists, in particular, worry about "injection effects" of expanding the money supply even merely to keep the price level from sagging in a technologically advancing economy. Their well-known theory of the business cycle focuses on the consequences of falsifying interest-rate signals through monetary expansion. George Selgin (1990: 277–81) stresses temporary widenings and subsequent painful narrowings of profit margins associated with delays in factor-price responses to spurts of productivity improvement under such a policy.

Arguments for price-level stabilization sometimes tacitly assume that gains in productivity come unanticipated. This assumption is usually inappropriate, Selgin suggests, as a basis for worry about how prices respond. Price-setters in directly affected markets will be alert to productivity improvements. Many will even have initiated them and will promptly pass cost cuts into prices. No pains demand avoidance through stabilizing the price level when productivity rises. Yet such a policy would expand money incomes, swelling profits temporarily unless it were perfectly understood and anticipated and promptly reflected in factor prices.

If productivity *falls*, monetary contraction to resist a rise in the price level shrinks nominal income and depresses profits. It discourages producers by making them bear "more than their fair share of the overall burden of reduced production"—until workers and other sellers of inputs belatedly accept painful cuts in wages and other factor prices (Selgin 1990: 279).

Avoiding abnormally high or low profits or profit expectations is more crucial to maintaining monetary equilibrium, Selgin insists, than price-level stability. Only under what he recommends as the "productivity norm," whereby the price level varies inversely with overall factor productivity, does aggregate demand remain adequate but not excessive for buying full-employment output at prices covering money costs of production. The productivity norm also avoids distorting interest rates away from their natural levels (Selgin 1990: 280–81).

Ways of avoiding price deflation without monetary injections are mentioned toward the end of this article—in case injection effects really are worrisome. Rather than repeat what I have said elsewhere on this issue, however, I turn to more fundamental issues.

Productivity, Equity, and the Price Level

Many economists have denied that a stable-valued money unit is desirable, even apart from the difficulties of achieving one. They go beyond acknowledging complaints about how unexpected price inflation or deflation redistributes wealth between creditors and debtors. Even the distributional effects of stability, especially in the face of changes in productivity, draw criticism. David Davidson (1906 and other articles listed in the references) invented hypothetical examples. Stable prices would keep a creditor from sharing in the gains from a general rise in productivity, while someone who had borrowed for productive purposes would unfairly keep the entire gain for himself. A rise in the productivity of land would tend to depress the prices of its products and so not unambiguously either raise or lower the value of the land itself. A monetary policy of stabilizing the product price level, however, would raise land's money value. A landowner who had leveraged his holding by debt would gain relative to a debt-free owner, which seemed unfair to Davidson.

Selgin (1990: 273–75), resurrecting related arguments, contends that when the price level falls because of generally improved productivity, debtors do not suffer, since their real incomes rise along with the real value of their debts. All they miss is an opportunity to enjoy an undeserved windfall at creditors' expense. In the opposite case of an adverse supply shock, preventing a rise in the price level would require an unfair *contraction* of all nonfixed money incomes.

Such arguments about the distributional unfairness of stable prices seem weak in the context of a long-term productivity uptrend. Investors, lenders, business firms, and other borrowers will allow for expected productivity gains in interest rates, in equity participations in loans, in issue prices and other features of corporate stocks, and in innumerable other terms of their financial transactions.

Worry about unfairness from adverse supply shocks seems more plausible. If, however, the monetary system is credibly committed to price-level stability even despite shocks, people will allow for their possibility in making contracts, including the mix of loan and equity elements in financial transactions. On this particular score, long-term loans will bear lower interest rates than they would in the absence of the price-level guarantee. In effect, long-term lenders pay an insurance premium for shock protection by accepting lower interest rates than if they bore the risk themselves. If an adverse shock does occur and creditors gain from a price level nevertheless kept stable, then they are in a position like that of a householder who "benefits" from having been insured (and having paid the premiums) when his house burns down. People and firms owing debts fixed in a stable unit of account do lose from an adverse supply shock, but they had presumably seen an advantage in borrowing at a lower rate of interest than they would have had to pay on loans denominated in a depreciation-prone unit; they are in the position of insurance companies.

To change the analogy, people who gain from holding claims denominated in a stable unit are in a position like that of stockpiles of oil who reap a "windfall profit" if an energy crunch occurs. In either case, do economists really recommend redistributing the gains and losses resulting from good and bad foresight and luck? (These are gains and losses judged relative to the distribution that would have emerged from a different course of events.) Do economists really recommend operating a monetary system to second-guess the parties to voluntary contracts?

A known and credible price-level policy at least provides a framework within which contracting parties can allow for contingencies as their own diverse circumstances, knowledge, and attitudes toward risk suggest. Can we really expect better results from centralized administration of foresight, risk-bearing, and their distributional consequences? The literature on rational expectations further suggests why the distributional case against stable money is a red herring.

Real and Monetary Influences on the Price Level

More narrowly economic considerations require closer attention. Critics of price-level stabilization sometimes agree about avoiding money-side disturbances but want to accord influences on the goods side their full natural scope. If rising productivity expands the supply of goods, a decline in prices is the natural response. Yet this distinction bears little weight. Growth in income and in the quantities of goods to be traded operates as much on the money side, expanding the demand for real cash balances, as it operates on the goods side.

I wonder whether the idea that money prices should reflect the "real" cheapening of goods in general does not rest on some inchoate illusion that money has a value of its own distinct from what it will buy. Earlier (Yeager 1988: 271–72), referring to David Davidson (1906) and Benjamin Anderson ([1917] 1922), I said that these economists had tried "to distinguish, though not in a way intelligible to me, between the value of money and its purchasing power, the reciprocal of the price level."

After further study of Davidson's writings (listed in the references), I now think I see what he meant. Gustav Cassel had forthrightly identified changes in the general price level with changes in money's value. A general rise in prices, Davidson objects, can reflect either a rise in the value of commodities or a fall in the value of money—or a rise in the value of both, with commodities gaining value in greater proportion, or a fall in the value of both, with commodities losing value in lesser proportion. Davidson (1923: 197) even presented a table purporting to show how much of the rise of prices in Sweden during World War I traced to an increased scarcity-value of commodities and how much to a decreased scarcity-value of money.

He accepted a real-cost theory of value and was even trying to improve Ricardo's mainly labor-input theory.[6] If increased productivity reduces quantities of labor and other primary factors necessary for a unit of output, then goods have really become cheaper, in Davidson's view; and their prices, expressed in money of stable value, go down.

Without going into detail, Davidson hints at how to reconcile this real-cost doctrine, more or less, with a marginal-utility theory of value. If goods become more abundant than before, then, precisely in accordance with the principle of diminishing marginal utility, their marginal utility and value decline. If effects like those of a decline in productivity occur, as when Sweden's international terms of trade worsened during World War I, then goods have higher marginal utility and greater scarcity value than before.

For money, too, lesser or greater scarcity (relative to population, as Davidson occasionally says) entails lesser or greater marginal

---

[6]His article of 1919 addresses theories of value in general, without special reference to money. It is a pity, says Thomas (1935: 47), that Davidson spent fruitless effort on revising classical value theory.

utility and value. Davidson warned against losing sight of how the values of goods and money might separately be changing. Concern only with their ratios of value would be like concern only with how the ratio of the average heights of women and men had changed over some period, neglecting what had happened to the average absolute heights of women and of men (Davidson 1909a: 12). To advocate money not of stable value of its own but of stable purchasing power as measured by some price index is as "metrologically absurd" as wanting to adjust the definition of the meter according to changes in the average absolute length of objects measured; it is like wanting a separate meter for children, shorter than the adult meter (Davidson 1922: 113).

Yet is it not true that all measurement is necessarily relative? There are no utterly absolute standards—are there?—of length or mass or value or anything else. Rising productivity cheapens some goods relative to others (notably, consumer goods relative to human effort), but it can hardly cheapen goods and services in general relative to goods and services in general. Each good's price expresses its value relative to others when prices are quoted in a unit of stable general purchasing power.

Letting the price level reflect changes in productivity seems more plausible when specific goods, not general trends, are in question. Suppose that technological progress cheapens some particular good and so reduces the average price level slightly as a matter of mere arithmetic (Selgin 1990: esp. 275). This decline evidences no excess demand for money undergoing perhaps sluggish correction. By hypothesis, producers have cut the affected good's price promptly and painlessly in line with its reduced cost. Its output presumably increases, perhaps along with outputs of other goods into whose production factors may have been released. The real volume of transactions to be lubricated increases and so does the associated demand for real cash balances. Money's rise in purchasing power automatically accommodates that increased demand (but accommodates it only more or less, for only by extreme coincidence would the pattern of interrelated price and quantity adjustments and of income elasticities of demand for real balances make the accommodation exact).

If only one particular good were ever to become cheaper through technical progress, that fact would argue against choosing it to define the money unit. (If only gold production kept gaining in technical efficiency, a gold standard would be inexpedient.) We would even want to omit that exceptional good from any bundle of commodities defining the unit or used to calculate a target price index. Rather than inflate other prices to stabilize the average, it would be simpler to let the price of the exceptional good fall.

More generally, whenever technical progress affects one good only, we might like its price to fall without disturbing any others. No unit is available, however, in which prices could behave that way. Substitutabilities and complementarities in consumption and production and other aspects of general interdependence keep any single price from changing *alone*. It is pointless to wish for a unit with impossible properties (like one whose adoption, besides offering all plausible benefits, would also prevent drug addiction and sloth among secretaries).

It is misleading, furthermore, to consider goods affected by technical progress only separately, one by one. Pervasive contributions to productivity, including capital accumulation and gains in knowledge, affect broad ranges of goods over long time spans. Goods cannot all fall in price relative to each other. The operational question becomes not "Why inflate other prices when a single price falls?" but rather "Why not absorb what would otherwise be a general downward pressure on prices?" Why express money prices in a way that requires most of them to fall even though relative prices are changing in diverse ways? It seems counterintuitive to suppose that individual price changes would be fewer when they were negative on average rather than zero.

Selgin (1990: 275–76), though not sharing my intuition on this issue, recognizes that no rigorous argument is available to settle it. How productivity gains may affect prices is far from straightforward, by the way, as Wicksell noted in 1909. Inventions or other developments promising to raise productivity may stimulate investment spending and so initially tend to raise prices. The question of the time pattern of productivity effects thus poses additional complexity for any notion of optimal responsiveness of the price level, as distinct from stability.

Productivity, Factor Prices, and Income Targeting

Considerations like Selgin's, perhaps along with Davidson-like notions of objective value, suggest defining the money unit by a bundle not of products but of labor and other primary factors of production. Davidson (1922) did have that idea, but practical difficulties recommended a rough equivalent to him—money managed to stabilize average nominal income per member of the population. David Glasner (1989: chap. 11) advocates money stabilized against an index of labor wage rates. While ideally preferring stabilization of money income per worker, Selgin (1990: 272) recognizes stabilizing per capita income as a practical approximation. That policy would come close to his productivity norm, making an adequately flexible price level vary in roughly inverse proportion to average productivity.

As Selgin (1990: 282) recognizes, his proposal loosely resembles currently popular ones for targeting monetary policy on nominal income. These proposals do not envisage fixing income per person, however. Instead, total nominal income or gross national product (GNP) would trend upward at a rate thought consistent with average price stability over the long run. Bennett McCallum (1987 and 1989: chap. 16) explains a rule aiming at this result. Michael Bradley and Dennis Jansen (1989) describe nominal GNP targeting as a straddle between price-level and real-output targeting, the latter being quite inappropriate for reasons one hopes are familiar. Nominal targeting would tend to stabilize "real GNP at its natural rate of output," and "automatically, without monetary policymakers having to know what the natural rate of output actually is" (Bradley and Jansen 1989: 40). James Hoehn (1989) claims further advantages for that policy.

The advantages of targeting on nominal GNP arguably extend to supply shocks. In McCallum's version, an automatic-feedback rule avoids reliance on episodic forecasting. Like any reform, however, such a rule implies a prediction of its operating properties, which implies a forecast about the economic environment and its interaction with features of the proposed institution.[7]

Several points seem to count against nominal GNP targeting. First, the target is conventional, constructed, less continuously available, more subject to delays in reporting, more open to revision, and less directly observable by the ordinary citizen than prices. (The underground economy contributes to inaccuracy.) A price index or the total price of a specified commodity bundle has its conventional

---

[7]Compare Viner (1962) on the long-run forecasting unavoidable in formulating any rule.

and constructed aspects, too, though in lesser degree; the ordinary citizen has a more nearly direct view of prices than of GNP. Second, by its nature, the GNP target must be pursued by a central monetary authority, which must be concerned with financial innovations that might loosen its control over its target. Alternative reforms could give freer rein to financial innovation. Third, centralized GNP targeting lacks the discipline of competition that would operate under private-enterprise-oriented reforms. It is easier for a central monetary authority to miss its targets by a little and eventually by a lot without coming under direct corrective pressure.

Adversity

Perhaps the most embarrassing case for advocates of stable money is a sharp drop in productivity or the equivalent—a supply shock worse than the oil shock of 1973—74, a war, or some other calamity. Such a shock is vividly imaginable in a small, economically specialized country depending on imports paid for by one or a few export products. The country is vulnerable to worsening of its terms of trade or, say, to failure of a major export crop. If a severe loss of income and wealth must be quickly allocated over its population somehow or other, an inflationary tax on cash balances and nominal incomes can hardly be ruled out a priori as a one method.[8]

Suppose, furthermore, that the shock directly raises some specific prices and others closely linked with them. The pattern of relative prices suffers initial distortion, which obstructs market-clearing. Mechanically, arithmetically, the average price level rises. Total real money balances shrink, and with them the volumes of transactions, production, and employment they can support. Trying, nevertheless, to hold the average price level steady by tightening the money supply to restrain the rise of the most directly affected prices and to strengthen downward pressure on other prices would worsen this recessionary shrinkage of real money balances.

An opposite policy might seem more sensible—resisting unemployment by partially restoring real balances through monetary accommodation of the inflationary shock. In the long run, it is true, such monetary accommodation would be unnecessary. Market pressures

---

[8]Such cases apparently persuaded Wicksell, towards the end of his life, to qualify his call for a stable price level (Uhr 1962: 300–05)

would in time overcome price and wage stickiness and would achieve declines in other prices averaging out the upward shocks to particular prices; maintaining the steady target price level would prove compatible with market-clearing. In the meanwhile, however, the economy would have suffered exceptional unemployment. Perhaps it would be reasonable, after all, to try to mitigate this consequence by tolerating and even monetarily ratifying the shock- imposed initial "arithmetical" rise of the average price level, at least temporarily.[9]

I see no logical or factual error in such a case. I even think it provides the strongest argument available against the goal of stable money. A valid argument is not necessarily decisive, however; other arguments may well pull the other way. An abandonable goal of price-level stability would less fully enlist the support of private expectations than a firm goal would. How sticky the "other" prices (and wages) are that would have to decline to average out the shock-imposed rise of specific prices is surely not independent of the policy rule and related expectations. A policy of accommodating price-raising shocks would increase people's reluctance to cut these other prices and wages that would otherwise come under downward pressure. (Why cut a price or wage if monetary expansion is likely to make the cut unnecessary?) A policy of accepting and supporting a shock-induced rise in the price level would thus worsen the very stickiness that seems to recommend that policy. A firm and credible commitment to a stable price level, on the other hand, would encourage price-setters and wage negotiators to yield to market pressures for market-clearing adjustments; and these responses would hold down the unemployment costs of price-level stability.

Worry about shocks applies less to a large, diversified country than to a small one, especially if a long-term productivity uptrend affords scope for absorbing moderate shocks through mere temporary slowdowns or interruptions in the growth of nominal incomes at a steady price level. A large, growing economy enjoys insurance, so to speak, from the law of large numbers: While at any time a few of its sectors may be suffering adversity, many other sectors are likely to be prospering.[10]

---

[9]The case for allowing temporary departures from a price-level target is a main theme of Hall (1986).

[10]Some considerations cited in the theory of optimum currency areas evidently also apply to choosing monetary institutions for an area taken as given.

No such considerations amount to claiming that any country's institutions can be made invulnerable to calamities. They cannot. Institutions should be chosen to serve and improve the relatively normal conditions in which they have a good chance of flourishing. Shaping institutions for the worse conceivable cases instead is perverse and reminiscent of the maximin criterion for income distribution recommended by John Rawls (1971).

One might even argue that stable money provides a better starting point for government borrowing and money issue in rare emergencies than money commanding little confidence in the first place. Such an argument was made in the late 19th century for putting Russia's floating paper currency onto the gold standard.

One general point demands emphasis. Ingenuity can produce innumerable particular cases in which price-level stability—like any other monetary rule or regime—brings results deemed inferior, on the specific grounds considered, to some alternative rule or regime tailored to the specific circumstances of a particular economic sector at a particular time. Yet monetary regimes can hardly be installed and altered to serve specific cases. Fundamentally, economic policy means choosing and modifying *institutions*—the rules and constraints within which individuals, families, firms, and government agencies act (Vining 1984). Policymakers have no direct handle on outcomes—prices, allocation of resources among different lines of production, geographic distribution of productive activities, patterns of employment and unemployment, and distributions of income and wealth.

For monetary regimes, the basic institutional choice concerns the unit of account—the unit in which prices are set, accounting conducted, costs and benefits estimated, and contracts drawn. Is the unit to be some particular commodity or composite of commodities, perhaps chosen for the expected behavior of its value relative to goods and services in general? Or is the unit to be some fiat currency whose value depends on its scarcity relative to the demand to hold it, a scarcity regulated by a monetary authority?

Adopting a fiat currency as unit of account implies choosing some principles for its management, but that adoption still cannot achieve some detailed pattern of economic outcomes. Of course, one may join Davidson in thinking up particular constellations of circumstances and propounding ethical judgments according to which fairness between debtors and creditors or among other groups might better be served by a fall (or rise) of the price level than by its stability. If, however, the balance of considerations favors institutions achieving monetary stability over alternative institutions, then it is simply irrelevant to think up particular cases in which some other price-level behavior might seem preferable. Institutions and rules cannot be switched on and off from case to case. It is unreasonable to expect a monetary system to achieve all sorts of good results, including economic justice as each person understands it, in the face of multifarious changes in conditions. Theories of rational expectations cast further doubt on the idea that the choice of monetary regime can reliably influence real economic outcomes, such as the distribution of real income and wealth.

No single set of institutions has advantages only, free of any disadvantages. Tradeoffs are unavoidable in institutional choice. Unwillingness to face them is paradoxical among economists, whose subject's most basic fact is the impossibility of having all good things at once.

A monetary system should do what it can reasonably be expected to do, leaving other institutions to undertake tasks more suitable for them. A stable unit of account at least facilitates economic calculation, planning, and contracting. As for fairness, savers need not restrict themselves to buying interest-bearing securities of fixed nominal value. They can try to take account of prospective changes in productivity in various industries by investing in equities. They can diversify their asset portfolios, directly or through mutual funds. Their portfolio choices can express their different degrees of willingness to bear risk. Business firms can raise funds not only by borrowing in nominal terms but also by obtaining loans with equity participations or by selling stock. A sound monetary system improves such opportunities by facilitating financial intermediation and innovation.

As a gesture toward completeness, we should briefly note some further leading arguments for and against a stable unit of account. No one argument, by itself, is decisive, and some arguments are disputed. First, inflation adds "noise" to nominal prices, it degrades the information they contain, and inaccuracies in price comparisons cause allocational inefficiencies (Gavin and Stockman 1988). Unpredictable, "ragged" inflation, especially, undermines economic calculation and long-run planning. The savings-and-loan mess provides an example. One aspect is that S&Ls found themselves locked into long-term assets at the old nominal interest rates of times before inflation speeded up. More generally, unexpected inflation and accelerations and decelerations redistribute wealth capriciously. Second, inflation interacting with the tax system and its depreciation rules distorts production and investment. Third, efforts to avoid losses of purchasing power on money and other dollar-denominated assets require spending real resources to keep down the size of these holdings. These efforts also breed new financial institutions and instruments that would otherwise be inefficient and unprofitable. Politics interacts with financial innovation, regulation, and deregulation in determining the details of the changes made. Fourth, by targeting on the price level and quickly moving to reverse any changes in it, policymakers would gain credibility and reduce uncertainty (Gavin and Stockman 1988; compare Bryan 1990).

Among other arguments against stable money besides those invoking adverse supply shocks, probably the one most commonly met nowadays does not actually condemn price stability; instead, it stresses the pains of squeezing a long-entrenched inflation out of the economy.[11] The desirability of a goal and possible difficulties of attaining it are, however, distinct topics. Furthermore, inflation as we know it is bound to occur at fluctuating rates: Relative disinflation from time to time, along with its actual or supposed pains, is unavoidable anyway. Steady inflation is a "mirage" (Okun 1971 and 1981: 283–84). Relatedly, a policy of keeping inflation steady at a positive rate is not credible and so can hardly serve as a focal point of private expectations, whereas there *is* something special about a rate of *zero*.

The Unit of Account and Free Banking

Rejecting price-level stability means rejecting a unit of account defined by a bundle of goods (and services), whether defined directly

---

[11]Rao Aiygari (1990) exemplifies an excessively narrow view of the costs of inflation. Briefly, he classifies them as the "shoe leather" costs of keeping cash balances smaller than otherwise, overtaxation through underappreciation, and confusion between changes in the price level and in relative prices. He overlooks the importance of a dependable unit of account for economic calculation and long-term planning and contracting. He does not identify, for example, the ways in which current disasters in the financial sector trace to the absence of such a unit. He overlooks the various costs of trying to cope with inflation, including the diversion of resources into seeking and providing supposed inflation hedges.

or defined indirectly through targeting on a price index.[12] What unit of account, then, does the critic recommend instead? The case is weak for a unit defined by gold or any other single commodity.

Anyone recommending some sort of productivity or money growth or nominal income rule—or, at the extreme, recommending the discretionary monetary actions deemed best case by case and day by day—must envisage application of the rule or exercise of discretion by a central authority equipped with the necessary powers. This means—unless I am committing some gross oversight—that the unit is nothing more definite than a unit of government fiat money managed, one hopes, in some satisfactory way. That choice of unit leaves the monetary system vulnerable to the government abuses to which the historical record testifies. It precludes a nongovernmental monetary system.

Choice of a commodity-defined unit of account, on the other hand—preferably one defined by a comprehensive bundle of goods and services—makes possible free banking as envisaged in several current proposals. Rather than again describe a proposal by Robert L. Greenfield and me [see Greenfield and Yeager 1983], I'll simply liken it to Irving Fisher's compensated dollar of 1920 modified as mentioned earlier in this article and further modified by placing the

[12]An exception is barely conceivable. At the present stage of discussion, however, possibilities of bypassing some difficulties of a stable price level while giving the unit of account a commodity-bundle definition seem worth only a footnote. The bundle of goods and services defining the unit or the target price index might be specified with a variable composition in the first place. "Outliers" might be removed automatically: Those particular goods bearing a specific aggregate weight in the bundle whose prices had risen most (and possibly, also, those whose prices had fallen most) over the previous x months might drop out of the bundle. While the price level of this variable bundle would thus remain steady, the broader price level would be allowed to rise to accommodate adverse supply shocks (and perhaps, also, to fall when supply developments were favorable).

Just conceivably, one might define the dollar as a certain (very small) fraction of nominal GNP, with the amount of redemption medium into which a one-dollar note or deposit is indirectly convertible being suitably adjusted. Since nominal GNP depends on conventions of definition and measurement and is not directly continuously observable and since such an approach requires a specific though growing total quantity of money, it is unclear whether the approach could be made compatible with competitive private issue of money and spontaneous adjustment of its total quantity. Credibility would be hard to achieve, furthermore, for a flexibly or completely defined unit. The idea of an adjustable unit or price-level target opens a can of worms, some of them political. Still, some such ideas (largely due to W.W. Woolsey) may be worth further thought.

issue and redemption of money on a decentralized, private, and competitive basis.

Under such a system, the unit of account has its value determined quite otherwise than by supply of and demand for money, whether base money or media of exchange more broadly conceived. No authority ever has to "inject" money into circulation (or sometimes withdraw it) to make its supply match the demand for it at a level compatible with a price-level target or any other principle of monetary management. The supply of money (however exactly money might be defined), as one aspect of the supply of financial-intermediation services, accommodates itself to the demand for it at the stable price level corresponding to the definition of the unit of account. The supposed problem of "injection effects" mentioned earlier is simply bypassed.

Bypassed also is any need for central forecasting. Any forecasting tasks that remain are dispersed among competing private money issuers and speculators. Speculation, along with the indirect convertibility of money and the operations of clearinghouses and arbitrageurs, keeps the commodity-bundle definition of the unit of account operational. "Macroeconomic entrepreneurs," as one might call them, will gather information about current or foreseeable aggregate demand and supply shocks and use it in their transactions in securities and other assets. Their activities will help determine market interest rates and a quantity of money consistent with the independent definition of the unit of account.[13]

Conclusion

"How would you define the unit of account?" Persons who reject a unit of stable purchasing power and dream up cases in which change in the price level would be preferable should have their noses rubbed in that question. What definition of the unit of account would make the price level behave as they deem optimal? Usually, I conjecture, those persons are at least tacitly envisioning the unit of a fiat medium of exchange ideally managed by a governmental authority. Such people would solve monetary problems by assigning them to a philosopher-king.

---

[13]Woolsey and I spell out this admittedly cryptic claim in our 1992 manuscript. Here I merely insist that government fiat money precludes this sort of decentralization and competition.

Ideally managed government fiat money is beguiling. Each person can imagine its being managed as he deems best for each imagined set of circumstances. Apart from this chimerical aspect, the sorry history of government fiat money, now reinforced by public choice theory, makes it doubtful that sound management would endure.

Fiat money managed to satisfy some macroeconomic criterion— its total or per capita quantity, total or per capita nominal income, a productivity norm, or whatever—precludes decentralizing and privatizing the issue of money. Free banking, however, could operate on the basis of a stable unit of account defined independently of any particular medium of exchange and instead defined by a comprehensive bundle of goods and services. The pressures of competition— competition from which a government monetary authority is exempt—would impose discipline on private money issuers, forcing them to keep meaningful the denomination of their bank notes and deposits (and checks) in the stable, independently defined unit.

Besides having other advantages, such a system would radically reduce the need for forecasting (whereas ambitious forecasting is necessary for ideal management of government fiat money, though less necessary for management bound to a price-level rule than management accorded greater discretion). Any forecasting functions that did remain would be healthily decentralized under free banking. Privatization of money seems to me, then, an attractive route toward forecast-free monetary institutions.

References

Aiyagari, S. R. (1990) "Deflating the Case for Zero Inflation." Federal Reserve Bank of Minneapolis *Quarterly Review* 14 (Summer): 2–11.

Anderson, B. M., Jr. ([1917] 1922) *The Value of Money*. Reprint. New York: Macmillan.

Boughton, J. M. (1989) "Commodity Prices and Inflation." *Finance & Development* 26 (June): 27–29.

Bradley, M. D., and Jansen, D. W. (1989) "Understanding Nominal GNP Targeting." Federal Reserve Bank of St. Louis *Review* 71 (November/ December): 31–40.

Bryan, M. F. (1990) "Inflation and Growth: Working More vs. Working Better." Federal Reserve Bank of Cleveland *Economic Commentary* (August 15).

Cassel, G. ([1927–28] 1951) "The Rate of Interest, the Bank Rate, and the Stabilization of Prices." *Quarterly Journal of Economics* 42: 511–29. Reprinted in *Readings in Monetary Theory*, 319–33. Selected by American Economic Association. Philadelphia: Blakiston.

Davidson, D. (1906) "Något om begreppet 'penningens värde.'" *Ekonomisk Tidskrift* 8: 460–68.

_____ (1909a) "Om stabiliseringen af penningens värde." *Ekonomisk Tidskrift* 11 (1): 1– 25.

_____ (1909b) "Replik." *Ekonomisk Tidskrift* 11: 67–68.

_____ (1919) "Några teoretiska frågor." *Ekonomisk Tidskrift* 21 (10–11): 231ff.

_____ (1920) "Valutaproblemets teoretiska innebörd." *Ekonomisk Tidskrift* 22 (3–4): 71– 123.

_____ (1923) "Till frågan om penningvärdets reglering under kriget och därefter." Two parts. *Ekonomisk Tidskrift* 24 (5–6): 89–114, and 25: 191–234.

_____ (1926) "Varuvärde och penningvärde." *Ekonomisk Tidskrift* 28 (1): 1–18.

Ellul, J. (1967) *The Political Illusion*. Translated by K. Kellen. New York: Knopf.

Fiedler, E. R. (1990) "The Future Lies Ahead." In P.A. Klein (ed.) *Analyzing Modern Business Cycles* 128–42. Armonk and London: M. F. Sharpe.

Fisher, I. (1920) *Stabilizing the Dollar*. New York: Macmillan.

Gavin, W. T., and Stockman, A. C. (1988) "The Case for Zero Inflation." Federal Reserve Bank of Cleveland *Economic Commentary* (September 15).

Glasner, D. (1989) *Free Banking and Monetary Reform*. New York: Cambridge University Press.

Greenfield, R. L., and Yeager, L. B. (1983) "A Laissez-Faire Approach to Monetary Stability." *Journal of Money, Credit, and Banking* 15 (3): 302–15.

Hall, R. E. (1986) "Optimal Monetary Institutions and Policy." In C. D. Campbell and W. R. Dougan (eds.), *Alternative Monetary Regimes* 224–39. Baltimore: Johns Hopkins University Press.

Hoehn, J. G. (1989) "Employment Distortions under Sticky Wages and Monetary Policies to Minimize Them." Federal Reserve Bank of Cleveland *Economic Review* 25 (2): 22–34.

Johnson, M. H. (1988) "Current Perspectives on Monetary Policy." *Cato Journal* 8 (2): 253–60.

Koppl, R. (2002) *Big Players and the Economic Theory of Expectations.* New York: Palgrave Macmillan.

Lutz, V. (1969) *Central Planning for the Market Economy.* London: Longmans.

McCallum, B. T. (1987) "The Case for Rules in the Conduct of Monetary Policy: A Concrete Example." Federal Reserve Bank of Richmond *Economic Review* 73 (September/October): 10–18.

_____ (1989) *Monetary Economics.* New York: Macmillan.

Marquis, M. H., and Cunningham, S. R. (1990) "Is There a Role for Commodity Prices in the Design of Monetary Policy? Some Empirical Evidence." *Southern Economic Journal* 57 (October): 394–412.

Nutter, G. W. (1983) *Political Economy and Freedom.* Edited by J. C. Nutter. Indianapolis: Liberty Press.

Okun, A. M. (1971) " The Mirage of Steady Inflation." *Brookings Papers on Economic Activity* 2: 485–98.

_____ (1981) *Prices and Quantities.* Washington: Brookings Institution.

Rawls, J. (1971) *A Theory of Justice.* Cambridge: Belknap Press of Harvard University Press.

Selgin, G. A. (1990) "Monetary Equilibrium and the Productivity Norm of Price-Level Policy." *Cato Journal* 10: 265–87.

Thomas, B. (1935) "The Monetary Doctrines of Professor Davidson." *Economic Journal* 45 (March): 36–50.

Uhr, C. G. (1962) *Economic Doctrines of Knut Wicksell.* 2d printing. Berkeley and Los Angeles: University of California Press.

Viner, J. (1962) "The Necessary and the Desirable Range of Discretion to Be Allowed to a Monetary Authority." In L. B. Yeager (ed.), *In Search of a Monetary Constitution,* 244–74. Cambridge: Harvard University Press.

Vining, R. (1984). *On Appraising the Performance of an Economic System.* New York: Cambridge University Press.

Wicksell, K. (1909) "Penningränta och varupris." *Ekonomisk Tidskrift* 11: 61–66.

_____ (1919) "Ett angrepp på kvantitetsteorien." *Ekonomisk Tidskrift* 21(3): 57–63.

Woolsey, W. W, and Yeager, L. B. (1992) "Is There a Paradox of Indirect Convertibility?" Manuscript. [Published 1994, *Southern Economic Journal* 61(1): 85–95.]

Yeager, L. B. (1988) "Domestic Stability versus Exchange Rate Stability." *Cato Journal* 8 (2): 261–77.

PART 4

ALTERNATIVES TO GOVERNMENT FIAT MONEY

14

GOLD AND SILVER AS CONSTITUTIONAL ALTERNATIVE CURRENCIES
Edwin Vieira Jr.

In his Inaugural Address of 1933, Franklin D. Roosevelt warned his fellow Americans that "in our progress towards a resumption of work we require two safeguards against a return of the evils of the old order: there must be a strict supervision of all banking and credits and investments, so that there will be an end to speculation with other people's money; and there must be provision for an adequate but sound currency." Nonetheless, Roosevelt proceeded to promote an exceedingly unsound currency—with the seizure of most Americans' gold, devaluation of gold coinage, removal of domestic redemption of Federal Reserve Notes in gold, and the nullification of gold clauses in both public and private contracts (Vieira 2002: 867–1235).

Subsequently, this country moved even further away from Roosevelt's professed desideratum (ibid.: 1235–40). To be sure, Americans' right to own gold was restored in 1973, gold clauses were once again permitted for private citizens in 1978, and starting in 1985 the U.S. Treasury began to mint large quantities of gold and silver coins denominated in "dollars" and impressed with the character of "legal tender" (ibid.: 1269–1311). Yet, it cannot be said that the United States now enjoys "an adequate but sound currency" based upon silver and gold in the manner the

Edwin Vieira Jr. is an attorney and author. This article is reprinted from the *Cato Journal*, Vol. 35, No. 2 (Spring/Summer 2015). It is adapted in part from Vieira (2010 and 2011).

Constitution requires (ibid.: 27–205). Rather, by providing financial aid and comfort to the overexpansion of the General Government, the operations of the Federal Reserve System—in particular, the use of Federal Reserve Notes, irredeemable in either gold or silver, as Americans' almost exclusive currency—have validated the prophecy of Justice Stephen J. Field, dissenting in *Dooley v. Smith*, that the fallacious arguments the Supreme Court employed to rationalize the constitutionality of irredeemable legal-tender paper currency

> tend directly to break down the barriers which separate a government of limited powers from a government resting in the unrestrained will of Congress. . . . Those limitations must be preserved, or our government will inevitably drift . . . into a vast centralized and consolidated government [80 U.S. 604, 607–8 (1872)].

But exactly what corrective is now to be applied? At least two alternatives for dealing domestically with the present situation are available: (1) reforming the Federal Reserve System by introducing a redeemable currency somehow "backed" by gold, and preferably by silver as well, because no monometallic gold standard can exist under the Constitution; and (2) replacing the present monetary regime with an entirely new system of economically sound, honest, and especially constitutional money. In this article, I shall focus on the second alternative, as I have shown in detail elsewhere the unconstitutionality and imprudence of attempting to salvage the Federal Reserve System by returning its notes to redeemability in gold or silver (Vieira 2002).

Replacing the Present Monetary Regime with Sound, Honest, and Constitutional Money

Replacement of the present monetary regime would begin with the introduction of alternative currencies consisting solely of gold and silver to compete with Federal Reserve Notes. Here, three possibilities exist:

- First, the American people could fashion such currencies for their own use, under the aegis of the Ninth and Tenth Amendments to the Constitution, and of certain statutes, with the hope that the General Government and the States would then adopt those currencies.

- Second, the General Government could provide such currencies for everyone's use, through the exercise of Congress's power "[t]o coin Money, regulate the Value thereof, and of foreign Coin" in Article I, Section 8, Clause 5 of the Constitution.

- Third, the States could adopt such currencies for themselves and their own people (with the hope that the General Government would then follow suit), on the basis of the States' explicit constitutional duty in Article I, Section 10, Clause 1 of the Constitution not to "make any Thing but gold and silver Coin a Tender in Payment of Debts"—and therefore of their implicitly reserved constitutional right and power *to* "make . . . gold and silver Coin a Tender in Payment of Debts."

Alternative Currencies through Private Action

The qualification *ultimately* to be recognized as official money by all public authorities takes into account that such a reform could be initiated by *private*, rather than governmental, action. In Article I, Section 8, Clause 5, the Constitution delegates to Congress the power "[t]o coin Money, regulate the Value thereof, and of foreign Coin", and in Article I, Section 10, Clause 1 imposes upon the States the duty not to "make any Thing but gold and silver Coin a Tender in Payment of Debts," and through the latter duty reserves to the States the right and power to "make . . . gold and silver Coin a Tender." Nothing in the Constitution, however, precludes Americans, as private individuals, from employing whatever honest media of exchange—in particular, gold and silver—as "Tender" in their private transactions. Indeed, besides the Ninth and Tenth Amendments, the very duty of the States to "make . . . gold and silver Coin a Tender in Payment of Debts" guarantees that private right and power. For most "Debts" arise out of private contracts, are made payable in currency of some sort, and are enforceable in the States' courts. So those courts are constitutionally required to enforce with the actual "Tender" of "gold and silver Coin" contracts that specify the payment of "Debts" in such "Coin"—no matter what other forms of currency Congress may have generated. The reserved duty, right, and power of the States to "make . . . gold and silver Coin a Tender" plainly limits the reach of Congress's power "[t]o coin Money, [and] regulate the Value thereof" (or any other power, for that matter) because the Constitution cannot be read to license Congress to override the very duty, right, and power it simultaneously reserves to the States.[1] In addition, Americans enjoy a statutory right under Title 31, United States Code, Section 5118(a) and (d)(2) to enter into private contracts that contain gold clauses or silver clauses[2]—which the States' courts must enforce pursuant to Article VI, Clause 2 of the Constitution. Thus, as a matter of law, nothing precludes common Americans from adopting gold and silver as their currencies in private transactions in preference to Federal Reserve Notes, even if the General Government and the States' governments were to continue to require people to employ those notes in financial interactions with public agencies.

As a matter of fact, however, powerful disincentives work against widespread adoption of alternative currencies by individuals on their own initiatives.

First, information costs. Before people can employ gold and silver clauses in their contracts, they must educate themselves about their legal rights and the economic advantages that might accrue from exercising them. Moreover, they must also learn how to draft legally binding and fully protective gold or silver clauses—or pay competent attorneys to do so.

Second, transaction costs. Economic actors who understand the advantages of gold and silver clauses must search out complementary partners who also know, or can quickly be educated, about those advantages; must convince them to consummate such arrangements; and must prepare the necessary documents to the satisfaction of various attorneys, accountants, corporate boards, and other supervisors and advisors. In addition, if those actors also enter into other deals pursuant to which they employ Federal Reserve Notes as their media of exchange, they must maintain complex systems of accounting which record receipts and expenditures sometimes in gold and silver,

---

[1]Compare Hostetter v. Idlewild Bon Voyage Liquor Corp., 377 U.S. 324, 332 (1964), with Dick v. United States, 208 U.S. 340, 353 (1908), and South Dakota v. North Carolina, 192 U.S. 286, 328 (1904) (White, J., dissenting), and with, e.g., United States v. Brignoni-Ponce, 422 U.S. 873, 877 (1975).

[2]See Bronson v. Rodes, 74 U.S. 229 (1869), and Butler v. Horwitz, 74 U.S. 258 (1869).

sometimes in notes, and which track exchanges of gold and silver for notes and vice versa.

Third, opportunity costs. In the absence of banks that pay interest in gold and silver on deposits of such currencies, people who employ gold and silver clauses can only "hoard" the gold and silver they receive but do not spend. This may prove economically disadvantageous.

Fourth, regulatory costs. Individuals who employ U.S. gold and silver coinage statutorily denominated in "dollars" as their media of exchange are typically required by tax gatherers and courts to report their gross receipts, incomes, sales, and other financial data, and to calculate and pay taxes, not on the basis of the face values of the coins in "dollars" as mandated by Congress, but instead on the basis of the much greater so-called fair market values of the coins expressed in Federal Reserve Notes (Vieira 2002: 1311–40). Although this requirement should be disallowed on both constitutional and statutory grounds, to challenge it is a costly and chancy endeavor.[3]

So, to expect individuals in large numbers spontaneously to adopt gold and silver as alternative currencies is unrealistic. Moreover, that many Americans did employ such alternative currencies in their private transactions would not by itself guarantee that the General Government and the States' governments would accept those currencies as media of exchange in the normal run of public transactions.

Alternative Currencies through the Federal Government

Pursuant to Title 31, United States Code, Section 5112(a)(7 through 10), (e), (h), and (i), the General Government already issues gold and silver coins as official currencies with the status of "legal tender." But it has not arranged for these coins to compete with Federal Reserve Notes in the marketplace on anything approaching equal terms (primarily because of the confusion surrounding how the "dollar" values of payments in such coins are to be determined). In the present political climate, the likelihood that any such arrangement will be made is essentially nil.

---

[3]Contrast Thompson v. Butler, 95 U.S. 694 (1878), and 31 U.S.C. § 5112(a)(7 through 10), (e), (h), and (i)(1)(B), with, e.g., IRS Notice 2008-14, Frivolous Positions, ¶ 15.

Moreover, although Congress has mandated in Title 31, Section 5119(a) that "the Secretary [of the Treasury] shall redeem gold certificates owned by the Federal reserve banks at times and in amounts the Secretary determines are necessary to maintain the equal purchasing power of each kind of United States currency", and although Congress has declared in Title 31, Section 5117(b) "the value (for the purpose of issuing those [gold] certificates . . .) of the gold held against" them to be "42 and two-ninth dollars a fine troy ounce," U.S. gold coins do not exchange against Federal Reserve Notes in the free market at anything close to that figure—and no one has called the Secretary to account for this discrepancy.

Alternative Currencies through the States

Not entirely unlikely, though, is that one or more of the States may recognize the economic necessity of adopting gold and silver as alternative currencies within their own territories. The constitutionality of such action is beyond question. The ultimate purpose of a State's adoption of an alternative currency would be to protect the economic, social, and political well-being of her citizens against the inherent instability of the Federal Reserve System and its paper currency. To this end, the States' "police power" is particularly well suited.

"The police power" "is a power originally and always belonging to the states, not surrendered by them to the general government, nor directly restrained by the Constitution of the United States, and essentially exclusive" (*In re* Rahrer, 140 U.S. 545, 554 [1891]). "The police power" "is not granted by or derived from the Federal Constitution, but exists independently of it, by reason of its never having been surrendered by the States to the general government" (*House v. Mayes*, 219 U.S. 270, 282 [1911]).[4] The States possess "the police power" "in their sovereign capacity touching all subjects jurisdiction of which is not surrendered to the federal government" (*Nebbia v. New York*, 291 U.S. 502, 524 [1934]). So "the police power" subsumes *all* of the sovereign powers of a State government reserved to it by the Constitution of the United States. It is, there-

---

[4]*Accord*, California Reduction Co. v. Sanitary Reduction Works, 199 U.S. 306, 318 (1905) ("the States possess, because they have never surrendered, the [police] power").

fore, the primary subject of the Tenth Amendment with respect to the States, because it embraces *all* of "[t]he powers not delegated to the United States by the Constitution, nor prohibited by it to the States, [which] are reserved to the States respectively." That being so, "the police power" is "one of the most essential of powers, at times the most insistent, and always one of the least limitable of the powers of government" (*District of Columbia v. Brooke*, 214 U.S. 138, 149 [1909]).[5]

In particular, "the police power of a State embraces regulations designed to promote . . . the general prosperity" (*Chicago, Burlington & Quincy Railway Co. v. Illinois ex rel. Grimwood*, 200 U.S. 561, 592 [1906]),[6] and "to enforc[e] the primary conditions of successful commerce" (*Noble State Bank v. Haskell*, 219 U.S. 104, 111 [1911])—and in a free-market economy "the general prosperity" cannot be advanced through "successful commerce" without a politically honest and economically sound medium of exchange.

The States possess "the police power" "in their sovereign capacity touching all subjects jurisdiction of which is not surrendered to the federal government" (*Nebbia v. New York*, 291 U.S. 502, 524 [1934]). The States' "jurisdiction"—that is, their legal authority—to employ gold and silver coin as alternative currencies is a "subject . . . which is not surrendered to the federal government." Rather, the Constitution itself explicitly reserves that power to the States. Article I, Section 10, Clause 1 of the Constitution provides that "[n]o State shall . . . make any Thing but gold and silver Coin a Tender in Payment of Debts." So, on the very face of the Constitution, the States *may* "make . . . gold and silver Coin a Tender"—and, according to the principle that the Constitution must always be read with an eye toward fully achieving its purposes, the States *should always* "make . . . gold and silver Coin a Tender" whenever the situation calls for it. For no one should "construe any clause of the Constitution as to defeat its obvious ends, when another construction, equally accordant with the words and sense thereof, will enforce and protect them" (*Prigg v. Pennsylvania*, 41 U.S. 539, 612 [1842]). True it is that the authority to "make any Thing *but* gold and silver Coin a Tender"

---

[5]Quoted in Eubank v. City of Richmond, 226 U.S. 137, 142–43 (1912).
[6]*Accord*, Bacon v. Walker, 204 U.S. 311, 317 (1907); Eubank v. City of Richmond, 226 U.S. 137, 142 (1912); Sligh v. Kirkwood, 237 U.S. 52, 59 (1915).

is drafted as an exception to the States' general disability to "make . . . Tender[s]"—that is, as an exception to an absence of power. But an exception to an absence of power is necessarily the recognition of that power to the full extent of the exception. And the exception in favor of "gold and silver Coin" knows no bounds in terms of the times at which, the circumstances in which, or the degree to which the States may apply it. So the States may and should "make . . . gold and silver Coin a Tender" under *all* circumstances considered appropriate *by them*.

"Tender" is generally defined as "[a]n offer of money; the act by which one produces and offers to a person holding a claim or demand against him the amount of money which he considers and admits to be due, in satisfaction of such claim of demand, without any stipulation or condition"; and "[l]egal tender is that kind of coin, money, or circulating medium which the law compels a creditor to accept in payment of his debt, when tendered by the debtor in the right amount" (Black's: 1637). So, perforce of Article I, Section 10, Clause 1, the States may not compel a creditor to accept, in payment of any "Debt]" solvable in money, "any Thing but gold and silver Coin," but *may* compel him—and certainly may allow him, and even assist him—to receive such "Coin" in fulfillment of a contract in which such "Coin" has been designated the medium of payment. On the other hand, if a creditor and a debtor have entered into an enforceable contract that specifies as the exclusive medium of payment something other than "gold and silver Coin," no State can compel them by some subsequently enacted law to substitute any other medium of payment, including "gold and silver Coin"—because Article I, Section 10, Clause 1 also declares that "[n]o State shall . . . pass any . . . Law impairing the Obligation of Contracts."

Because it is directed toward promoting "the general prosperity," the States' power to "make . . . gold and silver Coin a Tender" is necessarily a component of, and as exhaustive in its own domain as, their "police power" in general. Perhaps most important in this regard, except in one respect the Constitution in no way limits the ambit of the States' authority to "make . . . gold and silver Coin a Tender" with respect to the possible *sources* of such "Coin." The only "gold and silver Coin" excluded from the States' power to "make . . . a Tender" is the "Money" that *the States themselves* might purport to generate, because Article I, Section 10, Clause 1 declares that "[n]o State shall . . . coin Money." Otherwise, "where no exception is made in terms, none will be made by mere implication or construction" (*Rhode Island v. Massachusetts*, 37 U.S. 657, 722 [1838]). Therefore, the States may declare any and every domestic "gold and silver Coin a Tender," in addition to any relevant declaration Congress has put forth. The States may declare any and every foreign "gold and silver Coin a Tender," even when (as is the case today) Congress has refused to do so under Title 31, United States Code, Section 5103. And the States may declare even private "gold and silver Coin a Tender," too.

The *only* condition on the States' exercise of their power "to make . . . a Tender" is that they must apply it comprehensively to *both* "gold *and* silver Coin." Under Article I, Section 10, Clause 1, a State may not adopt a monometallic "gold standard" or "silver standard," but must always employ the two metals in tandem—and, of course, always in such a manner as to ensure that, in every particular transaction, "a Tender" required to be made in "gold . . . Coin" will deliver the same purchasing power as "a Tender" in "silver Coin," as the Constitution requires perforce of Article I, Section 10, Clause 1 ("[n]o State shall . . . pass any . . . Law impairing the Obligation of Contracts") and Amendment XIV, Section 1 ("nor shall any State deprive any person of . . . property, without due process of law"). This, however, would be quite easy to accomplish. For, under such a duometallic system, the required equivalence would be controlled by the free market. For instance, "a Tender" in gold of X grains could also be made with Y grains of silver, where Y equaled X *times* E (the market exchange rate between gold and silver). Or, "a Tender" in silver of Y grains could also be made with X grains of gold, where X equaled Y *times* the reciprocal of E. The matter would be entirely one of economic arithmetic, not of arbitrary political policy.

Besides being part of their "police power"—because it is "a power originally and always belonging to the states, not surrendered by them to the general government, nor directly restrained by the Constitution of the United States, and essentially exclusive" (*In re Rahrer*, 140 U.S. 545, 554 [1891])—the States' power to "make . . . gold and silver Coin a Tender" is, because of its placement in the Constitution, effectively *absolute* (Vieira 2002: 104–12). The States enjoy a right and power to "make . . . gold and silver Coin a Tender" *no matter what Congress may decree in the monetary field*.

The Supreme Court has arrived at the same conclusion on a different but complementary basis. In *Lane County v. Oregon* (74 U.S.

71 [1869]), the State courts had ruled that, as a matter of State law, certain county and State taxes were required to be collected in silver and gold coin. At issue in the Supreme Court was whether, notwithstanding State law, the taxes could be paid in U.S. Treasury notes that were at the time not redeemable in either gold or silver coin, pursuant to the congressional mandate that those notes "shall be receivable in payment of all taxes, internal duties, excises, debts and demands due to the United States, except duties on imports . . . ; and shall also be lawful money and legal tender in payment of all debts, public and private, within the United States" (74 U.S. at 75, quoting An Act to authorize the Issue of United States Notes, and for the Redemption or Funding thereof, and for Funding the Floating Debt of the United States, Act of 25 February 1862, Chap. XXXIII, § 1, 12 Stat. 345, 345). The Supreme Court held that the State could *not* be compelled to accept payment of taxes in those notes. "The people of the United States", the Court explained,

> constitute one nation, under one government, and this government, within the scope of the powers with which it is invested, is supreme. On the other hand, the people of each State compose a State, having its own government, and endowed with all the functions essential to separate and independent existence. The States disunited might continue to exist. Without the States in union there could be no political body as the United States.
>
> Both the States and the United States existed before the Constitution. The people, through that instrument, established a more perfect union by substituting a national government, acting, with ample power, directly upon the citizens, instead of the Confederate government, which acted with powers, greatly restricted, only upon the States. But in many articles of the Constitution the necessary existence of the States, and, within their proper spheres, the independent authority of the States, is distinctly recognized. . . . [T]o them and to the people all powers not expressly delegated to the national government are reserved. . . .
>
> Now, to the existence of the States, themselves necessary to the existence of the United States, the power of taxation is indispensable. It is an essential function of government. . . . There is nothing in the Constitution which contemplates or authorizes any direct abridgment of this power by national legislation. . . . If, therefore, the condition of any

State, in the judgment of its legislature, requires the collection of taxes . . . in gold and silver bullion, or in gold and silver coin, it is not easy to see upon what principle the
national government can interfere with the exercise, to that
end, of this power, original in the States, and never as yet
surrendered [74 U.S. at 76–78, followed in *Union Pacific
Railroad Company v. Peniston*, 85 U.S. 5, 29 (1873), and
Hagar v. Reclamation District No. 108, 111 U.S. 701, 706
(1884)].

The doctrine of *Lane County* recognizes that certain kinds of
monetary laws that Congress may make applicable to the government of the United States and to private individuals acting in their
personal capacities it cannot make applicable to the States or to individuals performing State governmental functions. The Supreme
Court later explicitly affirmed this interpretation in *Juilliard* v.
Greenman (110 U.S. 421, 448 [1884]), when it observed that
"Congress is authorized to establish a national currency, either in
coin or in paper, and to make that currency lawful money for all purposes, as regards the national government or private individuals"—
but, as the studied absence of any reference to the States makes
clear, *not* as regards the States' governments or individuals acting in
some official capacity on their behalf or under their auspices.

Thus, *Lane County* and related decisions laid down a wide
avenue for the States' self-emancipation from congressional media
of exchange other than "gold and silver Coin." For, although those
particular decisions all involved State taxes, their reasoning rested
on a principle that encompasses every monetary transaction arising
from a State's exercise of any and every one of her attributes of sovereignty. After all, taxation is no more "indispensable" to or "an
essential function of government" (*Lane County*), or an "attribute
of sovereignty" (*Peniston*), than (say) spending public moneys on
public functions, borrowing on the public credit, paying just compensation to persons expropriated under the power of eminent
domain, or awarding damages or collecting fines in judicial proceedings. All of these, and more, are quintessentially "sovereign"
activities, including:

- Taxation, which *Lane County*, *Peniston*, and *Hagar* so held;
- Public spending, as to which *Taub v.Kentucky* (842 F.2d 912,
  919 [6th Cir. 1988]) noted that "State sovereignty extends to the

total conduct of a State's fiscal affairs," and that "[a] sovereign must have the authority to determine how tax revenues are to be spent, or the power to tax is illusory";[7]

- Public borrowing evidenced in and enforceable through "binding obligations," which *Perry v.United States* (294 U.S. 330, 353 [1935]) held to be "a competence attaching to sovereignty";
- The power of eminent domain, which *Boom Company v. Patterson* (98 U.S. 403, 406 [1879]) described as "an attribute of sovereignty";[8]
- The jurisdiction of the courts, which *The Schooner Exchange v.McFaddon* (11 U.S. 116, 136 [1812]) treated as "a branch" of "independent sovereign power";
- All of the matters within the ambit of "the police power," which *Nebbia v. New York* (291 U.S. 502, 524 [1934]) held that the States may exercise "in their sovereign capacity touching all subjects jurisdiction of which is not surrendered to the federal government"; and
- The regulation and operation of the State's militia, which the Second Amendment declares to be "necessary to the security of a free State," and which therefore constitutes the ultimate embodiment and guarantor of *all* aspects of the State's sovereignty (Vieira 2012).

The Practicality of Electronic Gold and Silver Currencies

The practicality of having States offer alternative currencies based on gold and silver is also plain.

First, through the use of "Coin," a State could exercise her authority under Article I, Section 10, Clause 1 of the Constitution to

---

[7]*Accord, e.g.*, State *ex rel*. Walton v. Parsons, 58 Idaho 787, 792, 80 P.2d 20, 22 (1938) ("the power to levy and collect taxes and the power to appropriate public funds are coexistent and rest upon the same principle"); Mills v. Stewart, 76 Mont. 429, 438, 247 Pac. 332, 334 (1926) (same); Agricultural & Mechanical College v. Hagar, 121 Ky. 1, 14, 87 S.W. 1125, 1129 (1905) (same). See U.S. Const. art. I, § 8, cl. 1, which explicitly links the power "To lay and collect Taxes" with the power "to pay the Debts and provide for the common defence and general Welfare".

[8]*Accord*, Georgia v. City of Chattanooga, 264 U.S. 472, 480 (1924); Albert Hanson Lumber Co. v. United States, 261 U.S. 581, 587 (1923); Adirondack Railway Co. v. New York, 176 U.S. 335, 346-47 (1900).

"make . . . gold and silver Coin a Tender in Payment of Debts," and render such alternative currencies economically and politically by:

- Listing various domestic and foreign gold and silver coins—properly valued according to their actual contents of fine metal—as suitable for "Tender in Payment of Debts";
- Declaring that only those coins would be employed in certain (perhaps, eventually, all) financial transactions or other payments in the nature of "Debts" that involved the State, her subdivisions, and their employees, agents, and contractors;[9]
- Recognizing that everyone else in the State could enter into contracts payable in whatever currencies the parties agreed to use (including but not necessarily limited to "gold and silver Coin"), and specifically enforceable *in those terms and only those terms* in the State's courts;[10] and
- Facilitating the use of "gold and silver Coin [as] a Tender" by *inter alia*

  (i) creating a State depository which would establish and manage accounts in "Coin" for the State and her citizens, transfer ownership of gold and silver among these accounts (by such means as electronic assignments, debit-cards, and checks), and maintain appropriate accounting-records for depositors;

  (ii) providing businessmen in the State with the necessary computer-software and instructions to enable them to price their goods and services in terms of "gold and silver Coin";

  (iii) offering incentives to businessmen to encourage their customers to employ "gold and silver Coin [as] a Tender" in dealing with their businesses;

  (iv) simplifying the calculation and collection of State and local taxes by allowing (for example) transactions effected in gold

---

[9]Other payments that were not "Debts" in the strict constitutional sense of that term, such as taxes, could also be made subject to the "Tender" of "gold and silver Coin", under the constitutional rationale of *Lane County*. Although the legal explanations would differ, the practical effects would be the same.

[10]See Bronson v. Rodes, 74 U.S. (7 Wallace) 229 (1869); Trebilcock v. Wilson, 79 U.S. (12 Wallace) 687 (1872). On the valuation of such contracts where the currency is nominally valued in "dollars", *see* Thompson v. Butler, 95 U.S. 694 (1878).

and silver to be valued, and taxes on or related to those transactions to be paid, in gold and silver; and

(v) collecting selected taxes, fees, and other public charges in "gold and silver Coin" as soon as practicable, so as to familiarize as many citizens as possible with the existence, operations, and advantages of the alternative currency system (see Vieira 2002: 1664–66 for a model statue for this purpose).

Second, through the use of gold and silver in forms other than "Coin." Economically sound, constitutional, and honest alternative currencies consisting of gold and silver need not employ those metals only in the form of "Coin." For nothing in the Constitution prohibits a State from adopting *any* alternative currency as long as, in so doing, the State itself does not attempt to exercise any powers which the Tenth Amendment recognizes as "prohibited by [the Constitution] to the States," in particular the powers denied by Article I, Section 10, Clause 1 to "coin Money; emit Bills of Credit; [or] make any Thing but gold and silver Coin a Tender in Payment of Debts."

From a technological perspective, probably the best alternatives available today are so-called electronic gold and electronic silver currencies. Here, "electronic" refers to the method for recording and transferring legal title to specific amounts of gold or silver bullion actually held by an "electronic currency provider" in separate accounts for each depositor's use as money. Such "electronic" currencies offer numerous advantages both of and over gold and silver coins:

- *Security:* The gold and silver are owned by the depositors themselves and not by the "electronic currency providers" that hold those deposits. The depositors are bailors of the specie, the "providers" bailees. (With a typical bank, conversely, a deposit becomes the property of the bank, with the depositor merely a general creditor of the bank for the value of his deposit.)
- *Ubiquity:* Anyone maintaining an account with an "electronic currency provider" can easily acquire gold and silver through the "provider" and then deal with anyone else holding such an account, anywhere in the world.
- *Convenience:* transactions in gold and silver can be effected with debit cards or like instruments, so that payment is had immediately; but the actual specie may never have to leave the

"electronic currency providers'" vaults. (Transactions also can be effected on the basis of paper orders in the nature of checks and drafts, or actual physical delivery of gold or silver, if the parties so desire.)

- *Flexibility:* Transactions of very small and exact values can be made—down to thousandths of a grain or a gram, or even less—which is impossible with coins. And
- *Accuracy:* Details can be automatically recorded for purposes of accounting, including *inter alia* the date, the time, and the parties to a transaction; the location, nature, and purpose of the transaction; and its value in gold, silver, Federal Reserve Notes, or any other common media of exchange.

To implement such a system, a State would establish within her government an official "electronic gold and silver currency provider." This agency might develop its own "electronic currency," or license the necessary technology from some private vendor. The constitutionally as well as politically most secure arrangement would be to staff this agency with properly trained members the State's militia, and to secure the gold and silver bullion in a depository under the militia's direct supervision, operation, and physical control (Vieira 2012: 1208–33). This would provide the inestimable advantage of maintaining actual possession of the people's gold and silver in the people's own hands at all times. Particular depositors' gold and silver would be held in separate bailment accounts, so that the system could not be accused of operating on the basis of fractional reserves. This is critically important, inasmuch as any scheme utilizing "fractional reserves" would also necessarily implicate "Bills of Credit"—for if the State purported to credit a depositor's account with amounts of gold or silver bullion not owned by him, or not immediately subject to his order (either because they were not physically in the depository or were somehow legally encumbered), then those credits would amount at best to promises by the State to pay those amounts upon the depositor's demand at some future time, which is the essence of a "Bill of Credit" that functions as currency (*Craig v. Missouri*, 29 U.S. 410, 431-2 [1830]). Yet the depositors' gold and silver would always be impressed with the attributes of the State's sovereign authority, because the State had designated the metals as her own alternative currencies (*Ling Su Fan v. United States*, 218 U.S. 302, 311 [1910], and *Norman v. Baltimore & Ohio Railroad Co.*, 294

U.S. 240, 304 [1935]). Thus, the gold and silver in the State's depository would be serving, not only the particular purposes of the various depositors, both public and private, but also the overarching public purpose of guaranteeing the State's economic "homeland security."

Consequently, not only the gold and silver deposited by the State and all of the governmental bodies and agencies within her jurisdiction, but also the specie deposited by members of her militia in their capacities and pursuant to their duties as such—which would include essentially all of her adult population—would be protected by a intergovernmental immunity, arising out of federalism itself, from any form of interference on the part of rogue agents of the General Government. For, under Article I, Section 8, Clause 15 of the Constitution, Congress can "provide for calling forth the Militia" only "to execute the Laws of the Union, suppress Insurrections and repel Invasions." A State's adoption of an alternative currency involves neither an "Insurrection" nor an "Invasion." And, as no merely statutory "Laws of the Union" can interfere with the constitutional duty, right, and power of the States to "make . . . gold and silver Coin a Tender," the militia cannot be "call[ed] forth" on behalf of the federal government "to execute the Laws of the Union" with respect to such monetary matters *except to support the States in their fulfillment and exercise of that constitutional duty, right, and power.* Moreover, except for the president of the United States, no officials of the General Government can interfere by way of command in the operations of the militia within the States, because Article I, Section 8, Clause 16 of the Constitution "reserv[es] to the States respectively, the Appointment of the Officers." Even the president cannot interject himself into the matter, because under Article II, Section 2, Clause 1 of the Constitution he is "Commander in Chief . . . of the Militia of the several States" only when they are "called into the actual Service of the United States"—which "Service" can embrace only one or more of the three constitutional functions set out in Article I, Section 8, Clause 15. Indeed, this intergovernmental immunity would extend to the silver and gold used as media of exchange by *every one* of the State's citizens, whether members of her militia or not, because all such use would be in aid of preserving the State's economic "homeland security" by and through her militia.

Third, the constitutional equivalency of "Coin" and "electronic" currencies. The distinction between "electronic" gold and silver currencies, on the one hand, and actual "gold and silver Coin", on the other, is small in practice and inconsequential in principle. Instructive in this regard is the Supreme Court's decision in *Bronson v. Rodes* (74 U.S. 229 [1869]). At issue was whether a private contractual obligation of "dollars payable in gold and silver coin, lawful money of the United States" was, notwithstanding that stipulation, payable in United States Treasury notes which Congress had declared to be "legal tender" but were not redeemable in either gold or silver. In order to determine "the precise import in law" of the key contractual phrase, the Court reviewed the coinage acts of Congress from 1792 onwards, observing that "[t]he design of all this minuteness and strictness in the regulation of coinage . . . recognizes the fact, accepted by all men throughout the world, that value is inherent in the precious metals; that gold and silver are in themselves values, and being such . . . are the only proper measure of value; that these values are determined by weight and purity"—and that "[e]very . . . dollar is a piece of gold or silver, certified to be of a certain weight and purity, by the form and impress given to it at the mint . . . and therefore declared to be legal tender in payments" (74 U.S. at 247–50). From all this, the Court concluded that

> [a] contract to pay a certain number of dollars in gold or silver coins is, therefore, in legal import, nothing else than an agreement to deliver a certain weight of standard gold, to be ascertained by a count of coins, each of which is certified to contain a definite proportion of that weight. It is not distinguishable . . ., in principle, from a contract to deliver an equal weight of bullion of equal fineness. It is distinguishable, in circumstance, only by the fact that the sufficiency of the amount to be tendered in payment must be ascertained, in the case of bullion, by assay and the scales, while in the case of coin it may be ascertained by count.

Thus, "mak[ing] . . . gold and silver Coin a Tender" should not be distinguishable in constitutional principle from "mak[ing] . . . [an equal weight of bullion of equal fineness] a Tender". The only concern should be how to assure in practice that in either case a constitutionally "equal weight" of metal is delivered. This will depend, however, upon how "equal weight" is defined—whether physically or economically.

Traditionally, a coin containing a certain weight of gold or silver has been considered to be of somewhat greater market value than—that is, has commanded a "premium" over—gold or silver bullion of the same weight. This, because each coin is so designed as to certify its source, substance, content, and in most cases nominal legal value as money, and therefore on its face imparts more information than an equal weight of mere bullion. Also, coins are fabricated in sizes deemed convenient for commerce, and with a small amount of base metal added to the gold or silver in order to harden the resulting alloy so as to facilitate exchange in hand-to-hand transactions—and therefore are more useful than bullion in that context. Such design and fabrication add economic value to the bullion a coin contains.[11] And for quite a while the Treasury minted gold and silver coins according to the constitutional principle of "free coinage", whereby an individual who brought some weight of gold or silver bullion to the Mint would receive, after a time, coins containing the selfsame weight of metal, struck at no charge to him; or, if he preferred immediate receipt (and the Mint concurred), could accept coins containing some lesser weight according to a fixed formula. For example, the first coinage act enacted under the Constitution provided that "any person" might

> bring to the . . . mint gold and silver bullion, in order to their being coined; and . . . the bullion so brought shall be . . . coined as speedily as may be after the receipt thereof, and that free of expense to the person . . . by whom the same shall have been brought. And as soon as the said bullion shall have been coined, the person . . . by whom the same shall have been delivered, shall upon demand receive in lieu thereof coins of the same species of bullion which shall have been so delivered, weight for weight, of the pure gold or pure silver therein contained: *Provided, nevertheless,* That it shall be at the mutual option of the party . . . bringing such bullion, and of the director of the . . . mint, to make an immediate

[11]Some contemporary private purveyors of gold and silver bullion fabricate small bars stamped with such information, *except for a nominal legal value*. The absence of the latter distinguishes these bars from coins. Of course, if the legal unit of monetary value were a standard measure of weight—say, the troy grain or the metric gram—then a designation of weight on such a bar would simultaneously be a designation of its legal value in such units, and no practical difference would exist between bullion in that form and coin.

exchange of coins for standard bullion, with a deduction of one half per cent. from the weight of the pure gold, or pure silver contained in the said bullion, as an indemnification to the mint for the time which will necessarily be required for coining the said bullion, and for the advance which shall have been so made in coins ["An Act Establishing a Mint, and Regulating the Coins of the United States," Act of 2 April 1792, CHAP. XVI, § 14, 1 Stat. 246, 249].

The rationale for this statute was that the conversion of bullion into coinage has always been considered a prerogative of sovereignty that performs an indispensable public function (see *Ling Su Fan v. United States*, 218 U.S. 302, 311 [1910], and *Norman v. Baltimore & Ohio Railroad Co.*, 294 U.S. 240, 304 [1935]), and therefore the cost of which is rightfully chargeable to the public, unless some special benefit is to be provided to the purveyor of the bullion, in which case any excess charge that has to be incurred may fairly be laid upon him. The principle of "free coinage"—with its implicit recognition of the premium between coinage and bullion, and its allocation of the cost of generating new coinage to the public in the first instance—constitutes an integral part of Congress's constitutional power "[t]o coin Money" under Article I, Section 8, Clause 5 of the Constitution,[12] and therefore must be taken into consideration if a State chooses to employ bullion as alternative currency in conjunction with "Coin", so that nothing the State does in the course of "mak[ing] . . . gold and silver Coin a Tender" under the authority of Article I, Section 10, Clause 1 conflicts with that power.

A further consideration must be taken into account. With "electronic" gold and silver currencies, almost all transfers of ownership of bullion are effected, not "by count" as with coins, but by weight.[13] Nonetheless, these transfers do not require recourse to the cumbersome procedure of "assay and the scales," because the bullion is so controlled in the depository that its susceptibility to substitution or adulteration is for all practical purposes precluded. Therefore transfers of ownership of aliquots of bullion between account-holders can

[12]Compare Act of 2 April 1792, § 14, 1 Stat. at 249, with Myers v. United States, 272 U.S. 52, 174-5 (1926), and Field v. Clark, 143 U.S. 649, 691 (1892).
[13]Conceivably, a few transfers could be effected by actual physical delivery of some number of standard bars of bullion. These, however, would likely involve exceptionally large values of gold or silver.

be effected with speed, security, accuracy, and confidence through electronic accounting rather than anyone's physical involvement with the bullion. Indeed, the system can operate for most purposes without any disturbance of the bullion once lodged in the depository. Also, because an "electronic" currency can be subdivided into exceedingly small units, transactions of almost any value can be conducted—a flexibility impossible to achieve with coins, because coins of only a few different values are ever minted, which requires that so-called "token coinage" of base metals (or, worse yet, paper notes) be generated for use in small transactions and to "make change". So, with the advent of "electronic" gold and silver currencies, the former advantages of "Coin" arising out of special designs and fabrication have largely disappeared; and the few sizes of "Coin" available have become more of a liability than ever. As a result, any premium might now run in favor of gold and silver bullion in an "electronic-currency depository" over equal weights of such metals in the form of "Coin" held outside of such a depository. The weight of gold and silver in "Coin" held within such a depository could also be treated as bullion until the "Coin" were actually paid out, at which point some calculation involving a premium could come into play.

Obviously, investigation by experts will be necessary to determine whether any premium between bullion and "Coin" will arise, and if so what it may be and to the advantage of which it may accrue, when a State employs "electronic" gold and silver currencies as "Tender in Payment of Debts." In any event, a State must so arrange her system that the "Tender" for any "Debt[ ]" will, as a matter of both fact and law, be some actual "gold [or] silver Coin" or the amount of gold or silver bullion of weight and fineness "equal" to the weight and fineness of that metal in the "Coin," corrected for the premium (if any) in favor of either "Coin" or bullion, as the case may be. Moreover, the bullion in the State's depository must always be fully and freely convertible into "Coin," and "Coin" in the free market convertible into bullion in the depository, according to the same principle of relative valuation. A depository might also find it convenient to employ "Coin" as well as bullion as the basis for its "electronic" currency, because the problem of *inter*-valuation between the two would be merely a matter of arithmetic once the formulae for assigning and calculating any premium have been established. This, however, is a technical matter best left to specialists to sort out.

Implementation of an Electronic Gold and Silver Plan

Implementation of an electronic gold and silver currency plan would be highly advantageous.

First and foremost, adoption of alternative gold and silver currencies would be an act of foresight. It would recognize that resuscitation of the Federal Reserve System may prove impossible, and in any event is inadvisable.

Second, adoption of alternative gold and silver currencies would be an act of scientific insight, because it would introduce currencies the values of which could always be verified or falsified in terms of fixed amounts of gold and silver measured by universal standards of weight, not the fanciful names historically attached to various coins. Because a unit-weight of gold is always a unit-weight of gold, and no less for silver, these would be objective and permanent values everywhere and at all times throughout the world, no matter what economic, political, or social conditions happened to prevail here or there.

Third, under this plan, holders of these currencies not only would have some claim to, but would actually own, and at their discretion could themselves physically possess, the gold and silver that would constitute the currencies. Contrast this with Federal Reserve Notes: Even when those notes were redeemable in gold, some Federal Reserve Bank or the United States Government actually owned and possessed the gold that "backed" the notes; and holders of the notes had no more than a claim to redemption. Only upon actual redemption did actual title to and possession of the gold change hands. And that right of redemption was eventually cancelled, both domestically and internationally. As to gold, then, Federal Reserve Notes proved to be, as the late John Exter so trenchantly put it, "an I.O.U. nothing currency," because the notes and the gold were separate things, under the control of different people. But with actual weights of gold and silver as currencies, nothing is owed, and the holders of the currencies can always possess the actual gold or silver, so no promise of redemption can ever be repudiated.

Fourth, alternative gold and silver currencies would allow for more than one experiment to be conducted—indeed, as many as 50 separate experiments in each of the several States would be possible. Should any single trial fail in any particular, it would do so only locally, not nationally. If it succeeded, it could be expanded easily enough elsewhere. And by the process of judicious experimentation, constant improvements on initial successes would eventuate. Moreover, even if politically influential factions could succeed in frustrating the adoption of alternative currencies in one State, they would be unlikely to wield the political clout necessary to suppress such currencies in every other State as well. And if they could not stop the experiment everywhere, honest public officials and the free market would put the theory into practice somewhere, and then expand its application elsewhere.

Fifth, adoption of alternative gold and silver currencies could be accomplished incrementally and gradually, allowing the free market to set and equilibrate prices as more and more people employed the new currencies in preference to Federal Reserve Notes. No sudden, economically disorienting jump from Federal Reserve Notes to gold and silver would have to occur.

Sixth, quite unlike the Federal Reserve System and Federal Reserve Notes, alternative currencies of gold and silver would be fully constitutional. As explained above, the Supreme Court in *Lane County* v. *Oregon* has already ruled that the States constitutionally cannot be compelled to use a currency emitted by Congress—in particular, that they may choose to employ gold and silver in preference to irredeemable paper currency, even when Congress has declared that currency to be "legal tender." Thus, the adoption of alternative gold and silver currencies would return each State to the rule of constitutional law and federalism with respect to money.

Seventh, introduction of alternative gold and silver currencies would not depend upon a State's having any gold or silver in her treasury at the beginning of the process. To be sure, under Article I, Section 8, Clause 5; Article I, Section 10, Clause 1; and Article VI, Clause 2 of the Constitution, only Congress enjoys the power "[t]o coin Money"—that is, the "[*official*] Money" which all public agencies must recognize and employ for public purposes. But the Constitution is utterly silent as to purely "[*private*] Money" which individuals may create and exchange among themselves. Indeed, as "powers" with respect to the prohibition of "private Money" are "not delegated to the United States," and as the States' authority to "make . . . gold and silver Coin a Tender" is sufficiently broad to enforce "private Money" as "Tender" in private contracts so providing, under the Tenth Amendment the power to create and exchange "private Money" must be "reserved . . . to the people." Beyond that, inasmuch as alternative gold and silver currencies could—and initially should—consist of bullion, not coin, no State would find itself dependent upon the assistance of Congress and the U.S. Treasury for her adoption of such currencies.

Eighth, employment of alternative gold and silver currencies would not involve a State in the rat's nest of central economic planning. A State would not be required to attempt to regulate the supply of money against a so-called price level, to fix interest rates, or to engage in any of the other political-cum-economic manipulations characteristic of a central bank. Whatever amounts of gold and silver the people desired to use as their alternative currencies would become currency. The free market would then rationally establish and mutually adjust the prices in gold and silver of all goods and services, and competition in the free market between Federal Reserve Notes and the alternative currencies would control the rate at which the latter replaced the former.

Ninth, adoption of alternative gold and silver currencies would serve, not just one set of special interests, but instead all of society, by facilitating on a State-by-State basis the separation of private banking from government with respect to currency.

Tenth, if adoption of alternative currencies showed promise, with more and more people preferring those currencies to Federal Reserve Notes in more and more transactions, the banks would be forced to compete. Some of them might try to generate a new currency redeemable in or otherwise "backed" by gold, silver, or both. Exactly how they might do this one cannot predict, because such a new bankers' currency would have to be as secure as the alternative gold and silver currencies, which would require that it not be based on fractional reserves, or that it offered to its users some significant economic advantage, suitably enforceable by law, that offset the risk from fractional reserves—and that the right of the holders of the currency to its redemption in gold or silver were absolutely guaranteed, not only against default by the banks but also against any intervention by the government in favor of the banks which enabled them to default or otherwise prevented or delayed redemption. Yet even a few banks moving in that direction could facilitate the present system's orderly transformation or liquidation, rather than its sudden collapse.

Conclusion

Why, then, are the champions of sound money, limited government, and free markets not aggressively promoting the adoption of
alternative gold and silver currencies? The present economic crisis
presents the best opportunity since 1932 to free Americans from
their thralldom to the Federal Reserve System. Under the pressure
of this crisis, common people are awakening to their predicament,
and sensing what needs to be done—because, as Samuel Johnson
once reputedly quipped, nothing focuses a man's mind more than his
impending hanging. So, Americans can now be convinced that this
country's economy cannot be restored by some "Rube Goldberg" tin-
kering with the existing faulty edifice of money and banking, but only
by its total replacement. The present structure lacks the capacity to
survive—and, constitutionally speaking, can claim no right to be
saved. A new structure must be built from the ground up, on a new
site, according to a different plan. If this can be accomplished, then
for the first time in generations Americans will enjoy honest weights
and measures in the monetary field—and with that reform, will have
a realistic hope to restore honest commerce and even honest politics
as well.

References

Black's Law Dictionary (1968) Revised 4th ed. St. Paul, Minn.: West
    Publishing Co.
Vieira, E. Jr. ([2002] 2011) *Pieces of Eight: The Monetary Powers and
    Disabilities of the United States Constitution.* Gold Money Special
    Edition. Chicago: R. R. Donnelley & Sons.
_____ (2010), "A Cross of Gold." An address presented to
    the October 2010 Meeting of the Committee for Monetary
    Research and Education, New York City.
_____ (2011) *An Introductory Primer on the Constitutional
    Authority of the States to Adopt an Alternative Currency.*
    Available at www.knology.net/–bilrum/Alternative%20Currency%
    20Defense%202.pdf.
_____ (2012) *The Sword and Sovereignty: The
    Constitutional Principles of "the Militia of the Several States"
    (Constitutional Homeland Security).* Front Royal, Va. (Author's
    CD-ROM edition).

15

MAKING THE TRANSITION TO A
NEW GOLD STANDARD
Lawrence H. White

Suppose for the sake of argument that we all agree to the following proposition: If we could change the monetary regime with zero switching cost, merely by snapping our fingers, we would prefer the United States to be on a gold standard. In the most general terms, a gold standard means a monetary system in which a standard mass (so many grams or ounces) of pure gold defines the unit of account, and standardized pieces of gold serve as the ultimate media of redemption. Currency notes, checks, and electronic funds transfers are all denominated in gold and are redeemable claims to gold.[1] We then face the question: What would be the least costly way for the United States to make the transition to a new gold standard? We need to choose a low-cost method to ensure that the agreed benefits of being on the gold standard exceed the costs of switching over.

Two transitional paths suggest themselves (1) let a parallel gold standard grow up alongside the current fiat dollar, and (2) set a date after which the U.S. dollar is to be meaningfully defined as so many

Lawrence H. White is Professor of Economics at George Mason University, a Senior Fellow with the F.A Hayek Program for Advanced Study in Philosophy, Politics and Economics at GMU's Mercatus Center, and a Senior Fellow at the Cato Institute's Center for Financial and Monetary Alternatives. This article is reprinted from the *Cato Journal*, Vol. 32, No. 2 (Spring/Summer 2012). The author thanks George Selgin, Jim Dorn, and Ralph Benko for comments.

[1]For the generic definition and supply-demand analytics of a gold standard, see White (1999: chap 2).

grams of pure gold. This second, more conventional path, was followed after the suspension of the gold standard during the U.S. Civil War. It is more commonly described as establishing an effective parity stipulating so many dollars per fine troy ounce of gold. In our present situation, where Federal Reserve liabilities (book entries and currency notes) and Treasury coins constitute the basic dollar media of redemption for bonds and commercial bank liabilities, that implies converting the Federal Reserve System's liabilities and the Treasury's coins into gold-redeemable claims at so many grams of gold per dollar (or equivalently so many dollars per ounce of gold).

We see analogs to these two transitional paths when we observe how two countries have made the transition to using the U.S. dollar. In Ecuador in 1998–2000, a parallel unofficial U.S. dollar system emerged as the annual inflation rate in the local currency rose from low to high double digits, then to triple digits. The private sector of the economy was already heavily dollarized when the plug was finally pulled on the heavily depreciated local currency unit in 2000. In El Salvador in 2001, the government chose to permanently lock in the dollar value of the currency—by switching from a dollar-pegged exchange rate to outright adoption of the U.S. dollar—while inflation was low and the local currency still dominant. In a nutshell, when the official switch to the harder currency came in Ecuador, it was an act of necessity in the midst of a hyperinflation crisis. In El Salvador it was an act of foresight, to rule out such a crisis.

Allowing a Parallel Gold Standard

Clearing away the legal barriers to a parallel gold standard is fairly simple and can be done without immediately altering existing financial institutions. Rep. Ron Paul's HR1098, the Free Competition in Currency Act of 2011, represents one straightforward approach. It would (1) ensure the enforceability of contracts denominated in units other than fiat dollars by removing legal tender status from Federal Reserve notes and Treasury coins, (2) remove taxes on gold and silver coins that Federal Reserve notes do not face, and (3) remove sections of the U.S. Code that have been used to criminalize the victimless activity of privately minting distinctive pieces of metal intended to circulate as money (White 2011). If these steps seem unprecedented, note that Federal Reserve notes did not become legal tender until 1933. Bank of England notes are not legal

tender today in Scotland or Northern Ireland, where private banknotes (also not legal tender) predominate. Note also that in
Switzerland "the purchase and sale of Gold is not subject to taxes
(such as value-added tax or capital gains tax) under current Swiss
law" (Ledoit and Lotz 2011: 2).

Further legal and regulatory changes are necessary to allow
citizens who adopt the parallel gold standard to have access to gold-
denominated banking services. Banking services, including the issue
of gold-redeemable paper currency notes and token coins, are of
special importance for the success of a gold standard given the awk-
wardness of making small—or very large—transactions in physical
gold coins. Either existing bank holding companies would have to be
free to operate separate gold-denominated subsidiaries, or new gold-
based institutions would have to be free to open.

The case for a level playing field between the fiat dollar and
other monetary standards rests on the simple proposition that the
well-being of consumers is better served by competition than by
monopoly. Keeping alternatives to fiat dollar at a legal disadvantage, like silver- and gold-backed bank-issued monies, or foreign
currencies, limits the options of American consumers to their disadvantage. The option to use an alternative to the fiat dollar is naturally most valuable in an environment of high dollar inflation.
Consumers who don't like the ongoing shrinkage of the value of
the currency in their pocketbooks and wallets are then not limited
to complaining, or trying to lobby the Fed or Congress for better
policy, but can "vote with their pocketbooks" to protect their assets
by moving into less inflationary alternative currencies.

We should not expect a spontaneous mass switchover to gold, or
to Swiss francs, as long as dollar inflation remains low. The dollar
has an incumbency advantage due to the network property of a
monetary standard. The greater the number of people who are
plugged into the dollar network, ready to buy or sell using dollars,
the more useful using dollars is to you. Conversely, if you are the
first on your block to go shopping with gold coins or a gold-denominated debit card, you will find few stores ready to accept payments in gold. But like the benefit from using dollars in a peso
economy, the willingness to accept gold-denominated money in a
fiat dollar economy increases with the incumbent currency's inflation rate and its uncertainty. As Camera, Craig, and Waller (2004:
535–36) express the general theoretical proposition, "The local

currency sustains internal trade if the purchasing power risk is kept very low, but once that risk gets very high substantial currency substitution kicks in." Should the U.S. inflation rate return to double digits, consumers would find it very helpful to have an alternative currency network available. Potential competition might even help incentivize the Fed to keep inflation low.

Who is likely to produce private gold coins once they are recognized as legal? Gold medallions and biscuits in various sizes, from private producers around the world, are already widely held. Investors in coined gold normally pay a premium over the value of uncoined gold, which covers the cost of coining. In a recent working paper, Olivier Ledoit and Sébastien Lotz, two economists at the University of Zurich, raise an interesting possibility while discussing a proposal to allow private gold coinage in Switzerland. They envision that "Gold Francs would be minted by Commercial Banks, [and] the Banks would be allowed to put their brand name and/or logo on one side of the coin. The marketing benefits from having the bank logo in every citizen's wallet would clearly cover any minting costs, so these coins could be sold at par value with the market value of their weight in Gold" (Ledoit and Lotz 2011: 5). It is actually not clear that marketing benefits would cover minting costs. It is true that *if* the public prefers to use full-bodied coins, gold coins could circulate practically in larger denominations. Historically, however, the everyday circulation of gold coins became rare once people found banknotes more convenient and sufficiently trustworthy. At $1,600 per ounce of gold, full-bodied gold coins are completely impractical at perhaps $50 and below.

We can therefore expect most bank-issued coins to be tokens, essentially metallic banknotes, redeemable in gold (upon presentation of a minimum quantity) at the bank. Such tokens can carry the bank's logo, but they will pay for themselves by sparing the issuer the expense of using precious metal in coin production, and will save the system the burdens of incidental wear and tear and deliberate shrinkage that accompany full-bodied precious-metal coinage. As with paper banknotes, the float revenue rather than only the advertising value will cover the production and circulation costs. Ledoit and Lotz (2011) appear to overlook the standard historical solution to the problem of keeping small currency at par— redeemable tokens and banknotes—because they assume that payment services would be provided only by money warehouses, and do not consider that money-users might be induced by competing banks to prefer the lower-cost alternative of fractional gold-reserve bank liabilities.

Reestablishing a Gold Definition of the U.S. Dollar

The network property of a monetary standard supports the case for not simply legalizing a parallel gold standard, but reestablishing a gold definition for the U.S. dollar. Strong network effects imply that an uncoordinated piecemeal switchover to a superior standard would not occur except during a painful period of high and uncertain inflation in the incumbent standard. There is a strong practical case for avoiding that pain through a coordinated switchover before high inflation occurs. That is, we would do well to follow the Salvadoran model of transition rather than the Ecuadoran model.

In considering the reestablishment of a gold dollar now, more than 40 years after President Nixon closed the gold window, the question of the appropriate new parity (how many dollars per gold ounce) naturally arises. It is widely recognized that it would be foolish to try to relink the dollar to gold at the pre-1933 parity of $20.67 per ounce, the 1934–71 parity of $35 per ounce, or the post-1972 accounting price of $42.22 per fine troy ounce. It would be foolish because the U.S. price level has risen more than 5-fold since 1971, and the real price of gold has risen in addition, so that $42.22 per ounce or anything lower implies a massive deflation not anticipated in existing nominal contracts. Great Britain's painful deflation during Churchill's ill-considered attempt in 1925 to return to gold at the prewar parity, after the high inflation during the First World War, stands as a stern warning. The purchasing power of gold was greater in the rest of the world than in Britain at the prewar rate, gold accordingly fled Britain, and pound-sterling values faced inescapable downward pressure. Fortunately, this point is widely appreciated today, and nobody advocates returning to such a low parity.

By similar logic, it would be foolish to declare a new parity of (say) $8,000 per ounce, five times the current price. The result would be a sharp transitional inflation, and a very expensive *importation* of gold from around the world. Gold would rush in to take advantage of its higher purchasing power in the United States, until the U.S. price level rises approximately five-fold, to the point that $8,000 no longer buys more than one ounce of gold.

The gold parity that would avoid any transitional inflation or deflation is something close to the current price dollar price of gold. "Close to" because there will be some change in the real demand for monetary gold following the stabilization of the gold value of the dollar. On the one hand, with lower expected inflation, the cost of holding non-interest-bearing money will be lower, and hence the real demand to hold money in the form of M1 dollars will rise. On the other hand, with dollar inflation risk dramatically reduced, the dollar-inflation-hedging demand for gold Krugerrands and Eagles and bullion will fall dramatically. The latter effect is likely to dominate, seeing that inflation-hedging demand is the main reason why the real price of gold is higher now than it was when the United States abandoned the last vestiges of gold redeemability in 1971.

Does the U.S. Treasury own enough gold to return to a gold-redeemable dollar at the current price of gold? Yes, assuming that they have what they say they do. At a market price of $1,600 per fine Troy oz. (to choose a recently realized round number) the U.S. government's 261.5 million ounces of gold are worth $418.4 billion. Current required bank reserves are only $83 billion. Looked at another way, $418.4 billion is 19.9 percent of current M1 (the sum of currency and checking account balances), a more than healthy reserve ratio by historical standards.[2] Combined with the likelihood that U.S. citizens' inflation-hedging demand for gold will shrink by more than banks' reserve demand will grow with larger real demand for M1 balances, I expect that the denationalization and remonetization of the U.S. bullion stock at the current price would allow the U.S. economy to *export* some excess gold. There will be a small transitional windfall for U.S. citizens, getting imported goods and services in exchange for excess gold.

Expeditiously establishing a new gold definition for the U.S. dollar thus requires the following two steps:

1. Withdraw most of the $1.6 trillion in nonrequired reserves that banks have accumulated since September 2009 by eliminating interest on reserves and selling the mortgage-backed securities that the Fed acquired in QE1 (its first "quantitative easing" program), plus enough Treasuries to bring total bank

---

[2]In counting all the gold as bank reserves I am assuming that coins in circulation would become redeemable tokens, not become full-bodied gold coins. The current numbers update White (2004).

reserves down to the current value of the U.S. government gold stock.
2. Redeem Federal Reserve liabilities with the U.S. government's gold at the then-current market price.

Why Not Establish 100 Percent Reserves for M1?

The approximate figure we get if we divide October 2011's M1 (about $2.1 trillion) by the stock of gold held by the U.S. government (261.5 million ounces) is $8,000 per ounce of gold.[3] Some economists who favor 100 percent gold reserves for currency and checking accounts have offered this approach as the way to set a new parity. As already noted, however, such a high parity implies a large influx of gold from the rest of the world, a large loss of other U.S. wealth in exchange, and a sharp transitional U.S. inflation. The United States cannot establish 100 percent gold backing for M1 without great expense. To be specific, at $1,600 per ounce of gold, the difference between M1 (about $2.1 trillion) and the current value of the U. S. government's stock of gold (about $400 billion) is nearly $1.7 trillion. To ensure 100 percent backing of M1, American taxpayers would have to buy $1.7 trillion worth of gold—a very expensive proposition. And that is only the one-time cost. In an economy with 3 percent per annum real GDP growth, assuming a flat trend in the ratio of gold to GDP, a constant purchasing power of gold implies the importation each year of 3 percent of the gold stock. For a gold stock of $2.1 trillion (100 percent of M1), that would mean an annual expense of $63 billion. With a 20 percent fractional reserve against M1, the annual expense would be only one-fifth of that figure.

It should also be noted that with 100 percent reserves, the historically familiar sort of currency—circulating redeemable private banknotes and token coins—is infeasible. A money warehouse would be unable to assess storage fees on anonymous currency holders. Debit cards would still be feasible, but the warehouses issuing them would have to charge storage fees (White 2003).

[3]The Fed's gold certificate entry as reported on its balance sheet (H.4.1, October 6, 2011) is $11,041 million, the product of the bookkeeping price of $42.22 times 261.511 million fine troy ounces of gold. See also Federal Reserve Bank of New York (2008: 17), which notes: "A majority of these reserves are held in depositories of the Treasury Department at Fort Knox, Kentucky, and West Point, New York. Most of the remainder is at the Denver and Philadelphia Mints and the San Francisco Assay Office." I ignore the U.S. share of gold held by the International Monetary Fund.

What About the Central Bank?

Because the nation's stock of money becomes endogenous under a gold standard, no monetary policy is needed. Retaining a central bank committee to "manage" the gold standard undermines its automatic operation, creates uncertainty by opening the door to policies that lead to devaluation or suspension, and thus does more harm than good. A central bank inevitably faces political pressures to pursue monetary policies inconsistent with redemption for gold at a fixed rate. It can endanger or suspend redemption with legal impunity, and it faces no competitive pressure to maintain its reputation. When the central bank runs a policy inconsistent with maintaining the gold standard, typically the gold standard gives. Competing private banks, which do face legal and competitive constraints, have a better historical track record than central banks for maintaining gold redemption (Selgin and White 2005). The classical gold standard of 1879–1914 functioned quite well without a central bank in countries like Canada that did not weaken their commercial banks with legal restrictions. Even in the United States, despite several financial panics that (to judge from the Canadian example) could have been avoided by banking deregulation, the business cycle was not worse than it has been under the Fed's watch since 1914 (Selgin, Lastrapes, and White 2010).

Nor does the gold standard require a central bank for other purposes. Many of the banks that issue checking accounts may also be relied upon to issue gold redeemable circulating currency notes, as they did before the Federal Reserve monopolized banknote issue, and token coins. The Fed's other useful functions can be returned to private clearinghouse associations, namely the clearing and settlement of payments, the setting and enforcement of standards for solvency and liquidity, and the last-resort lending of temporary liquidity support to solvent member banks (see Timberlake 1993: chap. 14). Because their members' own money is at stake and they cannot simply print fiat money, clearinghouse associations do not and cannot bail out insolvent banks at taxpayer expense, whether through direct capital injections, asset purchases at above-market prices, or loans at below-market rates.

The journalist Martin Wolf (2010) has written:

> The obvious form of a contemporary gold standard would be
> a direct link between base money and gold. Base money—the
> note issue, plus reserves of commercial banks at the central

bank (if any such institution survives)—would be 100 percent gold-backed. The central bank would then become a currency board in gold, with the unit of account (the dollar, say) defined in terms of a given weight of gold.

Actually, although irredeemable central bank notes are base money today, under a gold standard only coined gold and bullion reserves are base money. Notes in circulation are redeemable liabilities of the issuers and not part of actual or potential bank reserves. And although a currency board is less likely than a central bank to undermine the gold standard, there is no need for either. The most efficient form of a contemporary gold standard makes gold the base money—that is, the medium of redemption and unit of account—while currency and other common media of exchange are the fractionally backed gold-redeemable liabilities of commercial banks.

Wolf (2010) rightly recognizes that "it is wasteful to hold a 100 percent reserve in a bank, if depositors do not need their money almost all of the time." However, he does not draw the obvious conclusion that a currency board in gold is therefore less efficient than fractional-reserve banking under a gold standard.[4] Wolf expresses the common worry that the later system is inherently unstable: "In good times, credit, deposit money and the ratio of deposit money to the monetary base expands. In bad times, this pyramid collapses. The result is financial crises, as happened repeatedly in the 19th century." Yet, the banking system is more robust than he suspects, as seen in Scotland, Canada, Sweden, and other less-regulated systems without central banks under the gold standard. Repeated financial crises were a feature of the 19th century banking systems in the United States and England, weakened as they were by legal restrictions, but not of the less restricted systems elsewhere (see Dowd 1992, Selgin 1996).

Eichengreen's Recent Critique of Reinstating the Gold Standard

In a recent critique of proposals for reinstating a gold standard, the economic historian Barry Eichengreen (2011) has repeated the often-made but nonetheless absurd claim that a gold numeraire is

[4]Wolf incidentally remarks that "economists of the Austrian school wish to abolish fractional reserve banking," but this is true only of a fraction of Austrian-school economists.

equivalent to a commodity price support, writing: "Surely a believer in the free market would argue that if there is an increase in the demand for gold, whatever the reason, then the price should be allowed to rise, giving the gold-mining industry an incentive to produce more, eventually bringing that price back down. Thus, the notion that the U.S. government should peg the price, as in gold standards past, is curious at the least." Surely Eichengreen understands that if there is an increase in the demand for gold under a gold standard, whatever the reason, then the relative price of gold (the purchasing power per unit of gold over other goods and services) will in fact rise, which will in fact give the gold-mining industry an incentive to produce more, which will in fact eventually bring the relative price back down. That one dollar, defined as so many grams of gold, continues be worth a specified amount of gold—or in other words that one unit of gold continues to be worth one unit of gold—does not involve the pegging of any relative price.

"More curious still," Eichengreen continues, "is the belief that putting the United States on a gold standard would somehow guarantee balanced budgets, low taxes, small government and a healthy economy." Of course "guarantee" is too strong a term, and a budget balanced each and every fiscal year is not the right goal. But a gold standard does help to ensure budget balance in the desirable present-value or long-run sense, by requiring a government that wants to sell its bonds in the international market to stay on a fiscal path consistent with full repayment in gold (see Sargent 2010).

"Most curious of all" to Eichengreen "is the contention that under twenty-first-century circumstances going back to the gold standard is even possible." This time is somehow different, apparently. But going back to the gold standard by reestablishing a dollar-gold parity requires today only what it has always required (1) a sufficient real gold stock, which the U.S. government already has on hand, and (2) the political will to do so. Developing a parallel gold standard, using present-day technologies for money transfer, would probably be easier today than it has ever been.

References

Camera, G.; Craig, B.; and Waller, C. J. (2004) "Currency Competition in a Fundamental Model of Money." *Journal of International Economics* 64 (2): 535–36.

Dowd, K. (ed.) (1992) *The Experience of Free Banking*. London: Routledge.

Eichengreen, B. (2011) "A Critique of Pure Gold." *The National Interest* (September-October). Available at http://national interest.org/article/critique-pure-gold-5741.

Federal Reserve Bank of New York (2008) "The Key to the Gold Vault." Available at www.newyorkfed.org/education/addpub/goldvault.pdf.

Ledoit, O., and Lotz, S. (2011) "The Coexistence of Commodity Money and Fiat Money." University of Zurich Department of Economics Working Paper No. 24 (August).

Sargent, T. (2010) "An Interview with Thomas Sargent," by A. J. Rolnick. Federal Reserve Bank of Minneapolis *The Region* (September). Available at www.minneapolisfed.org/publications_papers/pub_display.cfm?id54526.

Selgin, G. (1996) "Bank-lending 'Manias' in Theory and History." In G. Selgin, *Bank Deregulation and Monetary Order*. London: Routledge.

Selgin, G. A.; Lastrapes, W. D.; and White, L. H. (2010) "Has the Fed Been a Failure?" Cato Institute Working Paper No. 2 (November). Forthcoming in *Journal of Macroeconomics*.

Selgin, G., and White, L. H. (2005) "Credible Currency: A Constitutional Perspective." *Constitutional Political Economy* 16 (1): 71–83.

Timberlake, R. H. (1993) *Monetary Policy in the United States*. Chicago: University of Chicago Press.

White, L. H. (1999) *The Theory of Monetary Institutions*. Oxford: Basil Blackwell.

_____ (2003) "Accounting for Fractional-Reserve Banknotes and Deposits." *Independent Review* 7 (3): 423– 41.

_____ (2004) "Will the Gold in Fort Knox Be Enough?" American Institute for Economic Research *Economic Education Bulletin* 44 (9): 23–32.

_____ (2011) "Statement on HR 1098, The Free Competition in Currency Act of 2011." Available at http://financialservices.house.gov/UploadedFiles/091311white.pdf.

Wolf, M. (2010) "Could the World Go Back to the Gold Standard?" Available at http://blogs.ft.com/martin-wolf-exchange/2010/11/01/could-the-world-go-back-to-the-gold-standard/#axzz1aPjGlRV6.

16

CURRENCY COMPETITION VERSUS GOVERNMENTAL MONEY MONOPOLIES
Roland Vaubel

Currency competition for the established national central banks can come from foreign central banks or from private money suppliers (at home or abroad). At present, currency competition from both sources is severely restricted in many countries.

Barriers to Currency Competition

Currency competition from *foreign central banks* can be restricted in several ways:

- The currency issued by the national central bank can be prescribed as a private unit of account;[1]
- Contracts in foreign currencies can be prohibited by law or discouraged through discriminatory contract enforcement in the courts;[2]

Roland Vaubel is Professor Emeritus of Economics at the University of Mannheim. This article is reprinted from the *Cato Journal,* Vol 5, No. 3 (Winter 1986). It is a synthesis of Vaubel (1976, 1977, 1978a, 1978b, 1980, 1982a, 1982b, 1983, and 1984).

[1]For instance, the national currency is prescribed for the denomination of company capital in W. Germany, France, United Kingdom and for all obligations which enter the land register (W. Germany, France) or which have to be notarized (Belgium, France).

[2]In the United Kingdom, for example, the courts do not award foreign currency claims if the contract has been concluded between residents or in a "third" country.

- Governments can restrict or discourage the holding of foreign currencies by residents (or the holding of the domestic currency by foreigners) and thereby interfere with the choice of means of payments;
- Governments can refuse to accept any other currency than the one issued by their central bank.

Currency competition from *private money suppliers* is not admitted in any industrial country, but there have been many instances of such competition in monetary history (see Vaubel 1978a: 387–400). To the extent that money may be issued by private enterprises at all, it must usually be denominated in the currency issued by the central bank. Moreover, with minor exceptions, private enterprises are not permitted to issue currency (notes and coins). Their supply of deposits is subject to reserve requirements and many other regulations.

The existence of these barriers to entry raises three questions: (1) What welfare-theoretic grounds are there to justify restrictions of currency competition from foreign central banks? (2) If there is a case for free currency competition from foreign central banks, why doesn't this case extend to private banks as well? (3) If private banks should be free to supply currencies of their own, why should the government (its central bank) supply money, or a monetary unit of account, at all? These questions are the topics of the following three sections.

The Case for Free Currency Competition among Central Banks

The standard argument against barriers to entry is that they narrow the consumers' freedom of choice and that they raise the price, and reduce the supply and the quality, of the product in question. Prima facie, an increase in "price" and decrease of supply may seem to be desirable in the case of money. Do not a smaller supply and a higher "price" of money imply less inflation? No, because the argument confuses the price of acquiring money (the inverse of the price level) with the price (opportunity cost) of holding money[3] and overlooks the fact that the holding demand for money is a demand

---

[3]Harry Johnson (1969) has pointed out the same confusion in the work of Pesek and Saving (1967).

for real balances. Since money is an asset to be held, demand for it depends on the price of holding it. The yield forgone by holding a money that bears no interest, or is subject to non-interest bearing reserve requirements, is larger the higher the expected inflation rate. An inflation-prone central bank loses real money demand to less inflation-prone foreign central banks.[4] In this way, it loses both revenue and its power to affect the national economy through monetary policy. Thus, the removal of barriers to entry encourages less inflationary monetary policies. In real terms, the standard case against barriers to entry applies to the product money as well: the removal of barriers raises the *real* quantity of money and reduces the relative price of *holding* it.

If the standard case for competition applies, it implies not only removal of barriers to entry but also prevention of collusion among the public producers of money. Collusion is the international coordination of monetary policies.[5] In the extreme case, it takes the form of fixed exchange rates, an international holding-price cartel among money producers.[6]

Competition among central banks reduces inflation in at least three ways:

1. *"Exit"*[7] The world demand for money shifts from the currencies that are expected to depreciate and to be risky to currencies that are expected to appreciate and to be more stable.
2. *"Voice"* Even if exit does not help, public opinion in the more inflation-ridden countries is impressed by the example of the less inflation-ridden countries. It makes the government (the central bank) responsible for its inferior performance. In politics, too, competition works as a mechanism of discovery and imitation.

---

[4]In the absence of a forced or legal disequilibrium exchange rate, the less inflationary money prevails ultimately not only as a store of value but also as a means of payment. "Gresham's Law" operates only under very specific conditions created by government interventions. (Vaubel 1978a: 82–89).

[5]For a critical analysis of the welfare-theoretic arguments in favor of monetary-policy coordination see Vaubel (1983). Vaubel (1978b) shows that, in 1969–77, the average rate of European monetary expansion has always been negatively correlated with dispersion of national rates in the seven main countries.

[6]For a more detailed exposition, see Vaubel (1978a: 33f.). De Grauwe (1985) shows that, in 1979–84, the (full) members of the European Monetary System reduced their inflation less than the other major OECD countries on a weighted average.

[7]This is the terminology of Hirschman (1970).

3. *Acceleration Effect*—Even in the absence of exit and voice, an
inflationary monetary impulse in one country affects the price
level faster than a simultaneous monetary expansion of equal size
that is common to all, or several, countries. This is because the
uncoordinated national monetary impulse affects the exchange
rate, and to that extent the price level, almost immediately. By
rendering the causal connection between the money supply and
price level more transparent, international currency competition
reduces the likelihood of inflationary monetary policies.

In spite of these beneficial effects, free entry and, more generally,
international currency competition are not usually advocated by
national central banks, not even by the competitive ones. The
Bundesbank, for example, launched a campaign in 1979 to convince
the German public and foreign monetary authorities that everything
had to be done to prevent the mark from taking over a larger part of
the dollar's position as an international currency, especially as an official reserve currency (Deutsche Bundesbank 1979: 33).[8]

Typically, central bankers object to international currency competition on the grounds that it renders national monetary management
more difficult and risky, and it destabilizes exchange rates and the
whole international monetary system.

It is true that a spatial money monopolist enjoys a quieter life than
a competitive producer who must take into account not only the
changes in total money demand but also changes in its composition.
If the demand for money shifts among currencies, a simple x percent
rule for monetary expansion is not likely to be adequate. The forward
premium and a world portfolio growth variable will have to be
included in the money demand function[9] (or the monetary target has
to be formulated for the "world" money supply or some proxy
thereof).[10] Each central bank has to allow for the money supply decisions of other central banks.

Is international currency competition undesirable from an international point of view? It disciplines those who try to supply their

---

[8]For a detailed critique see Vaubel (1982a). In a more recent article, the
Bundesbank (1983) calls foreign holdings of DM assets "neither too large nor too
small."
[9]For a theoretical and econometric implementation, see Vaubel (1980).
[10]See the proposal by McKinnon (1983).

product at too high a price. For instance, if international shifts in the demand for money have been responsible for the dollar's and sterling's weakness in the 1970s and for the weakness of the French franc in the early 1980s, they have played a crucial role in bringing about a correction. International shifts in the demand for money are not the cause of monetary instability but its consequence and symptom. They are part of the corrective feedback mechanism. They impose a constraint which, in open economies, is more likely to be admitted than a constitutional money supply rule.

Why do even central banks that would be competitive object to international currency competition? It is tempting to adopt a public-economics approach: the benefits of currency competition accrue to private money holders and users (lower inflation tax and inflation risk) and to domestic taxpayers (larger external seigniorage), but the cost, the greater difficulty of determining the optimal rate of monetary expansion, has to be borne by the central bankers. After all, bureaucrats tend to be held responsible for the errors they commit rather than for the opportunities they miss.

In the theoretical literature (notably Kareken and Wallace 1981), we find the objection that competition among central banks (outside monies) renders the equilibrium exchange rate(s) indeterminate because all, and only those, exchange rates which promise to be constant, are compatible with a rational expectations equilibrium. This objection is misleading because it assumes that monies are only stores of value and that they can be perfect substitutes. First of all, different groups of people who consume different baskets of commodities prefer different standards of value: since money serves as a standard of value, they would prefer different monies—i.e., monies that are stable in terms of different commodity baskets. Moreover, if for this reason (or owing to past government intervention) different monies coexist, currency transaction costs will reinforce the tendency toward the formation of (overlapping) payments circuits or currency domains. Thus, if money is also viewed as a standard of value and means of payment, two competing monies will hardly ever be perfect substitutes. The Kareken-Wallace view is not relevant to this world.[11]

---

[11] Harberler (1980: 44) writes about the Kareken-Wallace view (in paraphrasing Keynes): "It is extraordinary example of how remorseless logicians can end up in Bedlam, if they get hold of the wrong assumptions."

Currency Competition from Private Suppliers: The Case for Free Entry

If free currency competition between the central banks of different countries has the salutary effect of reducing rates of inflation below the monopolistic rates, it is difficult to see why the case for a competitive supply of money should not also extend to competition from private banks of issue. From a present-day perspective, the suggestion of an unrestricted competitive supply of (distinguishable)[12] private high-powered money must be regarded as truly counter-revolutionary, and even Hayek needed more than half a year to proceed, in 1976, from the demand for "free choice in currency" to the case for the "denationalization of money."

Several justifications have been given for the prohibition of currency competition from private suppliers:

1. Profit-maximizing private issuers would increase the supply of their money until its price equals the marginal cost of producing it, namely zero; the result would be hyperinflation.[13]
2. Private competitive supply of money renders the price level indeterminate.[14]
3. The private banking system is inherently unstable.
4. Monopolistic production of money by the state is an efficient way of raising government revenue.
5. The supply of money is a natural monopoly because of economies of scale in production or use.
6. Money exerts positive external effects; money, or the currency unit, may even be a public good.

The first argument repeats the confusion noted above: it mistakes the price of acquiring money for the price (opportunity cost) of holding money. What private profit maximization reduces to almost zero is not the value of money but the opportunity cost of holding it.

Some authors have objected that private suppliers of money may choose to maximize their short-run profits rather than their long-run

[12]See Klein (1974).

[13]See Lutz (1936: 4f); Friedman (1959a: 7; 1969: 39); Pesek and Saving (1967: 129); Johnson (1968: 976); Meltzer (1969: 35); and Gehrig (1978: 454). This view has been criticized by Klein (1974: 428–31); Vaubel (1977: 449–52); and Girton and Roper (1981: 21–24).

[14]Gurley and Shaw (1960: 255ff.); Patinkin (1961: 116); and McKinnon (1969: 316).

profits, thus opting for hyperinflation at the time of their greatest success, when the present value of their confidence capital is at its maximum. Klein (1974: 449) and Tullock (1975: 496f.) have replied that private enterprises tend to have a longer planning horizon than democratically elected governments and their central banks. However, this answer implies that central banks act as profit maximizers as well—in some cases a debatable assumption. The answer is rather that, if there is a danger of "profit snatching," money holders will prefer currencies that offer value guarantees. This point will be further developed in the concluding section. It implies that private money is likely to be inside money. The first objection can only apply to outside money.

The second argument is correct in pointing out that the price level is indeterminate—indeed, under any system of money production, for the initial supply of nominal balances is an arbitrarily chosen number. To serve as an objection to private currency competition, the argument would have to show that the rate of change of the price level is indeterminate as well under such a system.

The third argument may justify money production by governments, but it does not justify barriers to entry. Whether claims on the private banking system are excessively risky is a question which each money holder can be left to decide on his own depending on his individual degree of risk aversion.

Fourth, even if a system of optimal taxation requires a tax on money balances in addition to the wealth tax, what reason is there to assume that the collection of government seigniorage is more efficient than the taxation of private money creation or of private money holdings?

Fifth, if money is a natural monopoly good, the central bank does not need a legal monopoly (although it may have to be subsidized).[15]

---

[15]Subsidies may be justified even if marginal cost pricing is not the aim (because the additional taxation required would create excessive distortions elsewhere in the economy). They may justified if the natural monopolist has passed the point of minimum average cost; for in this exceptional case, which Sharkey (1982: ch. 5) has emphasized, an efficient natural monopolist may be unable to produce the optimal quantity of output and to sustain himself against less efficient competitors if the government does not pay him a subsidy (which it should offer to all producers who supply at least as much output). Under Sharkey's assumptions, the subsidy must be sufficient to keep the net-of-subsidy average cost of the most efficient supplier of optimal output at the minimum average cost attainable for any smaller quantity of output.

Since we do not even know whether money is a natural monopoly good and what its optimal characteristics are (for instance, whether it should be of stable or increasing purchasing power), barriers to competition from private issuers prevent us from finding out; the mechanism of discovery is blocked. A governmental producer of money is not an efficient natural monopolist unless he can prevail in conditions of free entry and without discrimination.[16] Historically, the major central banks have not acquired their national monopoly position in this way.[17]

Finally, if money exerts positive external effects or is even a public good, there may be a case for subsidization, or even for governmental production, of money, but not for barriers to entry. The private supply of money would be too small, not too large.

Should Governments Supply Money?

The previous section has shown that governmental production of money may be justified, if (i) the private banking system is inherently unstable, and/or if money is (ii) a natural monopoly good or (iii) a public good. Whether arguments (i) and (ii) apply is an empirical question which cannot be answered as long as free currency competition from private issuers is not permitted.[18] Monetary history does not provide a clear answer (Vaubel 1978a: 387–401). Whether money is a public good, as has often been claimed, is largely a matter of definition and needs to be clarified.[19] There is no generally accepted definition of a public good. However, most authors seem to consider nonrivalness a necessary and sufficient condition.[20] Others regard

---

[16]Nondiscrimination also implies that the government is willing to accept or pay currency preferred by its private counterpart. Otherwise, a superior private money may not prevail in the market, merely because the government uses only its own money.

[17]The Bank of England, for example, was granted its monopoly not because it was gaining ground in the market but because it was losing out to other joint-stock issuing banks which had emerged after the Bank's joint-stock monopoly had been abolished in 1826 (for details see Vaubel 1978a: 389).

[18]See Vaubel (1984) for an econometric test of the natural monopoly hypothesis and a list of previous studies on this issue. The issues are not conclusive.

[19]The remainder this section is adapted from Vaubel (1984).

[20]The seminal modern contribution is Samuelson (1954).

nonexcludability as an alternative sufficient condition.[21] A few treat the term public good as synonymous with positive consumption externality.[22]

In this article, we shall retain the benefit of being able to distinguish between the general concept of consumption externality and the polar case of a (pure) public good which, in terms of production units, is equally available to all members of the group in a quantity or quality that is independent of the size of the group (nonrivalness).[23] We shall call a free good a good for which exclusion is not profitable (nonexcludability). The question of whether there are also more limited Pareto-relevant consumption externalities will not be pursued here because they would merely justify subsidies to money holders and users.[24]

One group of authors ascribe a public good nature to money because "any one agent, holding cash balances of a given average size, is less likely to incur the costs of temporarily running out of cash, the larger are the average balances of those with whom he trades" (Laidler 1977: 321f.).[25] However, money balances do not satisfy the nonrivalness criterion (nor the nonexcludability criterion): as long as one person holds a unit of money and benefits from its "liquidity services," nobody else can own it and benefit from it. If he gives it away, he increases his own risk of temporarily running out of cash. Therefore, he will ask for a quid pro quo—a good, service, or some other asset.

For the same reason, it is not true that "the provision of a convertible currency is an international 'public good'" because "a convertible currency can be held and used by foreigners" (McKinnon 1979: 3) or that "the dollar is an 'international public good'" because "the United States provides the world's reserve currency" (Schmidt 1979: 143).

---

[21]See notably Musgrave (1959: 9).

[22]Samuelson (1969).

[23]This is essentially Buchanan's definition (1968: 54).

[24]See Vaubel (1984: 32–45) for a discussion of confidence externalities, price level externalities, and transaction cost externalities. The analysis shows that there may, but need not, be Pareto-relevant externalities in the demand and supply of money.

[25]A similar view seems to be taken by Kolm (1972, 1977) and Mundell (Classen and Salin 1972: 97).

Otherwise, any exportable good or asset which happens to be supplied by a government would be an international public good.

Kindleberger refers to "the public good provided by money as a unit of account" (1972: 434) and "standard of measurement" (1983: 383) and applies the term public good to "money"(1978a: 9–10), "international money" (1976: 61; 1978b: 286), "an international unit of account," and "international monetary stability" (1972: 435). International monetary stability in the sense of stability of purchasing power or exchange rate stability is not a good but a quality characteristic of the product money. Quality characteristics, it is true, meet the nonrivalness test: enjoyment by one does not detract from enjoyment by others (nor can they be excluded from them) provided they have bought the good itself. However, this applies to the quality characteristics of all goods. If the publicness of its characteristics made a good a public good, all goods that are sold to more than one person would be public goods.

It might be argued that the benefits of a unit of account (and a price index) can be enjoyed by a person independently of whether he holds and uses the money which it denominates (Yeager 1983: 321). More specifically, a person or organization, by adopting a certain unit of account (and by publishing a price index for it), may convey information, a public good, to all others. This would imply that government should suggest a unit of account and publish a price index for it, but not that it should supply money, let alone the only (base) money[26] or monetary unit.

Brunner and Meltzer (1964, 1971) have emphasized that money itself is a substitute for information because it also reduces transaction costs, and because transaction costs can largely be reduced to the costs of information about possible transaction chains, asset properties and exchange ratios between assets. Since money is a substitute for information and since information is a public good, Hamada (1979: 7) and Fratianni (1982: 437) conclude, there is a "public good nature of money." However, to show that X is a substitute for a public good is not sufficient to prove that X is a public good. A fence, a dog, and an alarm system are all to some extent substitutes for police protection but they are not public goods. What has to be shown is not

---

[26]This conclusion is in fact reached by Engels (1981: 10f.); Hall (1981: 21); and Yeager (1983: 324f.).

that money is a substitute for information but that it provides the public good of information.

Several authors have argued that "public consensus" or "social agreement" on a common money is a way of creating generally useful knowledge and is thus a public good.[27] The knowledge in question is the predictability of individual behavior. What becomes predictable is not only the money which each individual accepts but also that each individual in the country accepts the same money.

Public decisions by definition meet the nonrivalness test. However, not all public decisions are public goods—they can be public bads (Tullock 1971). Since the aim of securing predictability of individual trading behavior, if taken to the extreme, may serve to justify the most far-reaching central planning by an omnipotent government (Hirshleifer 1973: 132), the mere fact that a certain act of government generates knowledge is not a sufficient justification. It has to be shown that the knowledge in question is worth its cost and that it is provided more efficiently by the government than by a competitive private sector. Both contentions are controversial.

The only operational proof that a common money is more efficient than currency competition and that the government is the most efficient provider of the common money would be to permit free currency competition. Whether the imposition of a common money or monetary unit is a public good or a public bad depends on whether money is a natural monopoly good or not. Hence, there is no independent public-good justification for the government's money monopoly. The public good argument is redundant.[28]

Forecasting Monetary Arrangements under Free Currency Competition

If currency competition is to serve as a mechanism of discovery, government must not prescribe the characteristics of the privately

[27]Hamada (1977: 16); Frenkel (1975: 217); Tullock (1976: 524); Tobin (1980: 86–87); and, with respect to unit of account, Hall (1983: 34); and Stockman (1983: 52).

[28]Currency competition might even be desirable if the process were known to converge to the government's money; for the government may not know in advance what type of money to converge to: "The monopoly of government of issuing money . . . has . . . deprived us of the only process by which we can find out what would be good money" (Hayek 1978b: 5).

issued currencies nor the organization of the private issuing institutions. Contrary to some proposals,[29] for example, it must not prescribe the monetary unit of account nor the types of assets that may be held by the issuing institutions.

Refusal to prescribe specific arrangements does not prevent us from trying to forecast monetary arrangements under free currency competition; even Hayek (1978a: 70ff., 122ff.) has done so. Hayek believes that private money would be stable in terms of "the prices of widely traded products such as raw materials, agricultural food stuffs and certain standardized semi-finished industrial products" (p. 71) and that "competition might lead to the extensive use of the same commodity base by a large number of issue banks" (p. 123). Vaubel (1977) has suggested that "value guarantees . . . are likely to be a necessary condition for acceptance of a competing money" and that "in the presence of unpredictable fluctuations in the determinants of the demand for money, value guarantees can only be maintained with precision and instantaneously, if they can be validated through exchange rate adjustment vis-a-vis another currency for which a price index is calculated" (p. 451). He believes that this reference currency, which cannot also be indexed (owing to the n-th currency problem), would be the outside money supplied by the government.

Another group of authors argues that the optimal money would appreciate relative to goods. Not all of them claim that the money which they regard as most efficient would also be most attractive to money users and prevail in the market, but this possibility should be considered. One variant is the so-called theory of the optimum quantity of money expounded by Friedman (1969), Johnson (1968), Samuelson (1963,1969), and others; as Mussa (1977) has emphasized and criticized, it views money only as a store of value and ignores its standard of value function. According to another variant, which is due to Alchian and Klein (1973), the optimal monetary unit is stable in terms of a price index of all assets because the money cost of a

[29]Engels (1981; 9f.) suggests that the government "has the task of defining the monetary unit . . . in terms of the market valuation of real assets . . . and of securing the solvency of issuing banks. Hall (1983) believes that private money must be denominated in an interest bearing reserve certificate which is issued by the government and indexed to the price level. See Vaubel (1982b) for a critical review of Engels.

given level of lifetime consumption utility ought to be held constant. Engels (1981) has recommended a real asset or pure equity standard because it would stabilize Tobin's q and thereby the business cycle. Engels suggests that such a unit would minimize the monetary risk for borrowers who invest in capital goods. However, the same is not likely to be true for all other debtors nor for all creditors. Bilson (1981) wants to transform money into an equity claim on a portfolio of real and nominal assets in order to render movements in the unanticipated rate of inflation countercyclical. A system of competing private mutual-fund monies is also envisioned by Fama (1982) and Greenfield and Yeager (1983). White (1984) predicts that they would not displace the government's outside money as a general medium of exchange.

Whether privately issued money would appreciate relative to, or be stable in terms of, some composite of goods, cannot be predicted with certainty. However, experience with hyperinflation shows that the value of alternative monies, some of them private monies, tends to be linked to the price of one or more commodities. At times, for example in Germany in 1922–23, several commodity standards were used side by side. Chen (1975) reports a case in which this occurred over two centuries. Whether convergence toward a common standard of value and money is efficient and occurs depends on how similar the purchase and sale plans of different market agents are and how variable they expect the relative prices among commodities to be (see Vaubel 1978a, 1982b).

What assets are private issuing institutions likely to hold if they are not restricted by government? They would minimize their balance sheet risk by having their assets and their money denominated in the same unit of account. The intermediation risk is zero in the case of equity or mutual-fund money. It is also zero in the case of commodity reserve money, however at the price of a zero real rate of return. The issuer of a money whose value is linked to a commodity price index can earn a positive real rate of return without incurring a monetary intermediation risk, if his assets are indexed as well; but he (and his creditors) cannot avoid a real intermediation risk. Thus, under free currency competition—even more than now—the composition of banks' assets will depend on the risk-yield preference trade-off of money users. Their degree of risk aversion is likely to differ, and it may vary over time. It cannot be reliably predicted—not even by governments.

References

Alchian, A. A., and Klein, B. (1973) "On a Correct Measure of Inflation." *Journey of Money, Credit, and Banking* 5(1): 173–91.

Bilson, J. F. O. (1981) "A Proposal for Monetary Reform." Manuscript, University of Chicago (September).

Brunner, K., and Meltzer, A. H. (1964) "Some Further Investigations of Demand and Supply Functions for Money." *Journal of Finance* 19 (2): 240–83.

_____ (1971) "The Uses of Money: Money in the Theory of an Exchange Economy." *American Economic Review* 61 (5): 784–805.

Buchanan, J. M. (1968) *The Demand and Supply of Public Goods.* Chicago: Rand McNally.

Chen, C. N. (1975) "Flexible Bimetallic Exchange Rates in China, 1650–1850: A Historical Example of Optimum Currency Areas." *Journal of Money, Credit, and Banking* 7 (2): 359–76.

Claassen, E. M., and Salin, P., eds. (1972) *Stabilization Policies in Interdependent Economies.* Amsterdam: North-Holland.

Deutsche Bundesbank (1979) "The Deutsche Mark as an International Investment Currency." *Monthly Report* (November).

_____ (1983) "The Deutsche Mark as an International Investment Currency." *Monthly Report* (January).

Engels, W. (1981) *The Optimal Monetary Unit.* Frankfurt Main: Campus.

Fama, E. F. (1982) "Fiduciary Currency and Commodity Standards." Manuscript, University of Chicago (January).

Fratianni, M. (1982) "The Dollar and the ECU." In S. Dreyer, G. Haberler, and T, D. Willett (eds.), *The International Monetary System: A Time of Turbulence*, 430–53. Washington: American Enterprise Institute.

Frenkel, J. A. (1975) "Reflections on European Monetary Integration." *Weltwirtschaftliches Archiv* 111 (2): 216–21.

Friedman, M. (1959a) *A Program for Monetary Stability.* New York: Fordham University Press.

_____ (1959b) "The Demand for Money: Some Theoretical and Empirical Results." *Journal of Political Economy* 67 (4): 327–51.

_____ (1969) *The Optimum Quantity of Money and Other Essays.* Chicago: Aldine.

_____ (1981) "Monetary System for a Free Society." Manuscript, Hoover Institution, Stanford, Calif. (November).

Gehrig, B. (1978) "Brauchen wir monopolistische Zentralbanken?" *Wirtschaft und Recht* 30 (4): 452–64.

Girton, L., and Roper, D. (1981) "Theory and Implications of Currency Substitution." *Journal of Money, Credit, and Banking* 13 (1): 12–30.

Grauwe, P. de (1985) "Should the U.K. Join the European Monetary System?" Treasury and Civil Service Committee, Subcommittee *Report on the European Monetary System*, London.

Greenfield, R. L., and Yeager, L. B. (1983) "A Laissez Faire Approach to Monetary Stability." *Journal of Money, Credit, and Banking* 15 (3): 302–15.

Gurley, J. G., and Shaw, E. S. (1960) *Money in a Theory of Finance.* Washington: Brookings Institution.

Haberler, G. (1980) "Flexible Exchange-Rate Theories and Controversies Once Again." In J. S. Chipman and C. P. Kindleberger (eds.), *Flexible Exchange Rates and the Balance of Payments: Essays in Memory of Egon Sohmen,* 29–48. Amsterdam: North-Holland.

Hall, R. E. (1981) "The Role of Government in Stabilizing Prices and Regulating Money." Manuscript, Stanford University (January).

_____ (1983) "Optimal Fiduciary Monetary Systems." *Journal of Monetary Economics* 12 (3): 33–50.

Hamada, K. (1977) "On the Political Economy of Monetary Integration: A Public Economics Approach." In R. Z. Aliber ed.), *The Political Economy of Monetary Reform,* 13–31. London: Macmillan.

_____ (1979) "On the Coordination of Monetary Policies in a Monetary Union." Paper presented at the conference on "New Economic Approaches to the Study of International Integration," Florence, Italy (May/June).

Hayek, F. A. ([1976] 1978a) *Denationalisation of Money.* Hobart Paper Special, 70. London: Institute of Economic Affairs.

_____ (1978b) "Towards a Free Market Monetary System." *Journal of Libertarian Studies* 3 (1): 1–8.

Hirschman, A. O. (1970) *Exit, Voice, and Loyalty.* Cambridge, Mass.: Harvard University Press.

Hirshleifer, J. (1973) "Exchange Theory: The Missing Chapter." *Western Economic Journal* 11(2): 129–46.

Johnson, H. G. (1969) "Problems of Efficiency in Monetary Management." *Journal of Political Economy* 76 (5): 971–90.

_____ (1969) "Pesek and Saving's Theory of Money and Wealth." *Journal of Money, Credit, and Banking* 1 (3): 535–37.

Kareken, J., and Wallace, N. (1981) "On the Indeterminacy of Equilibrium Exchange Rates." *Quarterly Journal of Economics* 96: 202–22.

Kindleberger, C. P. (1972) "The Benefits of International Money." *Journal of International Economics* 2 (3): 425–42.

_____ (1976) "Lessons from Floating Exchange Rates. In K. Brunner and A. H. Meltzer (eds.), *Institutional Arrangements and the Inflation Problem*, 51–77. Amsterdam: North-Holland.

_____ (1978a) *Manias, Panics and Crashes*. New York: Basic Books.

_____ (1978b) "Dominance and Leadership in the International Economy: Exploitation, Public Goods, and Free Rides." In *Hommage à François Perroux*, 283–91. Grenoble: Presses Universitaires de Grenoble.

_____ (1983) "Standards as Public, Collective and Private Goods." *Kyklos* 36 (3): 377–96.

Klein, B. (1974) "The Competitive Supply of Money." *Journal of Money, Credit, and Banking* 6 (4): 423–53.

Kolm, S. C. (1972) "External Liquidity: A Study in Monetary Welfare Economics." In G. P. Szego and K. Shell (eds.), *Mathematical Methods in Investment and Finance*, 190–206. Amsterdam: North- Holland.

_____ (1977) "Fondements de l'économie monetaire norma-tive: seignieurage, liquidity externe, impossibilité de remunérer les espèces." *Revue Economique* 28 (1): 1–35.

Laidler, D. E. W. (1977) "The Welfare Costs of Inflation in Neoclassical Theory: Some Unsettled Problems." In E. Lundberg (ed.), *Inflation Theory and Anti-Inflation Policy*, 314–28. London: Macmillan.

Lutz, F. A. (1936) *Das Grundproblem der Geldverfassung*. Berlin.

McKinnon, R. I. (1969) *Private and Official International Money: The Case for the Dollar*. Essays in International Finance, Princeton.

_____ (1979) *Money in International Exchange*. New York: Oxford University Press.

_____ (1983) *A New International Standard for Monetary Stabilization*. Washington: Institute for International Economics.

Meltzer, A. H. (1969) "Money, Intermediation and Growth." *Journal of Economic Literature* 7 (1): 27–56.

Mussa, M. (1977) "The Welfare Cost of Inflation and the Role of Money as a Unit of Account." *Journal of Money, Credit, and Banking* 9 (2): 276–86.

Musgrave, R. A. (1959) *The Theory of Public Finance*. New York: McGraw- Hill.

Patinkin, D. (1961) "Financial Intermediaries and the Logical Structure of Monetary Theory." *American Economic Review* 51 (1): 95–116.

Pesek, B. P., and Saving, T. R. (1967) *Money, Wealth and Economic Theory*. New York: Macmillan.

Samuelson, P. A (1954) "The Pure Theory of Public Expenditure." *Review of Economics and Statistics* 35 (4): 387–89.

_____ (1963) "D. H. Robertson (1890–1963)." *Quarterly Journal of Economics* 77 (4): 517–36.

_____ (1969) "Pure Theory of Public Expenditures and Taxation." In J. Margolis and H. Guitton (eds.), *Public Economics*, 98–123. London: Macmillan.

Schmidt, W. E. (1979) *The U.S. Balance of Payments and the Sinking Dollar*. New York: New York University Press.

Sharkey, W. W. (1982) *The Theory of Natural Monopoly*. Cambridge: Cambridge University Press.

Stockman, A. C (1983) "Comments on R. E. Hall's Paper." *Journal of Monetary Economics* 12(1): 51–54.

Tobin, J. (1980) "Discussion." In J. H. Kareken and N. Wallace (eds.), *Models of Monetary Economies*, 83–90. Minneapolis: Federal Reserve Bank of Minneapolis.

Tullock, G. (1971) "Public Decisions as Public Goods." *Journal of Political Economy* 79 (4):913–18.

_____ (1975) "Competing Monies." *Journal of Money, Credit, and Banking* 7 (4): 491–97.

_____ (1976) "Competing Monies: A Reply." *Journal of Money, Credit, and Banking* 8 (4): 521–25.

Vaubel, R. (1976) "Freier Wettbewerb zwischen Währungen?" *Wirtschaftsdienst* (Hamburg) 56 (8): 422–28.

_____ (1977) "Free Currency Competition." *Weltwirtschaftliches Archiv* 113 (3): 435–61.

_____ (1978a) *Strategies for Currency Unification: The Economics of Currency Competition and the Case for a European Parallel Currency.* Tübingen: Mohr.

_____ (1978b) "The Money Supply in Europe: Why EMS May Make Inflation Worse." *Euromoney* (December): 139–42.

_____ (1980) "International Shifts in the Demand for Money, Their Effects on Exchange Rates and Price Levels, and Their Implications for the Preannouncement of Monetary Expansion." *Weltwirtschaftliches Archiv* 116 (1): 1–44.

_____ (1982a) "West Germany's and Switzerland's Experience with Exchange-Rate Flexibility." In J. S. Dreyer, G. Haberler, and T. D. Willett (eds.), *The International Monetary System: A Time of Turbulence*, 180–222. Washington: American Enterprise Institute.

_____ (1982b) "Private Geldproduktion und Optimale Währungseinheit" (Review of *The Optimal Monetary Unit* by Wolfram Engels). *Weltwirtschaftliches Archiv* 118 (3): 581–85.

_____ (1983) "Coordination or Competition among National Macroeconomic Policies?" In F, Machlup, G. Fels, and H. Müller-Groeling (eds.), *Reflections on a Troubled World Economy: Essays in Honour of Herbert Giersch*, 3–28. London: Macmillan.

_____ (1984) "The Government's Money Monopoly: Externalities or Natural Monopoly?" *Kyklos* 37 (1): 27–58.

White, L. H. (1984) "Competitive Payments Systems and the Unit of Account." *American Economic Review* 74 (4): 699–712.

Yeager, L. B. (1983) "Stable Money and Free Market Currencies." *Cato Journal* 3 (1): 305–26.

17

THE MARKET FOR CRYPTOCURRENCIES
Lawrence H. White

Cryptocurrencies like Bitcoin are transferable digital assets, secured by cryptography. To date, all of them have been created by private individuals, organizations, or firms. Unlike bank account balances, they are not anyone's liability. They are not redeemable for any government fiat money such as Federal Reserve notes or for any commodity money such as silver or gold coins. The cryptocurrency market is thus a market of *competing private irredeemable* monies (or would-be monies). Friedrich A. Hayek (1978a) and other economists over the last 40 years could only imagine how market competition among issuers of private irredeemable monies would work. Today we have an actual market to study. In what follows I will discuss the main economic features of the market. I also discuss whether the market is purely a bubble.

As an introduction to the topic, I offer the following comic verse about the contrast between Bitcoin and the physical gold coins of the past:

> In the past, money's value was judged with our teeth;
> We *bit coins* to confirm they were real.
> Now a Bitcoin's just data, no gold underneath.
> That's okay if it buys you a meal.[1]

Lawrence H. White is Professor of Economics at George Mason University, a Senior Fellow with the F. A. Hayek Program for Advanced Study in Philosophy, Politics and Economics at GMU's Mercatus Center, and a Senior Fellow at the Cato Institute's Center for Financial and Monetary Alternatives. This article is reprinted from the *Cato Journal*, Vol. 35, No. 2 (Spring/Summer 2015). The author thanks Patrick Newman for research assistance and participants at Cato's 32nd Annual Monetary Conference for comments.

[1]The fourth line is mine. It refers to the news that Washington, D.C. now has a food truck that accepts Bitcoin payments. The first three lines are by Gary Crockett (2014). His original fourth line was: "Bitten bits don't make much of a meal."

The Size and Composition of the Cryptocurrency Market

Bitcoin rightly gets the lion's share of media attention, but it is not alone in the market for cryptocurrencies. The authoritative website CoinMarketCap.com tracks the US dollar price and total "market cap" (price per unit multiplied by number of units outstanding) for each of more than 500 traded cryptocurrencies. Bitcoin is the largest by far. On a recent day (March 9, 2015), the site showed Bitcoin trading at $291 per unit, with a market cap of $4.05 billion. The second and third largest cryptocurrencies, Ripple and Litecoin, had market caps respectively 8.5 percent and 1.8 percent as large. The entire set of non-Bitcoin cryptocurrencies (known as "altcoins") had a market cap of roughly $619 million, or 15 percent of Bitcoin's. Stated differently, Bitcoin had roughly 87 percent of the market, altcoins 13 percent. In percentage terms, altcoins do a higher share of Bitcoin's business than Bitcoin does of the Federal Reserve Note's business (currently $1.35 trillion in circulation). In trading volume the percentage share of altcoins (led by Litecoin and Ripple) has been similar.

The cryptocurrency market has grown about four-fold in market cap over the last 22 months, with altcoins growing faster than Bitcoin. This is seen by comparing recent data to the oldest snapshot of the CoinMarketCap site available via the Internet Archive "Wayback Machine," which reports data for May 9, 2013. On that date, Bitcoin had a price of $112 per unit, and a market cap of $1.2 billion. The two largest altcoins at that time, Litecoin and Peercoin (aka PPCoin), had market caps respectively 4.7 percent and 0.4 percent as large. Only 13 altcoins were listed. Jointly their market cap was about 6 percent of Bitcoin's, giving Bitcoin 95 percent of the market. Since then, the market share of altcoins has doubled, and their market cap has grown nine-fold. Trading volumes then were not reported.

At $4.05 billion, the market cap of Bitcoin, as of March 2015, was slightly smaller than the dollar value of the September 2014 monetary bases of the Lithuanian litas ($5.8 billion) and the Guatemalan quetzal ($5.5 billion), but larger than those of the Costa Rican colon ($3.3 billion) and the Serbia dinar ($3.3 billion).[2] The August 2014 figures from the Central Bank of the Bahamas do not provide the

---

[2]All figures to follow come from official central bank websites, converted to US dollars using the xe.com rates for September 30, 2014.

monetary base, but count Bahamian dollar currency in circulation at $210 million, less than two-thirds of Ripple's recent market cap of around $344 million.

Medium of Exchange, Store of Value, and Medium of Remittance Functions

The retail use of Bitcoin as a medium of exchange for goods and services is small to date, but is growing. In December 2014, Microsoft began accepting Bitcoin payments "to buy content such as games and videos on Xbox game consoles, add apps and services to Windows phones or to buy Microsoft software" (BBC 2014). In doing so it joined prominent online retailers Overstock, Dell, Expedia, TigerDirect, and Newegg, and the payment processors Paypal and Square. The list grows weekly. Payments processing firms Bitpay, Coinbase, Coinkite, and others, are enabling (and recruiting) brick-and-mortar retail shops to accept Bitcoin from any consumer whose smartphone "Bitcoin wallet" application can display a QR code. On its website Bitpay claims a clientele of "44,000 businesses and organizations"; Coinbase claims 37,000. These processors offer to purchase the consumer's Bitcoin as it is spent, paying the equivalent (minus a fee) in dollars or other preferred currency to the merchant. The merchant avoids all exchange rate risk of holding Bitcoin. For the retailer on the front end of the transaction, "accepting Bitcoin" via these services actually means receiving dollars (or euros, etc.), just like accepting a credit card or debit card does. Bitpay and Coinbase thereby remove the barrier against transacting in cryptocurrency posed by the incumbency advantage of the established domestic currency unit (Luther and White 2014), just as Visa and Mastercard enable merchants to accept credit and debit cards from a customers whose accounts are denominated in a foreign currency.

A potentially vast market for Bitcoin and altcoin use is international remittances. For example, workers abroad send an estimated $25 billion per year to the Philippines, where remittances contribute a remarkable 10 percent of national income. The established remittance services Western Union and MoneyGram commonly charge more than 10 percent in fees. Bitcoin remitters, by contrast, are charging only 1 percent. As the CEO of a recently launched Bitcoin remittance service remarked to a reporter: "We thought: with

Bitcoin we can do it cheaper." A Filipino working in Singapore or Hong Kong (say) doesn't need to have online access or a Bitcoin wallet. The worker can purchase Bitcoins at a BTM (Bitcoin teller machine), bring the QR code printout to the local "rebittance" provider's office, and the service delivers Philippine pesos as a direct deposit into a designated recipient's account at a participating bank back home or (for an addition fee but still much less than the legacy firms) as cash (Ferraz 2014, Buenaventura 2014).

Market Competition

The market for cryptocurrencies has always been characterized by free entry. A new development in the past two years is competition from profit-seeking enterprises. Free entry is exhibited by the remarkable growth in the number of altcoins, from the 13 listed in May 2013 to the 500+ listed in March 2015. Profit-seeking by new entrants is especially conspicuous in systems like Ripple (2nd behind Bitcoin in market cap as of March 9, 2015), BitShares (4th), Nxt (6th), and MaidSafeCoin (8th). In each of these systems a substantial share of "pre-mined" coins was initially held by their developer-entrepreneurs. The entrepreneurs hope to profit by raising the coin's market price through efforts to promote wider use of the coin and its associated proprietary payment network or trading platform, such that they can eventually realize a market value for their coin holdings greater than their expenditures on development and promotion.

Bitcoin, by contrast, was launched by a pseudonymous programmer (or set of programmers) apparently as a public-spirited experiment. Revenue from producing ("mining") new coins, the reward for validating peer-to-peer transfers, is open to anyone with the computing power to participate successfully. While Federal Reserve Bank of Chicago economist François Velde (2013) is thus right to contrast the non-profit Bitcoin system to the profit-seeking firms that Hayek (1978a) foresaw, the contrast does not apply to the new enterprises that are launching altcoins for profit.[3] In these new altcoin enterprises

---

[3]Velde also writes that Bitcoin does not "truly embody what Hayek and others in the 'Austrian School of Economics' proposed." But I would distinguish Hayek's *proposal*—to allow free choice and private competition in currency—from his *prediction* about what type of money would then dominate the field.

we see a working embodiment of competitive issue of irredeemable money by profit-seeking private firms. It is no longer correct—if it ever was—to say that Bitcoin is not "operating in a competitive environment." Bitcoin competes with altcoins in the same way that the giant non-profit YMCA competes with smaller non-profit and for-profit health clubs, or a large non-profit hospital competes with smaller non-profit and for-profit immediate-care clinics.

The Novel Implementation of Quantity Commitments

We should not be too surprised that the features of competing irredeemable privately issued currencies are different from what Hayek (and other economists) imagined, for two reasons. First, market competition is a discovery procedure as Hayek (1978b) elsewhere emphasized, in which successful entrepreneurs discover profit in overlooked or unforeseen ways of producing products and reconfiguring product features. Secondly and more specifically, Hayek imagined that the issuer of a successful irredeemable private currency issuer would retain discretion to vary its quantity. The issuer would promise (but not make any contractual commitment) to maintain a stable purchasing power per unit.[4] A naked promise of that sort unfortunately appears to be time-inconsistent (Taub 1985; White 1989: 382–83; White 1999: ch. 12). An issuer whose promise was believed could reap a large one-time payoff by spending a massive batch of new money into circulation until the public caught on. The one-time profit would exceed the normal rate of return from staying in business. By assumption, there would be no legal recourse against the decline of the money's value. Aware of the problem, the public would not believe the promise to begin with, giving the money zero value in equilibrium.

The traditional solution to the problem of giving a privately issued money a reliably positive value is a redemption contract, an enforceable money-back guarantee or *price commitment* (White 1989). Under the gold standard, a banknote was worth $20 when the bank of issue was bound to pay a $20 gold coin for it. Today a

---

[4]Benjamin Klein (1974), in a more formal model, supposed perfect competition among issuers on "rental price"—that is, the risk-adjusted rate of return to holding money—in an environment of perfect foresight or the equivalent (see White 1999: ch. 12).

bank deposit is worth $100 when the bank is bound to pay $100 in Federal Reserve Notes for it. A suitable medium of redemption has a value that is known and independent of actions by any particular bank of issue.

Ronald Coase (1972) identified an alternative solution to the problem—how an issuer is to bind himself not to run down the price of the thing issued—in the context of a monopolist selling a durable good priced above marginal cost. To get customers to pay $200 for an art print when the marginal cost of producing a duplicate copy is $1, the artist must convince them that she will not run off and sell lower-priced duplicates in the future. To commit herself, the artist produces the print in a numbered edition with a stated maximum ("this print is #45/200"), providing an enforceable *quantity commitment* that she will issue no more than a fixed number of prints. Despite discussing this solution years ago (White 1989), I did not foresee that a quantity commitment could be used in practice to launch a successful irredeemable private currency.[5]

It is this second solution that Bitcoin has creatively introduced to the field of private currency. The implementation uses an entirely new technology: the limit on the number of Bitcoin units in the market is not guaranteed by a contractual promise that can (with some probability) be enforced on an issuing firm, but rather by a limit having been *programmed* into the Bitcoin system's observable source code and being continuously verifiable through a public ledger (the "block chain") that is shared among all "miners" who participate in Bitcoin transactions processing.[6] Altcoins employ the same basic idea of a programmed quantity commitment verified through a public ledger, though sometimes implemented in a different way.

Altcoin Innovations

In order to compete with the market leader Bitcoin, the developers of altcoins have understandably emulated its best features (decentralized peer-to-peer exchange, quantity commitment embedded in

[5]I believed that redeemable claims to a commodity money would be preferred over any IOU-nothing as a medium of exchange. And perhaps they would be even today, if not for government suppression of the former. For recent examples of suppression, see Dowd (2014: 1–37) and White (2014b).

[6]On the mechanics of the Bitcoin system see King, Williams, and Yanofsky (2013), Velde (2013), and Dowd and Hutchinson (2015).

an open source code, and shared public ledger), while introducing various general improvements and customizations. Most of the emphasis has been on improving speed, robustness, and privacy. A few altcoins aim to serve niche constituencies.[7]

The first generation of altcoins are non-profit projects like Bitcoin, but tweak the Bitcoin code. *Litecoin* was introduced in October 2011 to provide faster transaction confirmation times (2.5 minutes versus 10 minutes). *Peercoin,* launched August 2012, increases the speed a bit more by using a newer protocol ("proof of stake" rather than Bitcoin's "proof of work") that is less computationally demanding. This protocol also promises to allow participants to share in the rewards from mining without joining mining pools or buying the expensive specialized equipment that it now takes, as the result of competition, to succeed at Bitcoin mining. Because Peercoin's protocol, unlike Bitcoin's, does not promote the merger of miners into ever-larger pools, it is said to be less vulnerable to a possible collusive attack by 51 percent of miners.[8] *Primecoin,* a later project from Peercoin's main developer, implements a newer proof-of-work protocol (finding prime numbers) to reduce confirmation times to 1 minute.

Darkcoin, a non-profit project launched in April 2014, in February 2015 introduced payment confirmation "within seconds." Darkcoin alters the Bitcoin code to provide greater anonymity to users. Where the Bitcoin ledger puts every transaction and transactor address on public view, Darkcoin transactions are "obfuscated." *BlackCoin,* supported by an active non-profit foundation and first listed in February 2014, uses a "proof of stake" protocol for speedy verification. It is connected to a proprietary trading platform, BlackHalo, that promises greater user anonymity than other systems. Blackcoin can now be spent (along with Bitcoin and Litecoin) at participating retail shops using the Coinkite debit card.

[7]While CoinMarketCap.com tracks market caps, the site CoinGecko.com ranks altcoins on a combination of market cap, trading volume, ongoing development activity, and social media buzz. In December 2014 it had Dogecoin at #2 and Darkcoin at #6, each four steps above its market cap ranking, based on their buzz factors. By March 2015 Darkcoin had risen to #5 in market cap.

[8]On this problem with the Bitcoin protocol, see Dowd and Hutchinson (2015) who predict that it will bring Bitcoin's demise. Whether or not they are right about that, many altcoin developers have recognized the problem and have made deliberate design changes to avoid what Dowd and Hutchinson call "inherent tendencies toward centralization, takeover and collapse."

Ripple, first traded in August 2013, is a cryptocurrency issued by the for-profit enterprise Ripple Labs. It does not rely on a mining protocol. A fixed stock of Ripples was "premined," though the developers have not released them all yet. To make the fixity of the Ripple stock credible, the system follows Bitcoin's lead in having a shared public ledger. The Ripple payment network confirms transactions through a "consensus" protocol that works *much* faster than mining protocols (5 seconds versus 1 to 10 minutes), so has a much better prospect of competing with ordinary credit and debit cards for point-of-sale transactions. The coin is only one part of the parent firm's efforts, which include building a wholesale remittance system for "real-time, cross-border payments" between banks, cheaper and faster than the legacy Automated Clearing House system (Liu 2014). *Stellar* is a non-profit project that emulates Ripple.

BitShares also promises greater anonymity and ease of use. Like Ripple, it is part of a larger for-profit enterprise funded by venture capital. In this case the larger project, according to the BitShares Wiki (http://wiki.bitshares.org/index.php/BitShares), is an "experiment," based on "a business model similar to existing banks or brokerages," to enable the creation and trading of "BitAssets," digital derivative contracts on "the value of anything from dollars, to gold," to exchange-traded equities, bonds, and commodities. The project exemplifies what two *Wall Street Journal* writers (Vigna and Case 2014) describe as "so-called Bitcoin 2.0 technologies – those bitcoin-inspired software applications that bypass financial middlemen and allow almost any asset to be digitized and traded over a decentralized computer network."

The niche-market strategy of *CannabisCoin* is to offer a payment service for medical marijuana dispensaries and other cannabis retailers whose access to bank accounts and credit cards is currently being blocked by the federal government even where their business has been legalized at the state level. In October 2014, the coin's promoters were seeking retailers willing to provide a specific type of cannabis to patients at one gram per one CannabisCoin. Whether this will lead to the institution of a new commodity money standard remains to be seen, however, as the number of participating retailers and their supplies were quite limited. The promotional effort appears to have helped the market cap of CannabisCoin to surge ahead of other cannabis-themed cryptocoins, such as the earlier-launched *Potcoin* and the more recent *MaryJaneCoin*.

Auroracoin is an Iceland-only altcoin introduced in February 2014 for the purpose of helping Icelanders evade the country's exchange controls. (The controls, which included a ban on Bitcoin purchases, were imposed during the financial crisis in October 2008 and are still in place.) *Scotcoin*, launched by an Edinburgh venture capitalist in May 2014, in advance of Scotland's independence referendum, is likewise a nationally specific enterprise. Its backer has expressed the hope (Hern 2014) that "introducing a voluntary cryptocurrency, which may in the future act as a medium of exchange for the Scottish people, can only benefit them should there be major disruption." A recent entry is *CzechCrownCoin*, launched October 2014, at least half of which is being distributed to Czech citizens. None of these national coins had a March 2015 market cap above $55,000.

But Aren't They All Just Bubbles?

A quantity commitment solves the problem of making a credible commitment not to over-issue. But it has a major shortcoming when applied to currency. Unlike a price commitment, it leaves the market price of the currency to vary with demand. This explains how it is possible for the prices of Bitcoin and other cryptocurrencies to be as volatile as they have recently been (Luther and White 2014). And it explains how it was possible for several altcoins, when enthusiasm for them evaporated, to decline to near-zero market cap in the past year.

The collapse of several altcoins is readily evident on CoinMarketCap.com. Three of the earliest thirteen altcoins have declined substantially in market cap. Terracoin, which at its peak had a market cap of at $7.1 million, is now (March 2015) down to around $23,000, a decline of more than 99 percent. Freicoin, which peaked at $16.1 million, has fallen to around $61,000, also a decline of more than 99 percent. The whimsically named BBQCoin, having peaked at $7 million, now trades around $21,000, another 99+ percent decline. All three had very sharp run-ups to their peaks in early December 2013, mostly reversed by month's end. Megacoin, first listed in July 2013, experienced the same December 2013 pattern, soaring from $1.2 million on

November 23, 2013, to a peak of $47.5 million on December 1, then sliding to around $328,000 today, a decline of more than 99 percent. Later-peaking examples of altcoins suffering 98 percent or greater peak-to-present declines have included Mooncoin, CryptCoin, Scotcoin, Bitgem, and CrtCoin.

Looking only at the market cap charts, the most remarkable case appears to be Auroracoin, which quickly climbed to chart a recorded market cap of $953 million, but is valued today at around $46,000, a drop of more than 99.99 percent. The incredible valuation of nearly $1 billion was, even at the time, a misstatement. The Auroracoin launch plan (Hern 2014) was to jump-start enthusiasm by giving away about 30 premined coins to every Icelandic citizen, for a total of 10 million units. (Such a giveaway is known, in honor of Milton Friedman's famous thought experiment, as a "helicopter drop" or "airdrop.") Dividing the CoinMarketCap.com peak valuation by the price on that day (March 4, 2014) indicates 10 million units in the market, when the number of coins actually available was one-hundredth of that figure (Torpey 2014), the airdrop having yet to be made. Multiplying the price by the actual number of coins, the true market cap was one-hundredth of the reported value, around $9.53 million. A drop from $9.53 million down to the current $46,000, however, is still a 99+ percent drop.

The repeated experience of crashing altcoins, in which the market valuation of a once-popular cryptocurrency all but evaporates, suggests in retrospect that the prices of *those* coins, at least, were simply bubbles. That is, such a coin's demand was unsupported by any price-independent usefulness that would put a floor under its equilibrium market price. (By contrast, industrial and ornamental uses support gold's market value.) To understand the argument, consider again the example of an artist's print. Some print buyers are presumably not just speculators who will put the print in storage and hope for its price to rise, but art-lovers planning to hang it on the wall and enjoy the real aesthetic pleasure it provides. That enjoyment is independent of its price. An irredeemable currency, by contrast, is presumed in standard monetary theory to be held only in order to be later spent or sold. It provides no service that is independent of its market value. People thus presumably have a positive demand price for any irredeemable currency, giving it a positive market value, only to the extent that they expect it to have a future market value. A market valuation anchored by *nothing* but expectations of market valuation is the definition of a bubble.[9]

Does this logic show that the prices of all cryptocurrencies are pure bubbles? No. We cannot rule out that the flourishing cryptocurrencies have some fundamental support.

As several economists have proposed, owning Bitcoin (or other cryptocurrency) may provide a kind of real pleasure to at least some of its holders, say anti-statists who like what it stands for,[10] tech enthusiasts who admire its ingenuity, or its own developers who gladly stake some wealth to help their project succeed (Luther 2013, Murphy 2013, Selgin 2014). For such an individual we can determine his affinity-based demand curve for Bitcoin by positing that he wants to own Bitcoin worth not just any old amount, but rather a specific amount of purchasing power, say 100 real US dollars. (A "real dollar" here means the equivalent in purchasing power to the dollar of a specified base year.) We can plot the individual's demand curve against the real price, i.e. the US dollar price of Bitcoin divided by the dollar price level. The individual's demand curve will be a rectangular hyperbola, a familiar construct in the basic theory of a fiat money's value. The market demand curve sums all the individual demand curves. At a given US dollar price level, if ten thousand individuals want to hold an average of $100 worth of Bitcoin each, just because Bitcoin is cool, then the market cap of Bitcoin must be at least $1 million.

This account does not explain day-to-day variations in the market price of Bitcoin, but it does potentially explain why the price is above zero. In this way real affinity demand provides an answer to economist-blogger Brad DeLong's (2013) rhetorical question: "Placing a floor on the value of bitcoins is . . . what, exactly?" Of course, if Bitcoin were to become completely uncool to *everyone*, the floor would vanish.[11]

---

[9]The same argument applies to any fiat money, to the extent that its market value exceeds whatever floor value it has due to exclusive tax receivability or other government compulsion. No cryptocurrency has *that* kind of support.

[10]A pseudonymous commenter on the reddit CryptoMarket page (Pogeymanz 2014) writes about Darkcoin: "I have some DRK because I like what it stands for."

[11]DeLong (2013) also writes: "Placing a ceiling on the value of bitcoins is computer technology and the form of the hash function . . . until the limit of 21 million bitcoins is reached." Actually, of course, Bitcoin's source code does not put a ceiling on the market cap or *value* of Bitcoins, only a limit on the *quantity*. The conceptual ceiling on *value* is Bitcoin achieving a 100 percent share of the real value of all money balances in the world (Luther and White 2014).

I previously (White 2014a) too hastily rejected this argument as an explanation of how Bitcoin first achieved a positive market price, on the grounds that it "does not deliver what the argument requires, namely, an account of how Bitcoins initially had a positive value *apart from their actual or prospective use as medium of exchange*. The value at every point in this scenario derives entirely from use or prospective use as a medium of exchange (only such use as a dollar competitor is what might [provide aesthetic pleasure], not the existence of untraded digital character strings)." I was mistaken to think that the argument has such a requirement. A positive affinity valuation of a cryptocurrency may well require the *possibility* of its taking off as a nonstate money, but that does not imply a chicken-or-egg problem. Affinity demand and hence market value can be positive before actual medium-of-exchange use begins.

The affinity account has the additional merit of being consistent with the great market cap of Bitcoin, esteemed for being the first mover, the middling market cap of altcoins that embody valuable technical improvements and have active support communities, and the low market cap of me-too altcoins. Five hundred altcoins are not all making a statement or breaking new technical ground. They have positive market caps, but most of them are slight.

A second grounding for fundamental value lies in the real demand for the sorts of payment services offered by a cryptocurrency. Ownership of a particular brand of cryptocurrency units is needed to make use of the brand's payment system, which may offer advantages over other systems (Tucker 2014).

With regard to the "bubble" element in cryptocurrency valuation, economist-blogger Stephen Williamson (2011) reminds us that official fiat money or a commodity money likewise trades well above its fundamental value. In a case where the surplus of a currency asset's market value over its fundamental value results from its solving a medium-of-exchange coordination problem, that surplus is a good thing because it represents value-added:

> Bubbles can be good things, as any asset which is used widely in exchange will trade at a price higher than its "fundamental," and the asset's liquidity premium—the difference between the actual price and the fundamental—is a measure of the asset's social contribution as a medium of exchange.

I would, however, qualify this claim by saying that the difference is a reliable measure of social contribution only insofar as it arises through voluntary trade rather than legal compulsion, and only after we subtract the costs of generating and maintaining the asset in question. It is from by adding such value that Ripple's entrepreneurs hope to profit. Unlike an official fiat currency, no part of Ripple's valuation is based on legal compulsion.

Is There a Problem of Monopoly? Is There Too Much Competition?

Milton Friedman (1960: 8) wrote of "the technical monopoly character of a pure fiduciary currency which makes essential the setting of some external limit on its amount." By "pure fiduciary currency" he meant an irredeemable or fiat currency. By "technical monopoly character" he meant that open entry into counterfeiting would drive the value of an irredeemable paper currency note down to the cost of paper and ink,[12] and all the way down to zero if ever-higher denominations could be introduced at no higher cost. Therefore, a single authorized issuer was needed to preserve the currency's value. As Benjamin Klein (1974) pointed out, however, Friedman here conflated monopoly with enforcement of trademarks. To ban the selling of knock-off perfume in bottles bearing a counterfeit Chanel trademark does not imply giving Chanel a monopoly except in the sale of Chanel-branded perfume. It does not require any restriction on the production of competing perfumes under different trademarks. Enforcing a ban on the counterfeiting of Federal Reserve Notes, or in other words having the Secret Service protect the Federal Reserve's trademark, does not require giving the Fed a monopoly on currency issue.

The counterfeiting of Bitcoins (also known as the problem of "double spending") is prevented not through police work and legal prosecution by any central authority, but quite elegantly by the decentralized verification process that prevents the transfer of any coin of unattested provenance from being accepted onto the public ledger. With such effective de facto counterfeiting protection, the quantity of Bitcoins remains on its programmed path.

---

[12]For a real-world example of this happening, see Luther (2012).

Velde (2013) states that Bitcoin has "a status of quasi-monopoly in the realm of digital currencies by virtue of its first-mover advantage." By "quasi-monopoly status" he may mean only that Bitcoin has a large market share, derived from its being the first mover into (that is, creating) the market. But such a status is distinct from the usual concept of natural monopoly (or quasi-monopoly) status due to economies of scale, which denotes the ability to serve every (or nearly every) part of the market at lower marginal cost than competitors. The main static danger of a monopoly in the usual sense, whether natural or state-granted, is that the monopolist firm may restrict output to raise price above marginal cost, thwarting efficiency by sacrificing potential gains from trade. Because the quantity of Bitcoin is predetermined by a program and not manipulable by a discretionary issuer, it poses no danger of any such monopolistic output restriction.

Competition from new entrants surrounds Bitcoin. The new entrants have the advantage of being able to introduce altcoins with improved features while the Bitcoin code was written five-plus years ago. The Bitcoin community can at most agree to patch the code, not to fundamentally revise it. Bitcoin does have the largest established network, but a dominant proprietary network does not imply monopoly pricing (in this context, transaction fees above marginal cost) when the market is contestable. Ripple, Litecoin, BitShares, and others entrants are vigorously contesting the market. The cryptocurrency market exhibits Schumpeterian competition from new business models rather than only static price competition.

DeLong (2013) raises an issue that is the opposite of monopolistic restriction. He worries that competition from more and more altcoins may expand the total quantity of cryptocoins without limit, and thereby—unless Bitcoin "can somehow successfully differentiate itself from the latecomers"—drive the market value of Bitcoin and all other cryptocurrencies to zero. He writes: "the money supply of BitCoin-like things is infinite because the cost of production of them is infinitesimal." To consider this possibility let us suppose, for the sake of argument, that the cost of introducing a me-too altcoin is indeed infinitesimal. The economic implication is that in a fully arbitraged equilibrium the marginal altcoin will have an infinitesimal real value (which is an approximate description of the marginal altcoins we do in fact observe). But this is not to say that the value of Bitcoin (or of established altcoins) will tend toward zero. Infinitesimally valued altcoins do not eat into Bitcoin's market share in real terms. Only valued altcoins can do that, as they have since May 2013 (reducing Bitcoin's share to 87 percent from 95 percent as noted; but at the same time Bitcoin's market cap in US dollars grew more than three-fold).

In the foreign exchange market for government fiat monies with flexible exchange rates, hyper-expansion in the nominal supply of dollar-like things, say Zimbabwe dollars or Venezuelan bolivars, does not drag down the purchasing power of the US dollar. Likewise, in the existing altcoin market with its completely flexible exchange rates, cheap altcoins simply have low exchange value against Bitcoin and do not drag down Bitcoin's real market value.

Cryptocurrency and Fiat Currency: Comparisons and Contrasts

DeLong likens Bitcoin to government fiat money in the following way: "BitCoin is like fiat money, and unlike 18th and 19th century Yap stone money, in that its cost of production is zero." In fact, although Bitcoin is similar to a government fiat money (and unlike gold) on the demand side, in that nothing supports its price if transaction and other money-related demand for it goes to zero, it is absolutely *unlike* a government fiat money on the supply side. It does not have an indefinitely expandable supply but the opposite. Just as monopolistic under-supply is ruled out (see above), so too is hyper-expansion. Bitcoin has a verifiably programmed commitment to a pre-specified quantity path.[13] In light of that commitment, the

---

[13]Blogger Charlie Stross (2014) colorfully comments that Bitcoin "wears a gimp suit and a ball gag, padlocked into permanent deflation and with the rate of issue of new 'notes' governed by the law of algorithmic complexity." That padlocked "gimp suit and ball gag" is Bitcoin's binding quantity commitment. It is a feature, not a bug.

cost of production beyond the scheduled quantity is extremely high, not zero.[14]

Noting that "improvements, bug fixes, and repairs" to the Bitcoin code have been "carried out by the community of bitcoin users, dominated by a small set of programmers," Velde (2013) downplays the prospects for Bitcoin to rival the fiat US dollar:

> Although some of the enthusiasm for bitcoin is driven by a distrust of state-issued currency, it is hard to imagine a world where the main currency is based on an extremely complex code understood by only a few, and controlled by even fewer, without accountability, arbitration, or recourse.

Substitute the phrase "bureaucratic agency" for the word "code" in this statement, however, and the hard-to-imagine world becomes a fair description of our current world of Federal Reserve currency. This fact completely overturns Velde's argument. If the prospects for Bitcoin against the dollar depended only on the public's choice between trusting an open source code with a public ledger and trusting a byzantine central bank, the prospects would look extremely good.

Bitcoin as a Vehicle Currency and Unit of Account

Finally, Bitcoin has an interesting role that is often overlooked or denied. A recent paper by a team of Bank of England economists (Ali et al. 2014), for example, declares that cryptocurrencies "are not typically used as media of exchange" and "there is little evidence of digital currencies being used as units of account." In fact Bitcoin is the vehicle currency (commonly accepted medium of exchange), and consequently is the unit of account, in most altcoin markets. With a few exceptions (Litecoin against US dollar, Chinese yuan, and euro; Chinese exchanges where altcoins trade against yuan; Peercoin

---

[14]In light of its programmed production limit, Selgin (2013) calls Bitcoin a "synthetic commodity money." He helpfully likens Bitcoin's quantity commitment to the quantity commitment of an artist who publicly destroys the engraved plates from which a known number of lithographic prints have been made.

against dollar), the vast majority of altcoin exchanges trade and quote prices in Bitcoins, not in dollars, euros, or yuan.[15]

The altcoin market is structured this way for the same reason that the US dollar is the vehicle currency for foreign exchange transactions (Kreuger 2012). To trade (say) Australian dollars for British pounds, the standard route is AUD for USD, then USD for GBP. Thicker markets enjoy lower bid-ask spreads. The US dollar currency markets are so much larger than others that for most almost all currency pairs that do not include the US dollar (euro-yen is an exception) the sum of bid-ask spreads is less for indirect exchange via the US dollar than for direct exchange. This pattern is self-reinforcing by bringing more volume to the US dollar markets.[16] Most non-USD to non-USD foreign exchange markets are missing.

The Bitcoin-US dollar market has much more volume and thus much lower spreads than any altcoin-US dollar market. To trade US dollars for an altcoin, often the *only* route in practice is to trade US dollars for Bitcoin, and then Bitcoin for the altcoin. Most altcoin-dollar markets are missing because volume would be too low to have attractive bid-ask spreads. With by far the thickest potential markets against any altcoin, even compared to US dollars, Bitcoin is naturally the vehicle currency and thus the unit of account in altcoin markets.

Policy Implications

The market for cryptocurrencies is still evolving, and (to most economists) is full of surprises. Policymakers should therefore be very humble about the prospects for improving economic welfare by restricting the market. Israel Kirzner's (1985) warning about the perils of regulation strongly applies here: Interventions that block or divert the path of entrepreneurial discovery will prevent the realization of potential breakthroughs such that we will never know what we are missing.

---

[15]See http://www.cryptocoincharts.info/main/priceBoxes.

[16]The positive network effect that makes the US dollar the common medium for inter-currency exchange echoes the self-reinforcing Mengerian process by which a common medium for inter-commodity exchange (money) emerged out of barter.

References

Ali, R.; Barrdear, J.; Clews, R.; and Southgate, J. (2014) "The Economics of Digital Currencies." Bank of England *Quarterly Bulletin* (Q3): 1–11.

BBC (2014) "Microsoft to Accept Payments made in Bitcoins" (11 December): www.bbc.com/news/technology-30377654.

Buenaventura, L. (2014) "The Rise of Rebittance: Reinventing Money Transfers in the Philippines with Bitcoin." *The Next Web* weblog (28 September): http://thenextweb.com/insider/2014 /09/28/rise-rebittance-reinventing-money-transfers-philippines-bitcoin.

Coase, R. (1972) "Durability and Monopoly." *Journal of Law and Economics* 25 (April): 143–49.

Crockett, G. (2014) "Bitcoin is Seen as an Ephemeral Currency." *Washington Post* Style Invitational Contest, Week 1062: Poems from the headlines (27 April): www.washingtonpost.com/enter-tainment/style-invitational-week-1069-big-thoughts-little-words-plus-more-from-recent-contests/2014/04/16/f556bf74-c331-11e3-b574-f8748871856a_story.html.

DeLong, B. (2013) "Watching Bitcoin, Dogecoin, Etc." *Equitable Growth* weblog (28 December): http://equitablegrowth.org /2013/12/28/watching-bitcoin-dogecoin-etc.

Dowd, K. (2014) *New Private Monies: A Bit-Part Player?* London: Institute of Economic Affairs.

Dowd, K., and Hutchinson, M. (2015) "Bitcoin Will Bite the Dust." *Cato Journal* 35 (2): TK.

Ferraz, E. (2014) "Send Home Your Wages Using Bitcoin and Avoid Hefty Money Transfer Fees? That's Now a Reality." *Tech in Asia* (3 July): www.techinasia.com/send-home-wages-bitcoin-avoid-hefty-money-transfer-fees-reality.

Friedman, M. (1960) *A Program for Monetary Stability*. New York: Fordham University Press.

Hayek, F. A. (1978a) *The Denationalisation of Money*, 2nd ed. London: Institute of Economic Affairs.

_____ (1978b) "Competition as a Discovery Procedure." In Hayek, *New Studies in Philosophy, Politics, Economics, and the History of Ideas*. London: Routledge.

Hern, A. (2014) "Bitcoin Goes National with Scotcoin and Auroracoin." *The Guardian* (25 March): www.theguardian.com

/technology/2014/mar/25/bitcoin-goes-national-with-scotcoin-auroracoin.

King, R. S.; Williams, S.; and Yanofsky, D. (2013) "By Reading This Article, You're Mining Bitcoins." *Quartz* webzine (17 December); http://qz.com/154877/by-reading-this-page-you-are-mining-bit-coins.

Kirzner, I. M. (1985) "The Perils of Regulation: A Market-Process Approach." In Kirzner, *Discovery and the Capitalist Process*, 119–49. Chicago: University of Chicago Press.

Klein, B. (1974) "The Competitive Supply of Money." *Journal of Money, Credit, and Banking* 6 (November): 423–53.

Krueger, M. (2012) "Money: A Market Microstructure Approach." *Journal of Money, Credit and Banking* 44 (September): 1245–58.

Liu, A. (2014) "Ripple Labs Signs First Two US Banks." *Rippleblog* weblog (24 September): https://ripple.com/blog/ripple-labs-signs-first-two-us-banks.

Luther, W. J. (2012) "The Monetary Mechanism of Stateless Somalia." Kenyon College Working Paper, http://papers.ssrn.com/sol3/papers.cfm?abstract_id=2047494.

_____ (2013) "Cryptocurrencies, Network Effects, and Switching Costs." Mercatus Center Working Paper No. 13–17, http://papers.ssrn.com/sol3/papers.cfm?abstract_id=2295134.

Luther, W. J., and White, L. H. (2014) "Can Bitcoin Become a Major Currency?" *Cayman Financial Review* (August): www.compass-cayman.com/cfr/2014/08/08/Can-bitcoin-become-a-major-currency.

Murphy, R. P. (2013) "The Economics of Bitcoin." *Library of Economics and Liberty* (3 June): www.econlib.org/library/Columns/y2013/Murphybitcoin.html.

Pogeymanz (2014) Comment in the thread "Darkcoin Is Going to Be a Behemoth," www.reddit.com/r/CryptoMarkets/comments/20t9nc/darkcoin_is_going_to_be_a_behemoth.

Selgin, G. (2013) "Synthetic Commodity Money." University of Georgia Working Paper, http://papers.ssrn.com/sol3/papers.cfm?abstract_id=2000118.

_____ (2014) "Mises Was Lukewarm on Free Banking." *Liberty Matters* (January): http://oll.libertyfund.org/pages/misestmc.

Stross, C. (2014) "Schadenfreude." *Charlie's Diary* weblog (25 February): http://www.antipope.org/charlie/blog-static/2014/02/schadenfreude-1.html.

Taub, B. (1985) "Private Fiat Money with Many Suppliers." *Journal of Monetary Economics* 16 (September): 195–208.

Torpey, K. (2014) "Auroracoin's Market Cap is Highly Inflated." *Cryptocoins News* (4 March): www.cryptocoinsnews.com/aurora-coins-market-cap-highly-inflated.

Tucker, J. (2014) "What Gave Bitcoin Its Value?" *The Freeman* (27 August): http://fee.org/the_freeman/detail/what-gave-bitcoin-its-value.

Velde, F. R. (2013) "Bitcoin: A Primer." *Chicago Fed Letter* 317 (December): www.chicagofed.org/digital_assets/publications /chicago_fed_letter/2013/cfldecember2013_317.pdf.

Vigna, P., and Case, M. J. (2014) "BitBeat: Ratings Firm Coinist Tackles Trust Problem with Bitcoin 2.0 Projects." *Wall Street Journal MoneyBeat* weblog (12 August): http://blogs.wsj.com /moneybeat/2014/08/12/bitbeat-ratings-firm-coinist-tackles-trust-problem-with-bitcoin-2-0-projects.

White, L. H. (1989) "What Kinds of Monetary Institutions Would a Free Market Deliver?" *Cato Journal* 9 (Fall): 367–91.

_____ (1999) *The Theory of Monetary Institutions*. Oxford: Basil Blackwell.

_____ (2014a) "Ludwig von Mises's The Theory of Money and Credit at 101." *Liberty Matters* (January): http://oll.libertyfund .org/pages/misestmc.

_____ (2014b) "The Troubling Suppression of Competition from Alternative Monies." *Cato Journal* 34 (Spring/Summer): 181–201.

Williamson, S. (2011) "Bitcoin." *New Monetarist Economics* weblog (24 June): http://newmonetarism.blogspot.com/2011/06/bitcoin .html.

18

MONETARY FREEDOM AND MONETARY STABILITY

Kevin Dowd

The single most important argument in favor of government intervention in the monetary system is that intervention is required to counteract the inherent instability of monetary laissez faire. In one form or another, this belief lies behind the justifications usually given for the need for a monopoly over the supply of base money, the lender of last resort function of the central bank, and government deposit insurance. As these are the principal pillars of modern central banking, it is probably fair to say that the case for central banking stands or falls on the idea that free-market money is naturally unstable.

This article rejects that claim. If it were correct, a stable laissez-faire monetary system would be self-contradictory. A hypothetical counterexample of a stable laissez-faire monetary system therefore suffices to refute it. In this article, I outline such a monetary system and explain why it is stable.[1] The underlying reason for its stability is

---

Kevin Dowd is Professor of Finance and Economics at Durham University and a Senior Fellow with Cato's Center for Monetary and Financial Alternatives. This article is reprinted, with minor revisions, from Dowd (1993: chap. 4). It was first presented at the Cato Institute's Seventh Annual Monetary Conference, "Alternatives to Government Fiat Money," Washington, D.C., February 23–24, 1989. The author thanks Mervyn Lewis and Genie Short for their helpful comments.

---

[1]Indeed, it is very difficult to think of plausible scenarios in which laissez-faire money is anything but stable. The famous case discussed by Friedman (1960: 8) implicitly assumes that different money issues cannot be distinguished, but the hyperinflation no longer takes place when this restriction is relaxed.

that the individuals operating within it demand stability and have the means to make those demands effective. Besides being stable, a free-market monetary regime is also efficient because all agents pursue their self-interest and all mutually beneficial trades are carried out. These features make the laissez-faire monetary system an attractive one, and far superior to our current government fiat system, which is neither stable nor optimal.

The question then arises how we managed to end up with a monetary system that is so patently unsatisfactory. The answer suggested is that our present monetary system, characterized by government power and discretion, is unstable and inferior *precisely* because it is not based on individual freedom under a genuine rule of law. This answer is confirmed by considering what would happen if we introduced an interventionist state into a previously laissez-faire system. Taking into account how and why the state would intervene, the outcome of the interventionist regime is a monetary system not unlike what we already have, which in turn suggests that the interventionist regime is itself the underlying cause of our monetary difficulties.

The Evolution of a Laissez-Faire Monetary System

Selgin and White (1987) and Cowen and Kroszner (1988) have provided accounts of the evolution of a laissez-faire banking system. I take a somewhat different approach by considering a hypothetical anarchist society. People have well-defined preferences and an advanced division of labor. All property is private, trades are decentralized, and contracts are enforced by an efficient private legal system.[2] There is no government, and everyone is motivated by their own self-interest.

Origins

In this environment, the monetary system originated from barter. Indirect trades were found to be more convenient than barter, and gold displaced other intermediary goods to become the dominant medium of exchange. Private mints evolved that converted lumps of

---

[2]The theory of private legal systems is discussed in D. Friedman (1978), Rothbard (1978), the Tannehills (1970), and Wooldridge (1970). Historical examples of well-functioning private legal systems are medieval Celtic Ireland (Peden, 1977) and the 19th century American West (Anderson and Hill, 1979).

gold into coins. Coins were minted in standardized units ("dollars"), which the public found to be more convenient exchange media than heterogeneous lumps of gold.[3] Competitive pressures then led traders to post prices in terms of gold dollars. Traders who posted prices in terms of other commodities imposed additional reckoning costs on potential trading partners, and therefore lost business (White 1984: 704). The gold dollar thus became both the medium of exchange and the unit of account.

The Development of Banks Issuing Convertible Media of Exchange

In time, individuals came to use exchange media issued by banks. These exchange media evolved from the receipts issued by earlier goldsmiths who used to accept deposits of gold for safekeeping. Because they were less expensive to move and store than gold, these exchange media eventually displaced gold entirely as a medium of exchange. They continued, however, to be convertible into gold as the old goldsmiths' receipts had been. This meant that the holder of a liability with a face value of $1 had the right to demand at any time that the issuing bank exchange it for $1.00 in gold.[4] Banks that had announced in the past that they intended to make their liabilities inconvertible had found that the public distrusted them. This outcome was predictable because these banks had proposed to dispense with the legally binding commitment to maintain the value of their notes and deposits against gold. Consequently, these banks lost their market shares to competitors who promised to maintain convertibility. Nor could the banks as a whole form an effective cartel and jointly abandon convertibility: they had no means of keeping out potential entrants who would undercut them by offering the public convertible media of exchange. Competition among the banks forced them to maintain convertibility because the public wanted it.

---

[3]The use of coins relieved the public from the need to weigh gold and assess its fineness. Since coins bore a premium, people were willing to pay mints to coin their gold, and competition among the mints kept down minting charges.

[4]To avoid unnecessarily lengthening the discussion here, I pass over the possibility that the banks may insert option clauses into their deposit and note contracts to give them the right to insist on notice. For more on the use of option clauses, see Dowd (1988).

The convertibility of note and deposit liabilities implied that banks would contract their issues of notes and deposits on demand by the public, at a given price in terms of gold. At the same time, the banks were always ready to issue new liabilities on demand, at the same fixed price, because they would make additional profits by doing so. In other words, the supply of liabilities was perfectly elastic, and the amount and composition of liabilities in circulation were determined entirely by the demand to hold them. The banks realized that their profits depended on their note and deposit issues, and they could only increase their issues if they increased the public's demand for them.

The banks also appreciated that the public would be more willing to accept a particular bank's notes if other banks were also willing to accept them. They therefore entered into clearing arrangements by which each bank accepted every other bank's liabilities at par. A central clearinghouse was then set up to organize the regular clearing sessions at which the banks returned each other's liabilities and settled up the difference in an agreed-upon medium. The establishment of the clearing system meant that a member of the public could redeem an unwanted note (or deposit) at any banks and not just the bank that issued it. Whenever note issues exceeded the demand to hold them, the excess issues were now returned more quickly to the banking system, the more rapid redemption process in turn reduced the disruptions to economic activity caused by occasional over-issues. The banks' attempts to increase the demand for their issues thus led them to create a clearing system that had the side effect of stabilizing the monetary system by returning excess issues more rapidly.

Bank Soundness and the Threat of Bank Runs

While gold was still the dominant medium of exchanges each bank would make a profit by lending out some of the gold deposited with it. It would hold gold to be able to honor demands for redemption, but it would economize its gold holdings because they represented foregone lending opportunities. Once bank liabilities replaced gold as a medium of exchange, a bank would create and lend out its own liabilities instead of gold, but it would continue to optimize its reserve holdings because it would still need to hold gold to meet demands for redemption. However, by issuing more liabilities than its keeps in gold reserves, a bank over any short period can redeem only a fraction of the liabilities that might be presented for redemption. It then faces the problem of how to avoid a situation where it would run out of gold and default on its promise to redeem its issues.

There are various ways in which the banks would protect themselves against this danger. A bank would supplement its stocks of gold by holding assets which could be sold relatively quickly and at little loss if it needed to obtain more gold, it would also cultivate a reputation for soundness to reassure liability-holders and potential creditors that they had no reason to fear losses. One way of doing this would be to maintain high capital ratios to demonstrate that it had the capital to withstand unexpected losses.[5] To reassure them further, a bank's shareholders might also adopt extended liability, or perhaps allow their managements to extend their liability if that was a precondition for a loan. A bank might also open its books or employ independent monitors to verify its soundness.

If a bank were faced with large unanticipated demands for gold, it would meet them by running down its reserves, and if necessary, by borrowing gold or selling assets to buy gold from those who have it. In most cases where this happens, those redeeming the bank's liabilities would have no wish to hold gold, but would convert them into other assets instead. Much of the gold would therefore be rapidly redeposited in the banking system. Other banks would then be flush with gold. Provided they were satisfied about the soundness of the bank wanting the loan, it would be in their individual interests to lend that gold to it. A sound bank should normally be able to demonstrate its soundness and thereby ensure that it could obtain whatever loans it required. It could then meet any drain of reserves from the public. Of course, once they appreciated its soundness, the public would have far less reason to'run on it in the first place. If a bank could not reassure creditors, on the other hand, they would have good reason to refuse to lend to it, and it may not be able to meet a run from the public. A run would then be much more likely to happen anyway, and such a run might well force the bank to default. In short, a sound bank is unlikely to face a run, and could meet one at relatively little cost even if it did occur, but an unsound bank is more likely to face a run and has much more to lose from it. The threat of a run is therefore a useful discipline against excessive risk taking by bank management.

[5]For more on the use of capital ratios, see Kaufman (1987) and Lewis and Davis (1987).

Financial Instruments Replace Gold as Banks' Reserves

While banks clearly want to protect themselves against demands for redemption, they also have an incentive to reduce the cost of maintaining the reserves they hold to meet such demands. These costs will fall anyway as the banking system develops, because public demands for redemption will fall as their confidence in the banking system increases, and the lower demands for redemption imply that the banks can operate on lower reserve ratios.[6] The banks will reduce the costs of holding reserves further by offering financial instruments as alternative redemption media. The costs of storing and protecting financial instruments are considerably lower than for gold, and many financial instruments have the benefit that they bear explicit returns. The banks would usually have little difficulty persuading the public to accept financial instruments rather than gold when they demand redemption. The public would normally prefer them because of their lower storage, protection and moving costs. To qualify as a suitable redemption medium, an asset must have a value independent of the bank that is using the asset to redeem its issues—that is, the bank must not use its own debt. Obvious examples are the debt or equity of other firms. Note that there is nothing to stop an individual bank using the debt of another bank to redeem its own liabilities. Indeed, banks will often find it particularly convenient to redeem their liabilities by giving out other banks' notes or by writing checks on other banks. But the banking system as a whole cannot redeem all its liabilities by writing checks on itself—there must be some "outside" redemption medium at the aggregate level. Of course, if the banks give out financial assets instead of gold there is a danger that the original issuers might default, the assets might fall in value, and so on, but they could always refuse a particular instrument and the banks would have to provide them with something else instead. If the public accepts a particular redemption medium, on the other hand, that implies they consider it at least "as good as gold," and that they are willing accept any risks it entails.

The banks' ability to obtain additional redemption securities on the market has the side-effect of protecting the monetary system

---

[6]We might also note that demands to convert bank liabilities into gold will also tend to be low because bank liabilities bear a liquidity premium over gold. Recall that gold is no longer used as a medium of exchange.

from the disruptions that would otherwise occur when there were largescale demands for redemption. Had they continued to redeem in sold, the banks could only have met a large loss of reserves by raising the interest rate they paid on deposits of gold, and arbitrage would then have forced interest rates up across the board. The banks would also have tried to maintain their solvency by recalling loans and cutting back lending. Many firms would then respond to the credit squeeze by dumping assets on the market, and asset prices would fall further and reinforce the rise in interest rates. Falling asset prices would inflict capital losses on many firms the banks included, and business failures would rise. Firms would also respond to the credit squeeze by curtailing production, laying off workers and dumping commodities at basement prices, and the falling commodity prices would increase business failures further. On the other hand, when the banks use financial instruments as reserves, they no longer have to raise interest rates and cut back their own lending to meet a reserve drain, they simply obtain reserves on the market. The prices of some reserve assets might rise, but that would cause no particular problems, and interest rates, lending, and so on would be substantially unaffected. The replacement of gold by financial instruments as banks' reserves therefore helps to insulate interest rates, bank lending, and economic activity generally from the effects of fluctuations in the demand for gold. This is a very important stabilizing feature of the laissez-faire monetary system.

The public's principal concern is that the exchange media they accept maintain their purchasing power and their general acceptability, and for this purpose it generally suffices that the banks guarantee to take their notes back in exchange for something of the same nominal value. This commitment pegs the nominal value of bank issues and forms the basis of the public's confidence in them. When demands for redemption do occur, the public will usually want to convert bank liabilities from one form into another (e.g., when they write checks against deposits), and the banking system as a whole will not lose reserves. Demands to convert bank liabilities into "outside" media will be unimportant in comparison, and in most of these the public would prefer to accept financial instruments to avoid the relatively heavy costs of handling gold. It will be relatively rare that a member of the public specifically wanted gold, and these demands would have little significance. The commitment to redeem specifically in gold then becomes more or less redundant, and the banks could easily replace it with a commitment to redeem their issues with alternative instruments of the same value as gold.[7]

The Fixed Price of Gold

It bears stressing that the abandonment of the commitment to redeem in gold does not mean that the price of gold would float. The banks would still be committed (for the time being) to maintain the price of gold at par. Given the high costs of handling gold, however, the banks would probably find it cheaper to peg the (spot) price of gold by intervening in the futures market. They would manipulate the futures price of gold to keep the spot price at par. To avoid having to take delivery of gold they would sell all futures contracts before they expired. Similarly, they would avoid having to deliver gold by buying back any contracts they had sold before they expired. Since operating in the futures market would relieve the banks of any need to handle physical amounts of gold, they could then dispense entirely with their stocks of gold. Any remaining "resource costs" would be eliminated.

The commitment to maintain the price of gold is of the utmost importance: it provides the anchor that ties down nominal prices. To see why, suppose that the banks as a whole overissue their liabilities. If there is a commitment to maintain the price of gold, then the overissue can have no lasting effect on the price level and the whole of the overissue must be returned to the issuing banks. Without that commitment, however, the overissue can permanently change the price level. In that case, some of the excess notes would stay in circulation to satisfy the higher nominal demand for notes at the higher price level. How many notes stay out and how many are returned to the banks depends on how rapidly the note reflux mechanism works and how flexible individual prices are. The more rapid the reflux, and the more "sticky" individual prices, the less the price level would rise.

---

[7]The system outlined here is very similar, and borrows much from, that of Greenfield and Yeager (1983). Obviously, the abrogation of the commitment to redeem in gold might cause *some* resentment, and a bank would not do it if it expected that the losses from the foregone business it would provoke were expected to outweigh the savings. One must bear in mind, however, that gold is no longer used for exchange purposes, and there is no obvious reason why the banks should find it worthwhile to redeem in gold when they do not find it worthwhile to redeem in any other physical commodities.

To modify Wicksell's analogy (1907), the price level would behave rather like a cylinder on a flat surface. Each overissue (or underissue) of bank liabilities would give the cylinder a push. The weight of the cylinder would correspond to the rapidity of the reflux mechanism, and the flexibility of prices would correspond to the smoothness of the surface. The lighter the cylinder, and the smoother the surface, the more it would move, and once it had moved, there would be no tendency for it to move back. Prices therefore drift from one period to another, and what give the system whatever price stability it possesses are the rapidity of the reflux and the inertia of individual prices. Short-run inertia notwithstanding, prices in the long run would be indeterminate. Fortunately, the commitment to peg a nominal price is not something that the banks can just abandon. If a bank announced that it intended to let the price of gold float it would suffer the same fate as the earlier banks that tried to abandon convertibility—with no guarantee about their value, the public would distrust its notes and it would lose its market share. The public desire the protection that a nominal peg gives them and competition among the banks forces them to provide it.

The Replacement of the Gold Peg

There is one last stage in the evolution of the monetary system. The system is still vulnerable to disturbances arising from changes in the relative price of gold. Since the price of gold is "fixed" at unity by the banks, the relative price of gold can only change if the prices of other goods change, this makes nominal prices dependent on conditions in the gold market. An improvement in the technology for extracting gold, for instance, would decrease the relative price of gold, and since the nominal price of gold is fixed its relative price can only fall if other (nominal) prices rise. The more variables the relative price of gold the less stable prices would generally be. This instability imposes costs on the general public—they find it hard to distinguish between true price signals and irrelevant price noise, and therefore make mistakes they would otherwise have avoided, they have less peace of mind about the future, and so on. The banks also have to live with these problems, but they have the additional problem that changes in the relative price of gold affect their net values. A bank's liabilities are indexed to the price of gold, but the value of its assets will depend to a considerable extent on prices generally. If the relative price of gold starts to rise, therefore, banks will find that the nominal values of their assets will fall, while their liabilities remain fixed in value. Changes in the relative price of gold can then undermine the banks' capital valuations.

To rectify these problems the banks will switch to a nominal anchor whose relative price is more stable. They will select an appropriate commodity (or commodity bundle) and announce that from a certain date on they will intervene to maintain its price instead of the price of gold. The price of gold would then be free to float and it would have no more monetary significance. Since both the banks and the public prefer more price stability to less, the new commodity (bundle) would be chosen to maximize (ex ante) price stability. Apart from unnecessarily exposing themselves to fluctuations in the relative price of gold, any banks that continued with the old gold peg would lose their deposit and note market shares because of the public's preference for media of exchange with more stable purchasing power. The same would apply to banks that adopted other commodity pegs that were considered to generate less price stability. Competition among the banks therefore leads not just to a commodity peg that generates price stability, but to one that generates the maximum possible price stability.

The banks could peg the price of a single commodity (or small set of commodities) whose relative price was stable, or else they could choose a large commodity bundle whose relative price was stable because the movements of the individual commodity prices tended to cancel each other out.[8] As they did previously with gold, the banks would avoid any physical handling costs by intervening in the futures market to maintain the spot price. On the date that the new regime came into force, the banks would peg the dollar price of the new commodity (bundle) at a rate given, say, by its previous day's market value. This would avoid any 'jumps' in the purchasing power of exchange media (and hence in prices) as the change took effect.

The simplest case would be where the banks selected a single commodity whose supply was perfectly elastic. Its relative price would then be constant, and price stability would be maximized.

---

[8]If the banks were to choose to peg a commodity basket, they would have to peg the price of the basket itself, and not the individual prices of the constituent goods. One way of doing this would be to peg a price indexed to that of the commodity basket—for example, a consumer price index (CPI).

A good example of a commodity that might satisfy this condition is the brick, as once suggested by Buchanan (1962). The brick has a very high elasticity of supply because it is produced under competitive conditions at a more or less constant marginal cost. If they decided that the spot supply of bricks was not sufficiently elastic, and therefore that the relative price of current bricks was not sufficiently stable, the banks might adopt a modified form of the "brick standard" and peg the price of future (or forward) bricks (e. g., bricks four months ahead) instead. Since factors are more mobile in the longer run, future bricks will have higher supply elasticity than current bricks, and therefore a more stable relative price. The brick is suggested purely for illustration, of course, but what matters is that the commodity whose price is pegged has a stable relative price and the brick might be as good as anything else.[9]

The Mature Free-Banking System

This completes our account of the idealized evolution of a free banking system. We can now assess its main features, and begin with its stability.

Stability

There are three main senses in which we can talk of the stability of a monetary system. The first is whether it is self-sustaining. To be stable in this sense, the system must leave no group able and willing to overturn it. The free banking system satisfies this condition because everyone already maximizes their own private utility (conditional on the external environment), and no one has any incentive to change their behavior. The free-banking system fares better on this criterion than current monetary systems because it does not rely on an outside "guardian" to protect it who might be inclined to undermine it instead. It also fares better because it does not try to foist

---

[9]It is interesting to observe how the role of gold changes as the system evolves. Gold originally emerges from barter as the dominant medium of exchange (and unit of account). Banks then issue liabilities denominated in gold dollars which gradually displace gold as a medium of exchange. After this the banks abandon gold as a medium of redemption and replace the gold peg. In the meantime, the bank dollar has long since replaced the gold dollar as the public's unit of account. Gold then ceases to have any monetary significance whatever. Gold is significant only in an underdeveloped monetary economy.

responsibility for any "social interest" on some institution that will not look after the "social interest" because it has insufficient private incentive to do so.

The second sense in which we can talk of the stability of a monetary system concerns its ability to respond to exogenous events while maintaining its integrity. In particular, there is the question of the ability of the banks to meet demands by the public to convert bank liabilities into other bank liabilities or into outside redemption media. Measured by this criterion, the laissez-faire monetary system performs extremely well: the supply of bank liabilities is perfectly elastic, and so their extent is determined by demand, if the public wish to convert one form of bank liability into another, the banking system contracts the issue of one and expands that of the other. The banking system accommodates public demands in the same automatic way that current banking systems convert one form of bank deposit into another. With the laissez-faire banking system, however, it makes no difference what kind of liabilities the public wish to convert, deposits can be converted into notes as easily as into another form of deposit, or vice versa. Nor do the banks have any difficulty accommodating demands to convert liabilities into outside redemption media. The banks simply run down their reserves and if necessary obtain more on the market, and there are no major disturbances to interest rates, credit markets or economic activity. The only exception is that banks which are judged to be unsound may not be able to meet a run, but the threat of a bank run will discourage bank managements from taking risks that could make their banks unsound.

The other sense in which we usually talk of the stability of monetary system refers to the stability of nominal prices. The laissez-faire system gets very high marks on this account as well. Since both the public and the banks benefit from price stability, the banks will peg their issues to a commodity chosen to maximize price stability. The old argument about competition in money leading banks to print it until it becomes worthless could not be more misleading. Competition will eliminate every money except the one that generates the most price stability.

Optimality

The mature free-banking system is optimal by virtually any criterion. All feasible and mutually beneficial trades take place because there are no barriers to prevent them. The banks provide the public with exactly the exchange media they want, and deposit interest rates, bank charges and other contract provisions (e.g., regarding liability) are competitively determined. The rents from issuing exchange media are therefore competed away to the public. Similarly, the banks' competition for loan business passes the rents from lending to their loan customers. The banks have an incentive to keep their reserves costs low, but not to reduce them to a level that threatens their solvency. A bank will use financial instruments rather than physical commodities to redeem its liabilities, and there will be no resource costs as such even though the currency is a convertible one. The costs of intervening to maintain the price of the pegged commodity (bundle) will be minimal. There are no free rider or externality problems, and therefore no discrepancies between private and social interests.[10] The problem of guarding guardians does not arise because there are no "outside" guardians to be watched. We do not have to worry about the incentives faced by the monetary authorities, the time consistency of their policies, and so on, because there are no authorities. There is no policy as conventionally understood, and therefore no "optimal policy problem." Everyone pursues his own self-interest, and all interests are harmonized by the market.

The Evolution of Our Current Monetary System

We have suggested that unfettered private interest could have produced a highly stable and attractive monetary system. To be complete, however, we must also explain why such a monetary system did not evolve, and why we ended up instead with the monetary system we have. The easiest way to do this is to introduce a state into our hypothetical anarchist society and see what happens. Once we introduce the state, we have to consider the rewards and penalties faced by the individuals who operate it (i.e., the politicians and civil servants). They differ from other individuals in that they have unique powers to compel other agents and to rewrite the rules

---

[10]Note that the benefits of information are privately appropriated (at least at the margin). Information is not a public good because it does not satisfy the nonrivalness and nonexcludability conditions that a public good satisfies. The same can be said for confidence in the banks,

under which everyone operates. We must presume that these powers will be used to further their own interests, as selfish or altruistic as they may be.

This new state will intervene in the monetary system for two main reasons. The first, and most basic, is to raise revenue from it. From a political point of view, the monetary system is often an attractive source of tax revenue. The costs are usually heavily disguised, and more often than not, the tax is not even perceived as such by those who pay it (e. g., inflation). Also, the public often fail to distinguish nominal and effective tax burdens, and are quite ready to acquiesce in taxes on the banks without realizing that much of the burden will be passed back to them. In addition, governments sometimes intervene in the monetary system to seize economic rents and transfer them to groups that have the political power to lobby successfully for them. This explains much of the regulation imposed on the banking system. An example is the separation of commercial and investment banking by the Banking Act of 1933 which cartelized the banking industry by preventing commercial and investment banks from encroaching on each other's territory. Finally, politicians are motivated to raise revenue from the monetary system because in that way they can by-pass the usual constitutional constraints against raising taxes. The inflation tax is perhaps the most conspicuous example, but subsidized loans are another.

The other principal reason for government intervention is to stabilize the monetary system. One of the state's primary responsibilities is to maintain (a semblance of) social order and perceived monetary instability usually leads to political pressure on the government to do something about it. The irony is that the instability can almost always be traced to earlier, interventions, but the first-best solution—to remove the earlier interventions is usually ruled out as being "politically unrealistic." The government therefore intervenes to correct the unintended consequences of its own earlier intervention, the new intervention later turn out to have unexpected side-effects of its own, and further intervention seems to be required to deal with them, and so it goes.

A good example of this "logic of intervention" is provided by U.S. monetary history. The United States had a reasonably adequate monetary system when the Civil War broke out, but during the war the federal government intervened to impose on it the regulations of the National Banking System. The principal motive was to raise revenue, but the consequence was to destabilize the banking system. Rather than abolish the restrictions that caused this instability, Congress instead established the Federal Reserve System to act as its lender of last resort. Unfortunately, in the early 1930s the Fed failed to function as lender of last resort and much of the U. S. banking system collapsed. Instead of abolishing the Fed and at least going back to the National Banking System, Congress responded to the banking crisis by establishing a system of federal deposit insurance that subsidized risk taking and prepared the way for the present banking crisis. It also relaxed and eventually abolished the Fed's commitment to maintain the gold standard, and in the process converted the Fed into an engine of inflation. Each of these interventions probably made the monetary system even less stable than it was before.[11]

We now examine in more detail some specific types of intervention and the effects they have.

Creation of Fiat Currency

A common form of intervention is to create a fiat currency. The process usually begins when the state intervenes to give privileges to one bank (e. g., it may establish a monopoly over the note issue).[12] The motive behind such intervention is usually to raise revenue by selling the privileges. Since the privileged bank has the protection of the state, the other banks typically view its liabilities as being "as good as gold," but cheaper to hold. They therefore start to use them as redemption media instead of gold, and in time they come to replace gold more or less entirely.[13] They continue for a while to be convertible into gold at the issuing bank, but in the end the state intervenes to suspend that commitment. It does so because it enables it to extract more revenue out of the banking system. The banks find

---

[11]This overview of U.S. monetary history is based on Dowd (1989: chaps. 5 and 6).

[12]This account is a stylized version of the establishment of the fiat currency in England.

[13]An interesting question is why the banks did not make much use of alternative redemption media issued by the private sector. In England, at least, part of the explanation seems to be related to restrictions against joint stock banking, which meant that all banks except the Bank of England were severely undercapitalized. As a result, no private financial assets could be considered "safe" in a crisis except Bank of England debt. Banks therefore used Bank of England liabilities (and gold) because the public would accept nothing else.

themselves using inconvertible redemption media issued monopolistically by a central bank (i.e., there is a fiat currency).

Once convertibility is abandoned, the value of the central bank's liabilities–and hence the price level—depend on how many of them it creates, that is, on central bank policy. We therefore have to examine what the central bank and its political masters have to gain and lose from price level changes. A perceptive analysis of this issue is provided by Barro and Gordon (1983). They suggest that unexpected inflation gives certain benefits to the government and central bank, but also imposes certain costs on them. One benefit is the reduction in the real value of the government's fixed interest nominal debt. Other benefits include greater tax revenues and lower unemployment payments when the "surprise" inflation increases output. The costs include the higher interest rates that the government must pay if inflationary expectations rise and the erosion of the central bank's reputation for monetary "good behavior." Barro and Gordon suggest that the central bank will aim to create that rate of inflation which equalizes the marginal costs and benefits of surprise inflation to it. Starting from a low rate of inflation (e. g., zero), the benefits from a surprise inflation are likely to be quite high, and the costs quite low. Consequently, the public will not rationally expect low inflation and the central bank will not deliver it. The public will instead expect that higher rate of inflation at which the central bank's marginal benefits and costs from inflationary surprises are equal. On average, this will also be the inflation rate that the central bank actually delivers. This inflation rate will change (usually unpredictably) as the costs and benefits of surprise inflation vary. A fiat money issuer will therefore produce a rate of inflation that is high relative to what the public want tie, presumably zero), and one that will tend to vary unpredictably. There will be no price stability because the central bank has no incentive to provide it.

Restrictions on Banks' Liabilities

Governments also intervene to restrict the issue of bank liabilities. These measures are often motivated by an intention to stabilize the monetary system. A good example was the 1844 Bank Charter Act in the United Kingdom, which gave the Bank of England an effective monopoly of the note issue but required that the Bank could only issue further notes if it kept equivalent values of gold in its vaults.

At the time, Bank of England notes (and deposits) formed the principal reserve medium of the other banks, and those notes were also used by the public as hand-to-hand currency. The motivation behind this measure was largely to stem the disturbances perceived to result from the "reckless" overissues of notes in the past. The solution proposed was to make the supply of notes behave as if it was a metallic currency—this was known as "the currency principle." The consequence, however, was to make it impossible for the banking system to satisfy largescale public demands to convert deposits into notes. Their knowledge that the banking system could only satisfy a limited demand for notes encouraged people to play safe and demand notes if they felt that they might become difficult to obtain. These preemptive demands for notes then sometimes provoked the very crisis that everyone was anxious to avoid. Such crises occurred in 1847, 1857, and 1866, and they only subsided when the government intervened to allow the Bank of England to issue more notes.

Another type of restriction on the note issue is to specify the redemption assets banks must use when they make issues. The classic example is where banks are compelled to redeem their issues for gold at a fixed price. This type of restriction is usually motivated by the fear that banknotes might otherwise somehow lose their value. This was certainly the case when such a restriction was imposed on U.K. banks by Act of Parliament in 1765. When faced with large demands to redeem their issues, the banks need to obtain gold but they are not allowed to pay more for it. They are therefore forced to raise interest rates and cut back their lending to protect their solvency, and economic activity falls. The restriction makes interest rates, bank credit and economic activity generally hostages to the vagaries of the demand for gold.

Lender of Last Resort and Deposit Insurance

A third sort of common intervention is to establish an agency to "protect" the banks. The classic examples are a lender of last resort and a system of liability (e. g., deposit) insurance. As our earlier discussion suggested, the "need" for a lender of last resort arises from the imposition of restrictions on the liabilities a bank may create. The usual case is where individuals want to convert deposits into currency, but the banks are not allowed to create the additional currency. The first-best solution is simply to abolish the restrictions on the note issue and let the banks issue the additional currency. Often, however, this option is dismissed or not even considered for political reasons. The only alternative is to establish a lender of last resort to print the additional currency end lend it to the banks that need it. Once the lender of last resort is created, it must resolve a variety of problems: it must know when to 'intervene' and issue emergency money; it must resolve the tension between its commitment to behave conservatively in normal times, and its obligation to create money freely during a crisis; and it needs a rule to tell it how much emergency money to create and at what terms to lend it. Most basic of all perhaps, some means has to be found to make the lender of last resort responsive to the desires of the banks. One would like to be reassured that the lender of last resort would actually function in a crisis. As the Fed demonstrated in the 1930s, having a lender of last resort that fails to lend can be worse than having no lender of last resort at all.[14]

The other example is deposit insurance, the principal justification for which is to protect banks against runs by removing the public's incentive to participate in them.[15] The problem with this thinking is that it mistakes the symptom (i.e., the bank run) with the underlying disease (i.e., banking instability), and applies a remedy that makes the disease worse. People run on a bank because they fear losses, and they have reason to fear losses when they hold deposits in banks of questionable soundness. The public have no reason to run on banks of obvious soundness, and such banks have no need for deposit insurance. Deposit insurance makes banks unstable in the longer run because it encourages them to take risks they would otherwise have avoided. Banks' managements take more risks because they no longer have to worry about a bank run, if they need more funds, they can simply raise deposit rates. They know that depositors will no longer need to monitor banks because their deposits are insured. Depositors will therefore tend to deposit their funds with the banks which promise them the highest return, regardless of the

---

[14]The reason for this is that since the Fed replaced the old system of private clearinghouse associations, the banks did not have their old support to fell back on when the Fed failed to help them.

[15]The literature on deposit insurance is vast. For a good introduction to it, see Kane (1985), Benston et al. (1966), and England (1988).

risks that such a bank might take. More cautious banks will have to raise their deposit rates to keep their deposits, and they may feel obliged to take more risks to cover their higher expenses. Banks then take more risks, and more of them will eventually become unsound. To make matters worse, inadequate failure resolution policies will often enable an unsound bank to fend off its creditors and remain in operation for a long time, during which it will have little left to lose and its management will be tempted to take extravagant risks at the expense of the deposit insurance agencies. Even though such behavior might greatly increase their ultimate losses, the insurance agencies frequently condone this behavior through excessively lenient forbearance policies motivated by short-term considerations.[16]

Conclusion

Contrary to widespread belief, monetary laissez faire is highly stable. For that reason as well as for others, it is also highly desirable. Our current monetary problems arise not because of free markets, but because markets are not free enough. They arise because of state meddling with the monetary system. The implications for reform are clear and unambiguous: if we really wish to put these problems right, we should be thinking about how to roll back the apparatus of state intervention to allow market forces to establish a stable and efficient monetary system.

References

Anderson, T. L., and Hill, P. J. (1979) "An American Experiment in Anarcho-Capitalism: The Not So Wild, Wild West." *Journal of Libertarian Studies* 3 (1): 9–29.

Barro, R. J. (1979) "Money and the Price Level under the Gold Standard." *Economic Journal* 89: 13–33.

Barro, R. J., and Gordon, D. B. (1983) "A Positive Theory of Planetary Policy in a Natural Rate Model." *Journal of Political Economy* 91: 589–610.

[16]Kaufman (1987: 22) notes that the most important determinant in the FSLIC's losses from thrift insolvency was the delay in closing down unsound institutions.

Benston, G. J.; Eisenbeis, R. A.; Horvitz, P. M.; Kane, E. S.; and Kaufman, G. G. (1986) *Perspectives on Safe and Sound Banking: Past, Present, and Future.* Cambridge, Mass.: MIT Press.

Buchanan, J. M. (1962) "Predictability: The Criterion of Monetary Constitutions." In L. B. Yeager (ed.), *In Search of a Monetary Constitution*, 155–83.. Cambridge, Mass.: Harvard University Press.

Cowen, T., and Kroszner, R. (1988) "The Evolution of an Unregulated Payments System." Unpublished paper, UC-Irvine and Harvard University.

Dowd, K. (1988) "Option Clauses and the Stability of a Laisser-Faire Monetary System." *Journal of Financial Services Research* 1 (3): 319–33.

_____ (1989) *The State and the Monetary System.* London: Palgrave Macmillan.

_____ (1993) *Laissez-Faire Banking.* New York: Routledge.

England, C. (1988) "Agency Costs and Unregulated Banks: Could Depositors Protect Themselves?" *Cato Journal* 7 (3): 771–97.

Friedman, D. (1978) *The Machinery of Freedom: Guide to a Radical Capitalism.* New York: Arlington House.

Friedman, M. (1951) "Commodity-Reserve Currency." *Journal of Political Economy* 59: 202–32.

_____ (1960) *A Program for Monetary Stability.* New York: Fordham University Press.

Greenfield, R. L., and Yeager, L. B. (1983) "A Laissez-Faire Approach to Monetary Stability." *Journal of Money, Credit, and Banking* 15 (3): 302–15.

Kane, E. J. (1985) *The Gathering Crisis in Federal Deposit Insurance.* Cambridge, Mass.: MIT Press.

Kaufman, G. G. (1987) "The Truth about Bank Runs." Federal Reserve Bank of Chicago Staff Memoranda SM-87-3.

Lewis, M. K., and Davis, K. T. (1987) *Domestic and International Banking.* Cambridge, Mass.: MIT Press.

Peden, J. R. (1977) "Property Rights in Irish Celtic Law." *Journal of Libertarian Studies* 1 (2): 81–95.

Rothbard, M. N. (1978) *For a New Liberty: The Libertarian Manifesto.* Revised ed. New York: Collier and Macmillan.

Selgin, G. A., and L. H. White (1987) "The Evolution of a Free Banking System." *Economic Inquiry* 25: 439–57.

Tannehill, L., and Tannehill, M. (1970) *The Market for Liberty*. Lansing, Mich.: Privately published.

Timberlake, R. H. (1984) "The Central Banking Role of Clearinghouse Associations." *Journal of Money, Credit, and Banking* 16: 1–15.

White, L. H. (1984) "Competitive Payments Systems and the Unit of Account." *American Economic Review* 74: 699–712.

Wicksell, K. (1907) "The Influence of the Rate of Interest on Prices." *Economic Journal* 17: 213–20.

Wooldridge, W. C. (1970) *Uncle Sam: The Monopoly Man*. New Rochelle, N.Y.: Arlington House.

INDEX

Note: Information in figures and tables is indicated by *f* and *t; n* designates a numbered note.

bank runs
  deposit insurance and, 284
  in free banking, 270–71, 278
BB&T, 53, 54, 56, 62–63
Bear Stearns, 44
Beckworth, David, 147n4,
    153n8, 162n10
Belgium, 229n1
benchmarks. *See also* forecasting
  inflation and, 34
  innovation with, 26
  interest rates and, 18, 32
Bernanke, Ben, 57–58, 135,
    144, 150, 155–56, 157
bimetallic standard, 79n1. *See
    also* gold standard
Bitcoin, xiv, 11, 128–29,
    247–51, 247n1, 248,
    249–50, 252–55, 252n6,
    253n8, 259–60. *See also*
    cybercurrencies
Bitgem (cybercurrency), 256.
    See also cybercurrencies
BitShares (cybercurrency),
    250, 254, 260. *See also*
    cybercurrencies
Black, Fischer, 69
BlackCoin, 253. *See also*
    cybercurrencies
BlackHalo (cybercurrency), 253.
    See also cybercurrencies
Blackman, Jules, 168n3
bond(s)
  and "Abrogation of Gold
      Clauses," 86
  Federal Reserve Act and,
      88n7, 89–90
  gold standard and, 226
  quantitative easing and, 157
  yields, 19f, 31f, 57–58

Boom Company v. Patterson,
    204
booms. *See* cycles
Bretton Woods system, 109
Broaddus, Al, 48
Bronson v. Rhodes, 196n2,
    205n9, 209
Brundesbank, 225
bubbles, 51, 53, 58, 134, 154,
    255–59. *See also* business
    cycle
Burns, Arthur, 135
Bush, George W., 54–55
business cycle, 21, 22f, 66, 153,
    154, 156, 173, 224, 241. *See
    also* bubbles; cycles
busts. *See* cycles
Butler v. Horwitz, 196n2

*California Reduction Co. v.
    Sanitary Reduction Works,*
    198n4
Canada, 33f, 145, 224, 225
CannabisCoin, 254–55. *See also*
    cybercurrencies
capital ratios, 271
capital requirements, 60–61.
    See also reserves
Cassel, Gustav, 168, 176
Centennial Monetary
    Commission, 2
central banking. *See also*
    European Central Bank;
    Federal Reserve
  abolishment of, 101
  credit allocation and, 45–46
  at crossroads, 2–4
  currency competition and,
      229–30, 230–33
  free currency and, 230–33

equilibrium (*continue*)
  monetary rules and, 117
  profit and, 173
  rational expectations and,
    233
Eubank v. City of Richmond,
  199n5
European Central Bank, 66
European Monetary System,
  231n6
European Union, 66
exchange rates
  currency competition and,
    231, 232
  cybercurrency and, 249,
    261
  financial crises and, 32
  fixed, 108–9
  monetary policy and, 66
  pegged, 120
  purchasing power parity,
    19f, 31f

Fama, Eugene, 69
Fannie Mae, 44, 47, 51, 53, 60
Federal Deposit Insurance
  Corporation (FDIC), 52–53,
  56–57, 60, 283–85
Federal Open Market
  Committee (FOMC), 110,
  111, 112, 119–20, 128, 136
Federal Reserve
  accountability of, 139–40
  credit allocation and, 43–44
  gold standard and, 224–25
  Great Depression and, 58
  and House Concurrent
    Resolution 133 of 1975,
    135–36
  inflation and, 157–58

interventionist impulse of,
  47–48
as lender of last resort, 47, 84,
  92, 101, 224, 267, 281,
  283–85
monetary policy and, 57–60,
  65–66
in payments system, 52
targeting and, 160–61
Federal Reserve Act, 84–92,
  136, 138
Federal Reserve Bank of
  Boston, 53
Federal Reserve Bank of New
  York, 84
Federal Reserve Policy Rule
  Act, 138
Federal Reserve Reform Act,
  136
Fed Oversight Reform and
  Modernization Act, 119–20
"feedback rule," 109, 126–27,
  179
fiat money. *See also* currency
  alternatives to, 9–12
  creation of, 281–82
  cybercurrency as, 257n9
  cybercurrency vs., 261–62
  forecasting and, 182–83
  parallel gold standard and,
    219
  rethinking of, 1–2
  taxes and, 257n9, 282
Field, Stephen, 83, 89, 194
Fifth Amendment, 86
final demand rule, 146n3
financial crises. *See also* Great
  Depression; Great Recession
  after booms, 25, 25n4
  and business cycles, 21, 22f

Walton v. Parsons, State ex rel., 204*n*7
Wang, Yichuan, 162*n*10
Washington Mutual, 52–53
West Germany, 229*n*1
White, Lawrence, 60, 123, 144*n*1
Wholesale Price Index, 84
Wicksell, Knut, 172*n*5
Wicksellian natural rate, 17, 30.
    See also interest rates
Williams, Gordon, 168–69
Williamson, Stephen, 258

Wolf, Martin, 224–25, 225*n*4
Woodford, Michael, 149
Woolsey, W. W., 162*n*10, 172*n*5, 185*n*12, 186*n*13
World War I, 5, 84, 86, 101, 145, 176
World War II, 45, 109

Yeager, Leland, 66
Yeager-Greenfield system, 69–73, 274*n*7
yield curves, 57–59

ABOUT THE EDITOR

James A. Dorn is Vice President for Monetary Studies, Editor of the *Cato Journal*, Senior Fellow, and Director of Cato's annual monetary conference. He has written widely on Federal Reserve policy and monetary reform, and is an expert on China's economic liberalization. He has edited more than ten books, including *The Search for Stable Money* (with Anna J. Schwartz), *The Future of Money in the Information Age*, and *China in the New Millennium*. His articles have appeared in the *Wall Street Journal*, *Financial Times*, *South China Morning Post*, and scholarly journals. He has been a columnist for *Caixin* and writes for *Forbes.com*. From 1984 to 1990, he served on the White House Commission on Presidential Scholars. Dorn has been a visiting scholar at the Central European University and Fudan University in Shanghai. He holds a PhD in economics from the University of Virginia.